GREAT LIVES OBSERVED

Gerald Emanuel Stearn, *General Editor*

EACH VOLUME IN THE SERIES VIEWS THE CHARACTER AND
ACHIEVEMENT OF A GREAT WORLD FIGURE IN THREE PER-
SPECTIVES—THROUGH HIS OWN WORDS, THROUGH THE OPIN-
IONS OF HIS CONTEMPORARIES, AND THROUGH RETROSPECTIVE
JUDGMENTS—THUS COMBINING THE INTIMACY OF AUTOBIOG-
RAPHY, THE IMMEDIACY OF EYEWITNESS OBSERVATION, AND
THE OBJECTIVITY OF MODERN SCHOLARSHIP.

SAUL N. SILVERMAN, *the editor of this volume in the Great Lives
Observed series, is presently engaged in research and consulting
in Canada. He has taught at the University of California,
Berkeley, and at the University of Prince Edward Island,
Canada, and has served as Science Advisor on the staff of the
Science Council of Canada. His writings range widely in the
fields of Soviet studies, international relations, and science and
technology policy.*

GREAT LIVES OBSERVED

LENIN

Edited by
SAUL N. SILVERMAN

"... [He was] a man who knew better than
any one else how to prevent people from leading
the life to which they were accustomed."

—MAXIM GORKY

A SPECTRUM BOOK

PRENTICE-HALL, INC., ENGLEWOOD CLIFFS, N.J.

Library of Congress Cataloging in Publication Data

LENIN, VLADIMIR IL'ICH, 1870–1924.
   Lenin.

   (Great lives observed) (A Spectrum book)
   Includes views on Lenin written by his contemporaries and other historians.
   Bibliography: p.
   1. Lenin, Vladimir Il'ich, 1870–1924—Addresses, essays, lectures. I. Silverman,
Saul N., ed.
II. Title.
DK254.L3.A5785   947.084′1′0924 [B]   72–2034
ISBN 0–13–529289–1
ISBN 0–13–529271–9 (pbk.)

© 1972 by PRENTICE-HALL, INC.,
Englewood Cliffs, N.J.

A SPECTRUM BOOK

PRENTICE-HALL INTERNATIONAL, INC. (*London*)
PRENTICE-HALL OF AUSTRALIA, PTY. LTD. (*Sydney*)
PRENTICE-HALL OF CANADA, LTD. (*Toronto*)
PRENTICE-HALL OF INDIA PRIVATE LIMITED (*New Delhi*)
PRENTICE-HALL OF JAPAN, INC. (*Tokyo*)

Contents

v

5

Lenin in 1917   148

6

Lenin in Power   162

PART THREE
LENIN IN HISTORY

7

8

9

10
Isaac Deutscher: Lenin's Moral Dilemmas

Acknowledgments

This book is only a small and initial repayment of debts accumulated over many years. Those who contributed to forming the critical judgments underlying the selection of material for this volume will, I hope, recognize the contribution they have made and will accept my work in the spirit in which it is offered.

Confining myself only to acknowledgments of direct contributions to the preparation of *this* volume, I would like to thank the series editor, Gerald Stearn, and my editors at Prentice-Hall, Jay Azarow and Marjorie Streeter, for both their patience and their gentle—but effective—prodding and encouragement, and Stephen Foster and Betty Thistle, for the ungrudging assistance they gave in the actual preparation of the manuscript.

The University of Prince Edward Island, Canada, helped defray certain costs through the generosity of its Dean's Fund. Special thanks are due to its library staff, and particularly to Mary Beth Harris, chief reference librarian, for aid in securing some of the material from which selections were made.

I am, of course, grateful to publishers, authors, and other holders of copyright for permission given to include their work in the anthology portions of this volume.

To Deanna and Ruth
who, as always,
sustained, encouraged,
criticized,
and diverted me

Introduction

Lenin was born in Simbirsk, on the Volga, in 1870. Over a century later, it is still difficult to put him into perspective as an historical figure. He is all but obscured by a variety of images that have been spawned by competing political ideologies.

In the West, many still see Lenin primarily as a destroyer—"the Grand Repudiator," as Winston Churchill called him. In a recent biography, Stefan Possony characterizes Lenin as a prototypical "compulsive revolutionary," who in his destructive career aimed mainly to establish a more viable base for further destruction.[1] Ironically, this view of Lenin aligns him, by implication, with those more anarchistic and nihilistic rebels whom he criticized consistently, both before and after 1917. True, the "Grand Repudiator" thesis does catch one aspect of Lenin's character and of his life's work—but how far does it go to explain him in historical context, in relation to the milieu with which he interacted as well as to what he achieved?

Was Lenin really the great destroyer? Or, was he a man who tried to impose order on a situation that was already degenerating into chaos?

The political myths of the Communist movements also distort our perception of Lenin. The Soviet slogan proclaims *Lenin s nami*—"Lenin is with us!" He becomes the transcendental symbol of everything that is good; he is invoked as guide and model in everything—from inculcating good wash-up habits in toddlers to inspiring young scientists to greater effort. History ends and political theology takes over. Embalmed, enshrined in his mausoleum, Lenin serves as a key symbol of an ongoing struggle for power and influence.

Yet there is considerable truth in the slogan *Lenin s nami*. More than any other political leader of the twentieth century, Lenin, through his ideas (both in their use and their misuse), continues to shape the conditions under which we live. Almost a half century after his death, the themes he dealt with and the problems with which he grappled are still very much with us. This, perhaps more than anything else, makes the problem of historical assessment an especially difficult one.

Lenin is prototypical of one kind of contemporary political man— the revolutionary intellectual. Hence, in assessing his significance, we are also holding up a mirror to our own lives. Because of this, three questions

[1] "But Lenin really did not destroy for destruction's sake. Lenin disorganized and destroyed in order *to seize power* and, in turn, used power to disorganize and destroy." (Stefan Possony, *Lenin: The Compulsive Revolutionary*, Chicago: Henry Regnery Co., 1964, p. 398).

1

are most relevant to the kind of inquiry that can be begun within the limits of a brief introductory essay:

—What led Lenin to devote his life to revolution?

—How did Lenin's ideas relate to what may be called his "revolutionary style"?

—Why, and to what extent, was Lenin successful as a revolutionary— and what were some of the implications of his success?

I

Lenin's development as a revolutionary was a function of time, place, and upbringing. He spanned the transition between two views of life, two forms of social action. Culturally, in his basic values, Lenin was a nineteenth-century Russian; politically, his career developed under the impetus of twentieth-century conditions, international in scope, that impinged upon the Russian milieu and produced radical changes within it. In his maturity, Lenin conceived an intellectual fascination for the more abstruse aspects of a dialectic that was more Hegelian than Marxist; this, perhaps, indirectly reflected some psychological and existential contradictions, difficult to resolve, in his own career and situation.

He was born Vladimir Ilyich Ulyanov; "Lenin" is a pseudonym (probably from the Siberian river, the Lena) adopted by him in the course of his revolutionary career. Simbirsk, his birthplace, was a sleepy provincial center of local trade and government; by virtue of its location, it epitomized the confrontation between the European and the Asiatic aspects of the Russian Empire. Simbirsk represented a different Russia from that of the two capitals—solid, conservative, Moscow and the newer, more westernized, and sometimes revolutionary city of St. Petersburg created by Peter the Great to be the center of government for the Empire.

Lenin grew up along the Volga; he did not come to St. Petersburg until he was twenty-three, and in all spent only a half-dozen years there during the remainder of his life. His outlook was shaped on the Volga, in the rural heartland of Russia, rather than in the great cities. A part of Lenin remained a countryman until the day he died. This manifested itself in various ways. To his associates, he seemed more relaxed when living in the country—near Longjumeau, in France, or at Poronino, in Austrian Poland, or later, after the Revolution, at a country villa some distance from Moscow. His favored recreations were hunting, walking, and mountain climbing. This influence of the countryside, however tangential and difficult to assess, seems to have had an underlying effect on Lenin's view of the world and, perhaps, on his style of action as well.

As a dominant theme in his earliest writings (till the late 1890s) and as a continuing thread in his later works, one may note the close attention that Lenin paid to socioeconomic conditions in rural Russia. By analyzing the growth of the network of production and trade that extended from the urban centers to the rural districts, Lenin sought to support his contention (against those who advocated a slower development of revolutionary activity) that "backward Russia" was already into a phase of fairly advanced capitalist development. In his conception of capitalism, he placed considerable emphasis on the absorption of a rural hinterland into the ambience of urban nodal centers of finance, production, and commerce, and on the superimposition of an industrially based exchange economy on the underlying pattern of rural life. In its most elaborated form (in *The Development of Capitalism in Russia,* 1898), this analysis, applied to urban-rural relationships in Russia, anticipates some of the underlying arguments that were to be applied to the wider international system when Lenin analyzed imperialism, almost two decades later.

Lenin developed a sensitivity to the potential role of the peasantry in revolution that was in advance of most of the Marxist analysts of his day. Especially after the unsuccessful revolution of 1905, Lenin turned increasingly to the question of the role of the peasant within a revolutionary alliance. He showed a pronounced tendency to divide and subdivide the rural population into classes, groups, and subgroups. The picture that he draws is one of a congeries of interests that could be brought together in various permutations, depending upon the particular requirements of specific revolutionary situations. His analysis of the peasantry arose out of close observation based on his experience in the countryside, buttressed by careful analysis of available economic and social data (particularly the rural district censuses undertaken by the *zemstvos,* or rural councils). Marx had railed against "the idiocy of rural life." Though Lenin feared the domination of the peasantry in a revolutionary situation gone out of control (see Gorky, p. 139 below), he did possess some real understanding, and, perhaps, an empathy, for the needs of the peasant, particularly the poorer peasant. More significantly, he could draw on this understanding in devising revolutionary strategy and tactics that would draw support from the peasantry or at least neutralize them. This extended beyond the peasant himself; his understanding of the peasantry gave Lenin added insight into the psychology, social relations, capabilities, and limitations of the Russian urban worker, who was only one step removed from the village and still closely linked, psychologically, to an age-old culture that he had left physically behind him.

But Lenin's understanding of rural Russia was placed in the context of the Marxist model of socioeconomic development and revolutionary action, which emphasized the role of the industrial proletariat. The rival Socialist Revolutionaries, who sought to implement an overtly peasant-oriented approach to sociopolitical change, were among the chief targets of Lenin's scorn. In the two decades prior to Lenin's own initiation into the revolutionary movement, Marxism had been imported into Russia and had developed there concurrently with the rise of industry in the main urban centers. Lenin's task, as he saw it, was to extend and apply Marxist theory in such a way as to meld it with certain characteristics of the specifically Russian situation.

Running counter to characteristics associated with the culture of rural Russia were traits that related more specifically to Lenin's upbringing, and, particularly, to the Ulyanov family itself. Ilya Ulyanov, Lenin's father, was a *raznochinets,* a self-made man—an intellectual who turned intelligence, discipline, and persistence to account in his rise from poverty to a high position in the Tsarist civil service. At the time of his death, in 1886, he had made a considerable reputation as educational chief of Simbirsk Province. With his rank, there came automatic admission to the lowest grade of the Russian hereditary nobility; Lenin and the other younger Ulyanovs inherited membership in the nobility from their father. Ilya Ulyanov was part Russian, part Kalmuk; it is believed that his father had been a serf. Lenin's mother, born Maria Blank, was part German and had been brought up in a manner that reflected the orderly way of life of the German settlers who had come to Russia a century before. She was the daughter of an army surgeon who had retired to become a prosperous landowner; her inheritance was apparently sufficient to maintain her family's middle-class way of life even after Lenin had reached maturity and embarked on his revolutionary career. Lenin was the third child and second son of this eminently respectable couple. The environment in which he was raised reflected the orientation of the hard-working, conscientious, demanding, culturally advanced, and liberal civil servant who was his father. The values of the Ulyanov household were similar to those associated with the Protestant Ethic in western countries: order, discipline, hard work, and a striving for excellence. Lenin was steeped in these values. Yet he and his brothers and sisters grew up to become revolutionaries, dedicated to tearing down the Tsarist order in whose ranks Ilya Ulyanov had found his niche.

Why? We will probably never know the answer. It is often suggested that Lenin's path to revolution was predetermined by the career and fate of his older brother, Alexander. The latter, a twenty-one-year-old science student in St. Petersburg, was arrested in 1887 and executed for his role in an abortive bomb plot against Tsar Alexander III. The fate of his brother may have served as a catalyst to Lenin's own actions, but just how much more Alexander's example helped shape Lenin's career is hard to determine. The fact that Lenin was the brother of an executed terrorist may have enhanced Lenin's status among student revolutionary circles in the period before he had developed his own claim to leadership. It may have been important in gaining access to the militant populist exiles who were scattered in towns on the middle Volga; here, prior to making his mark in St. Petersburg, Lenin was apparently initiated into the lore and basic outlook of the pre-Marxist revolutionaries. Whatever influence Alexander's career had on Lenin's political style was essentially negative. Throughout his life, Lenin was to hold back from making decisions in which emotion played an overt and significant part (his apparent coldness and superrationality are often noted); furthermore, he was to remain skeptical of the effectiveness of individual acts of terrorism and somewhat scornful of those who demonstratively engaged in revolutionary violence for its own sake, rather than with some overriding and explicitly political end in view. His brother's death did, indeed, leave its mark on Lenin. But one has to look elsewhere for the main causes of why Lenin became a revolutionary.

In the last half of the nineteenth century, a fundamental and multidimensional transformation occurred in Russian society. In the 1860s, under the "Tsar-Emancipator," Alexander II, a period of "reform from above" had been inaugurated. Emancipation of the serfs and a partial restructuring of the system of landholding and rural government were only part of a broader vista of projected change. Ilya Ulyanov, who was devoted to the eradication of the illiteracy and ignorance he had known in his own childhood in Astrakhan, was typical of many of the liberals of his day. Under Alexander II, these liberals saw a possibility of serving Russia by working within the existing system of government.

By the 1870s, however, the reforms had lost much of their earlier momentum and direction. The initial reforms had focused on basic social problems such as the emancipation and the development of primary education. A cumulative program of basic reform might have changed the basic life-style throughout a Russia that was still mainly agrarian. But basic social reform gave way to a concern for structural change within the administration and the armed forces. Furthermore, the attention of the Tsar and his aides shifted from domestic to foreign policy. Russia continued to expand in Central Asia, and revived its interest in extending its influence in the Middle East and the Balkans (in part under the guise of supporting the national liberation movements of fellow Slavs). The era of reform had begun in the wake of defeat in the Crimean War, as Russia recoiled from foreign entanglements to domestic concerns. It ended with Russia's reemergence as a major actor in European power politics, thus initiating a period of ever-increasing tension culminating in the outbreak of the First World War and the subsequent fall of the Tsarist monarchy.

The relative optimism of the men of Ilya Ulyanov's generation was increasingly difficult to sustain. Even in Lenin's father's day, many prominent literary-political critics were skeptical of the possibilities of real reform under Tsarism. From the early 1870s, the split between the state and society grew more intense. In part, this stemmed from an enhanced appreciation of the complexities and difficulties of the developmental process. The split was helped along by a worldwide depression that lasted intermittently from 1873 to 1896 and that had very real effects on Russia's economy and society. The Russian Empire was normally a net exporter of grains, timber, and various other primary products. Economic development, industrialization, the improvement of living conditions for the newly emancipated peasants, and the general prospect for social reform—all depended, to a considerable extent, on Russia's position in the world economy. The depression and the competition from new grain-producing areas in North and South America and Australia bore heavily during this crucial period on the economic, social, and political life of the Tsarist Empire. In particular, the generation that followed the emancipation lost hope that there would be significant improvement in the situation of the peasantry.

In the 1870s, the younger intellectuals made a serious effort to break through existing social and governmental structures and to establish direct links with the uneducated and unmobilized majority of the Russian people. In 1873, the abortive "movement to the people" saw waves of students and urban youth fan out through the countryside to engage the peasantry in radical dialogue. But few responded to the students' radicalism or were even able to understand it. In some instances, agitators were assaulted or turned over to the authorities. There followed a period of soul-searching and intensification of radicalism among the intellectual youth. This was exacerbated by the punitive measures of the police. Radical escalation occurred. Political terrorism—bombing and assassination—occurred in the aftermath of the failure of the peaceful movement of protest and agitation. Beginning with attacks on police officials, radical terrorism struck at the pinnacle of Russian society when, in 1881, Alexander II was assassinated.

By the mid-1880s, terrorism, to some extent, had been superseded by ideologically oriented attempts at mass political action. The question was whether a base for mass political action existed, as yet, in Russia. In 1879, a split occurred among the *narodniki* (populists). One group opted for terrorism. Others sought to develop an eclectic and programmatic socialism that was rooted in the needs of the Russian population (still overwhelmingly rural) and that could be the basis for a campaign of peaceful propaganda. The development of the peasant masses was emphasized; Russian radicalism was seen as potentially successful only if it could address itself to the direct needs and the long-term development of the peasantry. Though the populists stressed the virtue of evolving a communal democracy based on the primary traditions of village life, they were not completely anti-industrial; true, industry was considered secondary, but at least some of the *narodniki* put forward schemes to develop cottage industries and to establish mixed agricultural-industrial activities in the countryside.

Nor were the populists completely antithetical to Marxism. In Russia itself, and in the centers of emigré life, Marxist influence can be dated to the 1870s. In the 1880s, the most authoritative advocate and interpreter of Marxist ideas was Georgii Plekhanov, who was to be Lenin's mentor.

Plekhanov attacked the populist thesis that, in Russia, capitalism was not developing sufficiently to warrant the full application of the Marxist schema. He pointed out that Russia could not expect to transcend the capitalist experience and that the notion of a peasant-based socialism was a chimera. Eventually, Russia, like the European countries, would develop as an industrial society, and therefore its socialists would have to address themselves to the revolutionary potential inherent in industrial class conflict. The newly emerging industrial workers, rather than the peasantry, were the key to the future transformation of Russian society.

But Plekhanov realized that the revolutionary movement in Russia would have to move through a number of stages before it could be guided by the same kind of considerations that prevailed in Europe. This problem of developmental lag had already been faced by Marx. In the 1840s he had written that in Germany, in view of the lag in industrial development and in political maturity as compared to France and Great Britain, it would be necessary at first to work with the bourgeoisie in their struggle against the autocracy; only later would it be possible to shift to a struggle based on the proletariat and to establish socialism at the expense of the bourgeoisie. Plekhanov advocated a similar "two-stage" concept of revolution; this was dominant until 1905, when Lenin and Trotsky, in somewhat different ways, began to challenge it. Even as late as 1917, the two-stage concept was adhered to by the vast majority of Russian radicals; it came as a shock to hear Lenin advocate a rapid transition, without an intervening period of "bourgeois democracy," to the establishment of the bases of a socialist society.

This was the background of Lenin's involvement in revolutionary activity. His early experience in the heartland of rural Russia; his family background; the economic and social transition that was taking place in Russia; the emergence of a radical political culture running counter to Tsarism—these were the elements that shaped Lenin till, in the early 1890s, he emerged as an active participant in revolutionary circles in St. Petersburg.

Thus, if Lenin's becoming a revolutionary is closely associated with the fate of his brother Alexander, it was not just because of sibling emulation or desire for revenge, but because the same influences were operative in both cases. Their upbringing made for a sense of direction and of personal mission; they matured as inner-directed men into a society that was groping for a key to its future. Not only Alexander and Vladimir, but the other Ulyanov siblings were later to become involved, in the main, in revolutionary activity. Perhaps the role of Alexander should be subordinated to a consideration of the possible influence of Ilya Ulyanov. Is it too much to suggest that, to the degree to which he successfully instilled in his children the ideals of self-discipline and service to society, Ilya Ulyanov may have opened up the path to their later revolutionary

activity? Discipline, persistence, and devotion to Russia—the values inculcated by the elder Ulyanovs—were values which remained with Lenin
throughout his life and which sustained him in his revolutionary career;
they were projected by him as guidelines for his adherents in such works
as *What Is to Be Done?*.

During the years of Alexander II's reign, when apparently enlightened
policies seemed to favor the reform, Ilya Ulyanov could apply these
values to his chosen task of educational reform. A changed political context led to a shift in the direction posited by these values—towards acceptance of the rigors of revolutionary activity. As reform stagnated and
then, under Alexander III, gave way to outright and clumsily implemented reaction, an ever-widening gulf opened between the needs of
society and the policies of Tsarism. A strongly developed sense of duty,
a well-ordered, disciplined life-style, and a highly intellectualized sensitivity to the needs of society were the instrumental values that Ilya and
Maria Ulyanov had inculcated in their children; but the ends which
these values were to serve had now changed. Thus it was that Vladimir,
the second son of Ilya Ulyanov, set off on the path that was to lead him
to become the man we now know as Lenin.

II

For over twenty years, Lenin worked for the destruction of Tsarism.
Ironically, in 1917, his party, the Bolsheviks, played a virtually insignificant role in toppling the regime. What occurred, in March, 1917, was
essentially a collapse from within rather than a revolutionary uprising.
War-weariness, food riots, and the internal weaknesses and dissensions
of the regime were the decisive factors that, in immediate terms, produced
the fall of Tsarism.

Between Lenin's return to Russia, in April, 1917, and the Bolshevik
seizure of power (November 7, 1917), the main question was what kind
of political system would ultimately take the place of Tsarism and how
such a system would be brought into being. The enemy that Lenin confronted was the Provisional Government—really, a shifting series of coalitions; beyond that, there was a danger of societal drift into anarchy. Yet
the concepts which Lenin had formulated when his main target was
Tsarism were not entirely irrelevant to the new situation. True, the Bolsheviks came to power through a coup d'etat; it was a specific operation,
the technique of which had been delineated by Lenin in the preceding
months (see below, pp. 62–74), rather than the protracted revolutionary
struggle he had earlier envisioned would develop against Tsarism. But
the coup was a focal point in a broader process of revolutionary change.
The problem was not simply that of seizing power. Holding power and
holding together a society within which power could be meaningfully
exercised were far more intimidating problems.

Lenin had realized well before 1917 that to make a *political* revolution would not, in itself, suffice to meet the needs of Russia. Revolutionary transformation of society and economy were more significant and much more difficult to achieve. Industrialization under Tsarism had already brought Russia into the early phase of developmental takeoff. Further industrial development and the implementation of a Marxist program of social change ranked high on Lenin's agenda. An added dimension was that the Russian revolution occurred during a period of global socio-political transformation, epitomized by the First World War. To disengage from the military imbroglio and to find a place for Russia in rapidly changing world politics: this, too, was a key aspect of Lenin's strategic thought and action.

Like other ideologies, Lenin's operated on a number of levels. Leninism derived its basic ideology, at the metaphysical and teleological levels, most directly from classical Marxism (and, ultimately, from Hegel). Ultimate historical and sociopolitical processes were envisaged as the dialectical interpenetration and transmutation of opposites. At the teleological level, the Leninist ideology interpreted social development as an historical process whereby emerging contradictions in a social system reflect strains in the economic structure as it attempts to absorb new material and technological developments. Such contradictions can be resolved only by conflict in the socioeconomic system (primarily, class conflict), which results in a shift to a synthesized, presumably more advanced, socioeconomic order. But this ultimately sets in train even more complex processes of socioeconomic development through contradiction, breakdown, and resynthesis on a changed base. This developmental teleology is codified in the Marx-Engels conception of stages of historical development. Stages are identified according to whatever class allegedly dominates in the social structure during a given historical period. A sequence of successive stages is delineated: from primitive, to feudal, to bourgeois capitalist society, and thence (ultimately) via socialism, in various substages of development, to communism—the "classless society."

Nineteenth-century Russian intellectuals had searched for an ordering concept that could be applied to a society caught in a bewildering process of multidimensional change. Marx's schema was attractive even to Russian radicals conscious of the difficulties inherent in applying it outside of the Western European framework. Lenin, like Plekhanov before him, seemed initially little concerned with the problems that the application of Marxism would engender in a predominantly peasant country. In his view, capitalism had already made significant inroads on Russian agrarian society. Later, however, though he retained the main outlines of the Marxist schema, he made considerable modifications to its content. Thus, his theory of revolutionary strategy accorded more significance to the peasantry and to nationalist movements than seemed consistent with classical Marxism.

Further changes were foreshadowed by Lenin's efforts to come to grips with the bases of Marxist theory. They were initiated on the eve of the First World War and continued whenever he could spare the time from more immediate organizational questions of the following few years. Lenin was led back to a reconsideration of the metaphysical foundations of Marxism and, in particular, to a personal reevaluation of the Hegelian dialectic. His notes, however, are fragmentary; moreover, the outbreak of the revolution aborted the possibility that Lenin might have developed a well-articulated position on the fundamentals of Marxist theory.

Lenin sought (see, for example, his summary of dialectics, pp. 30–31 below) a broad theoretical underpinning for a voluntaristic, only partially determined, conception of revolutionary action and transformation. In his summary of dialectics, he associates everything from the plus-minus relationship in mathematics to the class struggle in society. He concludes that "the condition for the knowledge of all processes of the world . . . in their real life, is the knowledge of them as a unity of opposites. Development is the 'struggle' of opposites," and Lenin sees the ability to differentiate these opposites and to discern their reciprocal relation as "the key . . . to the 'break in continuity,' to the 'transformation into the opposite,' to the destruction of the old and the emergence of the new." By inference, this is also the key to the delineation of revolutionary strategy. Thus, Lenin's study of Hegelianism is something more than abstraction for the sake of abstraction. It was an intrinsic part of his intellectual preparation for revolution.

Metaphysics and teleology (as theory, in its purer sense) were at the core of the ideological process. Derivative from this core, three levels of ideology—"situational," "operational," and "instrumental" (in our terms)—constitute the ideological bond that links theory to action. For Lenin, as for Marx, the first step is the metaphysical analysis of motive forces of history; next comes teleological analysis—the delineation of various phases of the historical process, forming, dissolving, and giving way, ultimately, to the new. These are preliminaries to the formulation of strategy and tactics. To make the leap from theory to the revolutionary process, one must be able to look at history in terms of "where it's at," i.e., to make an appraisal of the situation. The dialectic, in itself, may not have been the key to history; but, confronted by revolutionary change, Lenin, as a student of dialectic, was psychologically armed for action—and this was at least as important. He was confident that he could discern the relationship of a projected course of action to basic historical givens and, hence, to a desired target in the future.

Lenin's earliest analyses of the Russian situation were based on the premise that economic transformation under Tsarism had already brought Russia to the point where her evolution could be evaluated according to criteria reasonably close to those appropriate to capitalist

Europe. For a time, Lenin could see himself as operating within a frame of action essentially consistent with that of the mainstream European socialists—even though he did not agree with them on all points. Lenin's controversies with his more democratic opponents in the Russian Socialist movement sharpened the differences between Bolshevism and the Western mainstream. Despite this, Lenin maintained the essentials of his original position until the aftermath of the Russian Revolution of 1905.

The experience of 1905 led Lenin to believe that the preparation for revolution was not necessarily dependent upon a long period of bourgeois transformation. In the decade that followed, Lenin developed a modified situational analysis, as a consequence of which other changes ensued in his total ideology. Ultimately, the theory of imperialism enabled Lenin to place his analysis of the Russian situation in the context of a fundamentally revised conception of the international system. International society was now viewed in twofold perspective. On the one hand, it had evolved highly advanced and readily transferable structures and processes for socioeconomic organization (as embodied in monopoly capitalism); as "monopoly" or "finance capitalism," imperialism represented a higher substage of that capitalism which allegedly laid the basis for socialism. On the other hand, in geopolitical terms, the international system was wracked by irreversible crises (the First World War and the dislocations in the colonial and semicolonial world).

In Lenin's view, it was now possible to force the pace of revolution in such "backward" countries as Russia, for these comprised the "weak links" in the system of imperialism. Furthermore, because of the transferability of new technologies and new systems of organization, and because of the possibility that once the "weak links" showed the way the advanced countries would also succumb to revolution, the initial revolutions in countries such as Russia could be sustained and further developed. This series of propositions differed fundamentally from the original Leninist model that had been taken over almost bodily from orthodox European Marxism.

From this there stemmed the operational and instrumental aspects of Lenin's ideology. Basing himself until 1905 on the situational appraisal made in the late 1890s, Lenin saw revolutionary strategy as turning on the need for Russian socialists to act as critical collaborators of the bourgeoisie in making the "democratic revolution." As a result, a structure of political liberties would emerge within which it would be possible to prepare for the ultimate transition from capitalism by engaging in widespread organizational and propaganda activity. Meanwhile, further development of capitalist economy and society would occur under the aegis of the new bourgeois-democratic regime; the infrastructure for socialism would be created, and contradictions between the bourgeoisie and the working class would be exacerbated.

After 1905, Lenin's radicalism was intensified and his strategic concept became increasingly voluntaristic. The timespan envisaged for revolution was condensed (though, as late as January, 1917, he still expressed the view that socialist revolutions might not occur in the lifetime of his own generation). In the aftermath of 1905, Lenin developed the concept of "uninterrupted revolution" (somewhat different conceptually from Trotsky's "permanent revolution," though the thrust of the two doctrines was similar). The proletariat, and the more disadvantaged peasantry, led by the Bolsheviks, would still be active partners in a phase of the revolution that would be initially dominated by the bourgeoisie. (This conception of the first phase remained essentially unchanged until Lenin's return to Russia in April, 1917.) But in the course of the "bourgeois" phase of the revolution, the proletarian revolutionaries would constantly press for ever more radical measures, extorting these as the price for their support. Particular emphasis would be placed on the need, during the bourgeois phase, to extirpate the remnants of the old order. The bourgeois democrats, having won a victory over the autocracy, would be forced under pressure from their radical "allies" to destroy the props of the social order; ultimately, they would find themselves bereft of support from potential allies on the right, stripped of a structure for maintaining public order, and facing an increasingly radicalized mass of the population.

Rather than wait for a new phase of revolution to begin, in order to push forward with their own program on the basis of a matured capitalist society, the proletariat and its peasant allies would (under Bolshevik direction) press on with a revolution of its own within the context of the broader political revolution. In the pre-1905 version of Lenin's strategy, the proletariat were radical allies of the bourgeoisie, seeking to promote political revolution as a preliminary to their own; now they were transformed into the central core of a Bolshevik-dominated mass alliance embodying discontented elements wherever they could be found—particularly among the poorer peasants and the national minorities. This revised conception, further modified in the direction of even greater accommodation (temporary though it might be) of the peasantry, made Bolshevik doctrine transferable to the Third World. At the same time, this became one of the features which differentiated Leninism from the Marxism of the West.

A number of specific elements which had developed piecemeal were fitted into the general framework of the operational ideology. Thus, the notion that the proletariat should work in tandem with bourgeois liberals to establish a democratic republic, as the initial phase of a revolution, had entailed some residual faith in the value of civic liberties. Though his authoritarianism had been manifest at an early date (particularly in his concept of the party, where it was excused on the grounds that Tsarist police methods rendered a democratic party ineffectual), it was not until World War I that Lenin moved completely to the position that bourgeois democracy offered few liberties worth having. As the war progressed, suppression of dissent in the European countries enhanced Lenin's cynicism about Western democracy. In his writings, he effectively used these aberrations from prewar liberal democracy to push his attack against the moderates; the Bolsheviks could no longer be dismissed as Russian extremists reacting to the "barbarism" of Tsarism; instead they constituted a model for dissident socialists in the West who were forced to consider, or to adopt, extraparliamentary and underground methods.

Thus, such works as *State and Revolution* and, later, *The Proletarian Revolution and the Renegade Kautsky* make the case, among others, for aborting the development of a "bourgeois-democratic phase" of the Russian Revolution. From 1915, various of Lenin's writings stressed the transferability to Russia of new forms of organization and administration that had emerged under advanced capitalist conditions in the most highly developed countries. Techniques used in big business management, particularly in Germany and the United States, could provide possible shortcuts for the transition to socialism. Cost accounting, as the key to administrative control, and time and motion studies, as a basis for imparting standardized operations to a mass of uneducated workers and peasants, appealed to Lenin's penchant for logic and practicality. He evidently thought that, by superimposing such techniques on revolutionary Russia after the *political* revolution had been carried out, it would be possible to establish at least a rudimentary socialist state and to keep such a state in existence until the capitalist West, as a result of its own revolutions, crossed over to an advanced form of socialism.

The role of the Bolshevik Party was emphasized at the instrumental level of ideology; the party was the key to direction and organization in the society. Lenin's view of the significance of the party changed but little from the early 1900s. Lenin's "party of a new type" consisted of disciplined professional revolutionaries who would provide the organizational base to apply an arsenal of strategic and tactical instrumentalities to the making of revolution. The party was a two-edged sword: on the one hand, it sought to divide the forces of the enemy; conversely (and especially in the later statements of Lenin's position), it formed, and then sought to control, alliances of the discontented.

The role of the party in the revolutionary alliance was central to Lenin's strategic concept of both the political revolution and the postrevolutionary transformation of society. Without the tight discipline and continuity of purpose that was enshrined in Lenin's notion of the party, the party itself would be weakened by the wider and more "spontaneous" revolutionary alliance. Only by hewing rigidly to the basic purpose and organization of the party could Lenin afford the necessary tactical flexibility, operational relativism, and freedom to form alliances that were required for both the seizure of power and the postrevolutionary maintenance of the Soviet system.

It is at this point that theory and action join. Here again, we refer to those abstruse, and—at first glance—purely theoretical notes on dialectics:

> The unity (coincidence, identity, resultant) of opposites is conditional, temporary, transitory, relative. The struggle of mutually exclusive opposites is absolute, just as development and motion are absolute.

> N. B. The distinction between subjectivism (skepticism, sophistry, etc.) and dialectics, incidentally, is that in (objective) dialectics the difference between the relative and the absolute is itself relative. To objective dialectics there *is* an absolute even *within* the relative. To subjectivism and sophistry the relative is only relative and excludes the absolute.

The notion of an "absolute within the relative" is central to Lenin's revolutionary style; it is epitomized by his ability to maintain a strategic end in view even while executing tactical flip-flops. The view that Lenin, as revolutionary activist, was simply a successful opportunist is maintained by dismissing his theoretical concepts as irrelevant to his politics. It might be argued, however, that it was precisely the nature of his theoretical insights that prepared Lenin to cope with the demands that would be made on him by the complexities of a revolutionary situation. The doctrinal consistency which he maintained at the core of his ideology contributed to a self-confidence that enabled him, on essentially tactical issues, to indulge in the kind of "battlefield flexibility" required by a rapidly changing revolutionary situation. Nevertheless, on certain basics —for example, the need to take Russia out of the war—Lenin never deviated from a position arrived at long before this stance became politically opportune. Also, though details varied with circumstances, Lenin's essential approach to the peasantry and the nationalities had been prepared, long in advance of the Revolution, by years of theoretical consideration and ideological disputes.

Many of Lenin's colleagues and opponents were awed by the immensity of the challenge posed by the revolution and were swallowed up in events. Lenin succeeded because he was prepared to *act* in the revolution; this ability to act developed not in spite of, but because of, his supposed ideological-organizational rigidity. In 1917, Lenin was much more than the spoiler who is seen to have destroyed the prospects for democracy in Russia. Rather, he was the man who was prepared, after the seizure of power, to do what he felt was necessary to prevent a slide into social chaos and, however warped the result, to attempt to establish a reconstructed social order.

III

The dualism of Lenin's objectives necessitates a corresponding two-fold approach to the task of assessing his success. He created and directed the Bolshevik party with an immediate objective in mind: the seizure of power. But his long-range goal was more basic: the radical transformation of Russia's economy and society, a transformation that was, in turn, related to an even more far-ranging program of global change. Thus, *political* revolution was an end in itself only in the most immediate sense; in the broader context, Lenin's success in 1917 can only be regarded as instrumental.

It is now generally agreed that Lenin's active participation in the Bolshevik revolution was necessary to his party's success in seizing power. Between April and November, 1917, Lenin played a vital role—often against the opposition of his closest associates—in pointing the Bolsheviks toward the coup. On his return to Russia, Lenin unveiled a more radical program in opposition to the Provisional Government than his colleagues had anticipated. In the last few weeks before the coup, Lenin, from his hiding place in Finland, peppered the Bolsheviks with secret and detailed memoranda, and, after his return to Petrograd, outargued those who cautioned further delay; in the end, he took over the close strategic direction of the rising. For months, then, he had goaded his followers to a test of strength on which the fate of the revolution was seen to depend. But he was equally capable of counselling restraint when this was required to secure the survival of the revolution. This was particularly evident in the months following the seizure of power, when, once more against intense opposition from his colleagues, Lenin advocated making the drastic concessions necessary to secure peace with the Germans.

We have already suggested that the ideological preparation that took place before 1917 contributed significantly to Lenin's success as a revolutionary. Beyond this, one should assess factors inherent in the nature of the Provisional Government, the context within which the struggle for power took place, and, finally, Lenin's own qualities of leadership. Adam Ulam assessed the Bolshevik role in the revolution as follows:

> The Bolsheviks did not seize power in this year of revolutions. They picked it up. First autocracy, then democracy capitulated to the forces of anarchy. Any group of determined men could have done what the Bolsheviks did in Petrograd in October 1917: seize the few key points of the city and proclaim themselves the government. . . . It is not in the maker of the revolution that we can see Lenin's genius in its fullest; far greater is his achievement as its conqueror.[2]

[2] Adam B. Ulam, *The Bolsheviks* (New York: Macmillan, 1965), p. 314.

The Provisional Government against which Lenin and the Bolsheviks conspired was, in reality, a series of coalitions of factions and individuals, inherently unable to develop a coherent and consistent program. It failed to fill the vacuum of power and authority that resulted from the fall of Tsarism and was tragically myopic and indecisive in its policies. Though clearly little or nothing could be done to prevent the peasants from seizing the land, the provisional regime procrastinated in adopting a viable land policy; it refused to conciliate the peasants by giving some legal recognition to the *fait accompli* of land seizure. This could only play into the hands of the more radical opponents of the government. A segment of the peasant-based Socialist Revolutionary party, whose support was vital to Premier Kerensky, became alienated from the government and aligned itself, *de facto,* with the Bolsheviks. Furthermore, the forlorn effort to prosecute the war against Germany was continued long after it became clear that this could only contribute to a drastic erosion of support for the government among both the troops and the civilians in a war-weary country.

The Provisional Government was weak from the moment of its inception. The suddenness and completeness of the collapse of Tsarism, together with its supporting structures, occurring in the midst of a disastrous war, created an almost impossible situation for *any* would-be successor. This is not to say that the actions of the Provisional Government's opponents were irrelevant to its decline. The Bolsheviks placed great burdens on the government's capacity to survive, but they were not the only contributors to its collapse. Attacks on the provisional regime were launched not only by the Bolsheviks, but by non-Bolshevik left-wing groups and, militarily, by the right. The attempted *putsch* by General Kornilov, in September, 1917, set in train the weakening of the Kerensky government, and drove a wedge between the government and the officers' corps, which was a necessary prelude to Bolshevik victory. Russia's allies made selfish, short-sighted, and, ultimately, impossible demands on her to actively continue the war. They did not appear to realize that, in seeking Russian military pressure on the Germans as a way of gaining some respite in the West, they were intensifying the domestic pressures on Kerensky and his associates and thus easing the path to further revolution.

A number of basic factors contributed to Bolshevik success in the revolution and civil war:

1. Russian society had been sapped by the World War; its underlying structure for maintaining authority had, by and large, eroded beyond the point where it might have helped sustain the Provisional Government.

2. The continuation of the war in the West during the year following the Bolshevik coup precluded a really effective intervention by foreign

powers in Russia's affairs. Such intervention as did occur was not pushed with sufficient vigor to seriously affect the outcome of the civil war. After November, 1918, a desire to return to "normalcy" quickly enveloped the Allied countries and there was increasing reluctance to continue military action in Russia.

3. Bolshevik antiwar propaganda found fertile ground in Russia, especially within an army that had suffered casualties mounting into the millions in the course of three years of war. Lenin successfully used this against the Provisional Government; with Trotsky's aid he was able—but just barely—to counter war-weariness when the Bolshevik regime was faced with civil war from mid-1918 on.

4. The Russian peasantry was a potentially powerful force which any serious claimant to power had at least to neutralize. During the civil war anti-Bolshevik forces alienated the peasants, who believed that the "Whites" intended to restore the old landholding system. The peasants were not, in fact, enamored of the Bolsheviks: they resisted government requisitioning of food and, in some districts formed partisan bands which fought against both the Reds and the Whites. Nevertheless, the Bolsheviks managed their policy in the countryside more effectively than the Whites, and, in balance, were the gainers from the peasants' desire to hold onto the land they had seized.

5. Strategically, the Bolsheviks were in a favorable position during the civil war, since they were defending the "interior lines." Moreover, Tsarist centralization was reflected in a countrywide communications infrastructure so organized that whoever controlled Moscow and Petrograd would have an advantage in any long, drawn-out struggle. This was augmented by the degree of support for the Bolsheviks, however grudging it was at times, on the part of railwaymen and other workers in transport and communications.

Yet ultimately, beyond the factors listed, one must recognize the significance of Lenin's political personality and the nature of his political leadership. Over the years, tempered by party struggles, Lenin had attained a position of considerable authority among his followers. This did not mean that he faced no opposition; the days when "democratic centralism" meant unchallenged rule, à la Stalin, were yet to come. In April, 1917, when his program was more radical than that of his main supporters; in the fall of 1917, when he was pushing the party to dare the seizure of power; after November, when he had to go so far as to threaten resignation to gain acquiescence to peace on the terms forced on the Soviets by the Germans—on all these occasions, Lenin strove against considerable opposition in Bolshevik ranks. But, in the end, he was able to push through policies substantially his own and to impose a unity of purpose on his party. This was largely the result of his own charisma. In contrast to the relative unity of Lenin and the Bolsheviks, both the domestic and the international enemies of Bolshevism during the revolution and civil war were divided in their counsels and half-hearted in their efforts to attain their objectives.

Some of Lenin's personal traits (as illustrated in many of the documents in this volume) may be summarized at this point; they constituted decisive weights in the revolutionary struggle: his instinct for the creation of alliances and his skill in fragmenting, through propaganda and tactical shifts, the unity of his opponents; his decisiveness as regards both ultimate goals and the timing and mode of action for a particular move; his ability, especially under pressure, to organize himself and his adherents for effective action; his persuasiveness and ability to dominate his associates and make them accept the course of action he desired; his charisma; his skill in communicating his ideas to people of widely varying levels of sophistication; his flexibility; his willingness, if necessary, to surrender the appearance of power in the short run for the sake of long-term gains. Many of these are the desired attributes of a successful political figure of any place and time; they were particularly important for the revolutionary leader whose society was undergoing a rapid process of change.

But success in the *political* revolution was only one aspect of the task that confronted Lenin. How successful was Lenin in addressing the broader problems of societal transformation? An ultimate answer to this must await the historian who has gained sufficient perspective to assess the long-range validity of the political system that Lenin helped to create; the two questions are, of course, interwoven.

The criteria for weighing success in the revolutionary "politician"—the man whose concern is to gain power—are not necessarily the same for the revolutionary "statesman," i.e., the *user* of the power thus gained in pursuit of certain ends. For the political revolutionary, the key to success lies in the qualities of thought and action that enable him to reflect and transmute fundamental tendencies in his society so as to bring about a change in the configuration of power. Politically, the revolutionary politician acts as a prism, gathering and focusing basic aspirations, resentments, and frustrations, and coordinating them in a program of revolutionary action.

The revolutionary statesman deals with dimensions of transformation that are more fundamental. Here, Lenin's task was twofold. On the one hand, he continued the processes that had been at work in Russia for some considerable time. Early biographers compared Lenin to Peter the Great, and, while the analogy is not complete, nevertheless it is not totally inappropriate. Historically, Lenin was one of the great "modernizers from above"; but he based his effort not on dynastic continuity, but on the harnessing of a primary revolutionary force. On the other hand, as a prototypical radical intellectual in the twentieth century, Lenin did not completely fit into the chain of historical continuity in the Russian drive for modernization; he was a radical innovator, a would-be implementor of dreams that had not yet been tested elsewhere.

The very factors that contributed to Lenin's success in gaining power in the revolution may have hampered his efforts in the more complex areas of social change. Political revolution calls for daring on the part of the leaders, for an optimism that may even be misplaced about the prospects for change in a complex and crisis-ridden society. Lenin's confidence in undertaking the task of political revolution may have clouded, for a time, his awareness of just how difficult the postrevolutionary transformation would be. A similar contradiction may be noted when we consider the milieu within which Lenin operated. The deterioration of Russian society at the end of the Tsarist period and its virtually complete disruption by 1917 undercut the authority first of Tsarism and then of the Provincial Government, and paved the way for the Bolshevik conquest of power. But once Lenin had gained power, these same conditions worked against him: he was now confronted by the almost complete breakdown of the components on which the reconstruction of Russia would have to be based.

Lenin's conception of how Russia might be transformed was based on his perception of what had been achieved under the most advanced forms of capitalist organization in the West. He believed that the organization and administrative practices of corporate capitalism were transferable and transmutable and could serve to shorten the developmental process if harnessed to socialist objectives and techniques for social mobilization. His argument in *State and Revolution* (particularly when he refers to administration as being analogous to running a post office—something that anyone can learn to do) has sometimes been interpreted as a harkening back to anarchism. In the light of Lenin's appreciation of political organization and his long-standing antipathy to anarchism, it would have been strange if this were the case. Such an interpretation would require that we regard *State and Revolution*, the last of Lenin's major writings prior to the seizure of power, as an aberration in his thinking. But Lenin was not, in fact, repudiating his earlier emphasis on the importance of organization. Rather, if we read *State and Revolution* together with other writings of the time and with his notes on political and economic questions, it appears that Lenin arrived at his conclusions on the basis of a somewhat overenthusiastic interpretation of the significance of early theorists (primarily American) of management and organization. In extrapolating from the work of Frederick Taylor and others, and applying their ideas to political organization, Lenin was guided by the Marxist interpretation of the division of labor as well as by his own conception of the ability of an organized elite party to mobilize and direct the more talented members of the working class. He concluded that administrative tasks which, in aggregate, were complex and sophisticated could be subdivided into easily learned routines; these could be mastered, if the techniques of mass education were effectively applied, by large numbers of people only recently raised from illiteracy. Capping the whole structure, an organized party of the Bolshevik type would keep the system so conceived in working order and direct it to the achievement of ideologically-defined policy objectives.

Lenin drastically underestimated the difficulties, even in the Western countries, inherent in the attempt to apply the new concepts of management and organization. He was willing to make an imaginative leap from the avant-garde bourgeois theories of business administration to the realm of practical politics partly because of the need to grasp at any straw that held out hope for a rapid development of an advanced and efficient social system once the revolution had been achieved. Once his optimism proved to be grounded on misconceptions about the applicability of these and other techniques to the Russian situation, Lenin was left bereft of any transcendent plan of operations; he was thrown back on the more immediate imperatives of keeping the regime going and safeguarding it against challenges inside and outside the country. Parts of his basic conception remained, but these were fragmentary and were abstracted from the original theoretical framework. His economic planning derived less from Marxism than from wartime planning experiences, particularly in Imperial Germany; he was also aware of the studies of resource development undertaken during the last years of the Tsarist regime by the Imperial Academy of Sciences.

In the aftermath of 1917, Lenin had also counted on the short-range prospects for socialist revolution in Western and Central Europe. The Russian example, combined with war-weariness abroad, would lead to the internationalization of the revolutionary process. If such external revolutions did not occur and succeed, the Russian revolution would not be able to survive for long—or, at least, Russia would be unable, in isolation, to go very far toward socialism. Here, Trotsky was not alone in his assessment. But though the wave of revolution in the aftermath of the war reached as far west as Germany, Europe, in the end, held firm against revolutionary change. Lenin was left to be the helmsman of an isolated revolutionary state, its survival assured, at least temporarily, but its prospects for development in the short run severely curtailed.

Out of these disappointments, the paradigm of post-Civil War Leninism emerges. The retreat to the New Economic Policy was a sign of Lenin's political realism and his willingness to put survival ahead of other considerations. But retreat was not easy to accept. And the retreat did not put an end to the problems of the Bolshevik regime. To evolve on the basis of the New Economic Policy required the capability of maneuvering amidst a welter of contradictory political, social, and economic forces, both internal and international.

In that brief period of power between the end of the civil war and his final illness and isolation from the active direction of Soviet policy, Lenin gradually became aware of the degree to which, in the process of trying to create a new society, he had become the prisoner of a complex dialectic of forces. What was required to halt stagnation of the Revolution and a drift into personal dictatorship were the talents of a new Lenin—and even these might not have sufficed. In his illness, Lenin came to realize that the system he had created, and, in particular, the "party of the new type," had failed to bring forth an heir adequate to the situation. The man most likely to win the already emerging battle for the succession, Stalin (against whom Lenin issued explicit warnings), was already showing precisely those characteristics of autocracy and fanaticism that Lenin saw as the worst features of the old regime. Isaac Deutscher has characterized these last days of Lenin as a period in which his "moral dilemma" came to the fore. The conditions exploited by Lenin in his drive for political power had persisted as underlying forces and frustrated the achievement of the social and, ultimately, moral transformation that was the eventual objective of the revolution. The revolution was in the process of being conquered by the men whom it had brought to power, and distorted Leninism was coming to the fore as Lenin himself passed from the scene.

Chronology of the Life of Lenin

1870	Born April 10/22 [1] in Simbirsk. Given name: Vladimir Ilyich Ulyanov.
1883	Beginnings of organized development of Russian Marxism; in Switzerland, Plekhanov and other emigrés form Liberation of Labor group.
1886	Death of Ilya Ulyanov, Lenin's father.
1887	Older brother, Alexander, arrested and executed for his role in plot to assassinate Tsar Alexander III.
	Enters University of Kazan; expelled in December for participating in student demonstration.
1888–93	Member of revolutionary study groups, Kazan and Samara.
1891	Passes extramural law examinations.
1893	Moves to St. Petersburg; participates in Marxist study and propaganda groups. Meets Nadezhda Krupskaya.
1895	Goes abroad, meets Plekhanov. Returns to St. Petersburg, and joins Martov to establish St. Petersburg Union of Struggle for the Liberation of the Working Class. Arrested in December.
1896–1900	Prison, followed by Siberian exile. Writes *The Development of Capitalism in Russia* (completed 1898).
1898	Marries Nadezhda Krupskaya.
1900	Completes period of exile, goes abroad. Reestablishes contact with Plekhanov. Plans publication of revolutionary newspaper as core of party organization; first issue of *Iskra* ("The Spark"), December, 1900.
1902	*What Is to Be Done?* sets forth his concept of revolutionary party.
1903	Second Congress of Russian Social-Democratic Labor Party. Two factions emerge: Bolsheviks (led by Lenin) and Mensheviks.
1904–05	Russo-Japanese War: Russia suffers major defeat.
1905	Revolution in Russia.
	January 9/22: "Bloody Sunday"—troops in St. Petersburg fire on peaceful demonstration led by Orthodox priest, Georgii Gapon.
	Fall: extensive strikes, culminating in general strike in St. Petersburg. Trade unionists organize "soviets" (workers' councils).

[1] Where dual dates are given, the first is according to the prerevolutionary calendar; the second according to the familiar Western calendar, adopted in Russia in February, 1918. The Russian calendar lagged twelve days behind the Western in the nineteenth century, thirteen days in the early twentieth.

	October: Tsar promises to consider reforms, and to establish Duma (parliament).
	November: Lenin returns to Russia.
1907	Lenin goes abroad; does not return until 1917.
1908–10	Philosophical and cultural controversies among Bolsheviks. Lenin writes *Materialism and Empirio-Criticism* (1908), the beginning of the "party line" in the areas of philosophy and culture.
1912	Prague conference of Bolsheviks. Lenin consolidates his position as the leader of a truly separate party.
	Strikes and peasant unrest in Russia. Lenin moves to Poronino, in Austrian Poland, just across the border from Russia.
1914	August: outbreak of war; Lenin arrested by Austrians, but allowed to go to Switzerland after intercession by Austrian Social-Democratic parliamentarians.
	Most European Social-Democratic parties split over question of support for national war efforts. Lenin adopts militant antiwar position.
1915	Lenin's propaganda stresses need to convert "imperialist war" into "revolutionary war."
	September: conference of antiwar socialists from various countries, Zimmerwald, Switzerland; Lenin's influence rises in the international left.
1916	Completes *Imperialism* and begins work on *State and Revolution*.
1917	February/March: fall of Tsarist regime, formation of Provisional Government.
	April 3/16: Lenin and other emigrés arrive from Switzerland after having been allowed to pass through Germany. "April Theses."
	July: abortive left-wing uprising; Lenin in hiding.
	August/September: abortive coup by General Kornilov; Provisional Government gets aid from railway workers; in aftermath, left wing begins to recover momentum.
	Late October: in face of opposition from such colleagues as Zinoviev and Kamenev, Lenin persuades Bolshevik leadership that the time is ripe for armed rising.
	October 25/November 7: Bolsheviks seize power in Petrograd. Soviet government proclaimed, followed by Decrees on Peace and on land reform.
	November 12/25: elections for Constituent Assembly; Bolsheviks receive only one-quarter of vote.
	December 2/15: Soviet-German armistice, followed by peace negotiations at Brest-Litovsk.
1918	January: Constituent Assembly meets one day and then is dispersed.
	February 19: nationalization of land.
	March 3: after bitter debate, Lenin persuades colleagues to accept Brest-Litovsk peace; heavy losses of population and territory.

23

	Beginning of Civil War and Allied intervention (to 1920–21)
	August 30: Fanya Kaplan attempts to kill Lenin.
1919	Third International (Comintern).
1920	Tide turns in favor of Bolsheviks in Civil War.
	Treaties with some neighboring states; beginning of negotiations
	to reestablish trade and diplomatic links. Publication of
	"Left-Wing" Communism: An Infantile Disorder.
1920–21	War with Poland; Soviets advance as far as Warsaw, but
	Poles force them to retreat behind original frontier
	(Western aid to Poles).
1921–22	Widespread famine and epidemics.
	Peasants resist food seizures. Other signs of failure of
	stringent economic policy ("War Communism").
1921	Uprising at Kronstadt naval base.
	New Economic Policy: retreat from economic stringency.
1922	Treaty of Rapallo (Germany-Soviet Russia): major
	breakthrough in diplomatic relations with West.
	May: brain hemorrhage; Lenin makes partial recovery by fall.
	Resumes normal activity (November).
	December: second stroke.
1923	Generally incapacitated; confined to country estate near Gorki.
	Dictates "testament" on Party policy and succession to leadership;
	break with Stalin.
1924	January 21: final stroke; dies.
1956	In aftermath of Khrushchev's speech attacking Stalin,
	Lenin's "testament" is published openly for the
	first time in the U.S.S.R.

LENIN LOOKS AT THE WORLD

Lenin was both a man of action and a deeply committed revolutionary theorist. It would be futile to assign priority either to the activist or to the theorist in Lenin; in his view, theory and action were intimately interwoven—theory fed action, while action created new demands for analysis and explanation. Attempts to structure Leninism into a rigid operational code do less than justice to Lenin, unless one keeps in mind that his ideas were subject to the test of revolutionary action.

From the 1890s through 1923, Lenin wrote millions of words for publication; in addition, the texts of many of his speeches survive, particularly those made after 1917. A few dozen books and major pamphlets are supplemented by thousands of articles and speeches and by a vast outpouring of letters, minutes, and memoranda; beyond this, notes and preliminary drafts survive in sufficient number to account for over thirty volumes of miscellania, aside from the fifty-odd volumes of the latest Russian-language edition of Lenin's works.

Thus, any selection from Lenin's works is, of necessity, far from adequate. What follows, it is hoped, will introduce the reader to Lenin's intellectual style, and tempt him to dip into the material that is now available in English. Three kinds of material have been chosen: basic writings on the themes (e.g., Marxism, theory of imperialism) that form the basis of Lenin's view of the world around him; his concepts of revolutionary strategy and tactics, including his theory of the revolutionary party, and the application and modification of these concepts as illustrated in some of his writings of 1917 and 1918; finally, material dealing with problems of domestic and international policy after the establishment of the Soviet state.

1

On Marxism and Imperialism: Some Foundations of Leninism

LENIN ON MARXISM

Throughout his career, Lenin periodically returned to the question of defining classical Marxism and relating it to the needs of revolution in Russia. Even while he was transmuting Marxist doctrine, adapting it to the needs of an underdeveloped country dominated by the peasantry, he attempted to show that the ideology that was evolving under his aegis was in the true spirit of the theories of Marx and Engels. He justified the changes that he introduced on the grounds that Marxism was "not a dogma, but a guide to action"; at the same time, he denounced both his Russian opponents and Western European "revisionists" as perverting the heritage of the founders of "scientific socialism."

In 1913, in an historical sketch of the evolution of Marxism, Lenin argued that Marxist theory was appropriate for the guidance of nationalist revolutionary struggles in underdeveloped countries, as well as for class conflict in industrially mature countries.[1]

The chief thing in the doctrine of Marx is that it brings out the historic role of the proletariat as the builder of socialist society. . . .

Marx first advanced it in 1844. The *Communist Manifesto* of Marx and Engels, published in 1848, gave an integral and systematic exposition of this doctrine, an exposition which has remained the best to this day. Since then world history has clearly been divided into three main periods: (1) from the revolution of 1848 to the Paris Commune (1871); (2) from the Paris Commune to the Russian revolution (1905); (3) since the Russian revolution. . . .

I

At the beginning . . . Marx's doctrine by no means dominated. It was only one of the very numerous groups or trends of socialism. The

[1] From V. I. Lenin, *Marx, Engels, Marxism*, 7th rev. ed. (Moscow: Progress Publishers, 1965), pp. 70–73.

26

forms of socialism that did dominate were in the main akin to . . .
Narodism: incomprehension of the materialist basis of historical movement, inability to single out the role and significance of each class in
capitalist society, concealment of the bourgeois nature of democratic reforms under diverse, quasi-socialist phrases about the "people," "justice,"
"right," and so on.

The revolution of 1848 struck a deadly blow at all these . . . forms of
pre-Marxian socialism. In all countries, the revolution revealed the various classes of society *in action*. . . .

. . . The craven liberals grovelled before reaction. The peasantry
were content with the abolition of the survivals of feudalism and joined
the supporters of order, wavering . . . occasionally between *workers'*
democracy and bourgeois liberalism. All doctrines of *non*-class socialism
and *non*-class politics proved to be sheer nonsense. . . .

In all . . . European countries, . . . a bourgeois society . . . had
taken definite shape. Towards the end of the first period (1848–71), a
period of storms and revolutions, pre-Marxian socialism was *dead*. Independent *proletarian* parties came into being: the First International
(1864–72) and the German Social Democratic Party.

II

The second period (1872–1904) was distinguished from the first by
its "peaceful" character. . . . The West had finished with bourgeois
revolutions. The East had not yet risen to them.

The West entered a phase of "peaceful" preparations for the changes
to come. Socialist parties, basically proletarian, were formed everywhere
and learned to use bourgeois parliamentarism and to found their own
daily press, their educational institutions, their trade unions and their
co-operative societies. Marx's doctrine . . . *began to spread*. The selection and mustering of the forces of the proletariat and its preparation for
the coming battles made slow but steady progress.

The dialectics of history were such that the theoretical victory of
Marxism compelled its enemies to *disguise themselves* as Marxists. Liberalism, rotten within, tried to revive itself in the form of socialist *opportunism*. They interpreted the period of preparing the forces for great
battles as renunciation of these battles. Improvement of the conditions
of the slaves to fight against wage slavery they took to mean the sale by
the slaves of their right to liberty for a few pence. They cravenly preached
"social peace" (i.e., peace with the slave-owners), renunciation of the
class struggle, etc. They had very many adherents among socialist members of parliament, various officials of the working-class movement, and
the "sympathising" intelligentsia.

III

However, the opportunists had scarcely congratulated themselves on "social peace" and on the non-necessity of storms under "democracy" when a new source of great world storms opened up in Asia. The Russian revolution was followed by revolutions in Turkey, Persia and China. It is in this era of storms and their "repercussions" in Europe that we are now living. No matter what the fate of the great Chinese republic, against which various "civilised" hyenas are now whetting their teeth, no power on earth can restore the old serfdom in Asia or wipe out the heroic democracy of the masses in the Asiatic and semi-Asiatic countries.

Certain people . . . were driven to despair and to anarchism by the lengthy delays in the decisive struggle against capitalism in Europe. We can now see how short-sighted and faint-hearted this anarchist despair is. The fact that Asia, with its population of eight hundred million, has been drawn into the struggle for these same European ideals should inspire us with optimism and not despair. . . .

After Asia, Europe has also begun to stir, although not in the Asiatic way. The "peaceful" period of 1872–1904 has passed, never to return. The high cost of living and the tyranny of the trusts are leading to an unprecedented sharpening of the economic struggle, which has set into movement even the British workers who have been most corrupted by liberalism. We see a political crisis brewing even in the most "diehard," bourgeois-Junker country, Germany. The frenzied arming and the policy of imperialism are turning modern Europe into a "social peace" which is more like a gunpowder barrel. Meanwhile the decay of *all* the bourgeois parties and the maturing of the proletariat are making steady progress. . . .

In 1899, Lenin presented a concise synopsis of what, to him, appeared to be the most salient features of Marxist theory.[2]

. . . Marxism was the first to transform socialism from a utopia into a science, . . . and to indicate the path that must be followed in further developing and elaborating [it] . . . It disclosed the nature of modern capitalist economy by explaining how the hire of the labourer, the purchase of labour-power, conceals the enslavement of millions of propertyless people by a handful of capitalists, the owners of the land, factories, mines, and so forth. It showed that all modern capitalist development displays the tendency of large-scale production to eliminate petty produc-

[2] From V. I. Lenin, "Our Differences" (1899), *Marx, Engels, Marxism*, pp. 104–105.

tion and creates conditions that make a socialist system of society possible and necessary. It taught us how to discern, beneath the pall of rooted customs, political intrigues, abstruse laws, and intricate doctrines—the *class struggle,* the struggle between the propertied classes in all their variety and the propertyless mass, the *proletariat,* which is at the head of all the propertyless. It made clear the real task of a revolutionary socialist party: not to draw up plans for refashioning society, not to preach to the capitalists and their hangers-on about improving the lot of the workers, not to hatch conspiracies, *but to organise the class struggle of the proletariat and to lead this struggle, the ultimate aim of which is the conquest of political power by the proletariat and the organisation of a socialist society.*

Lenin's interest in dialectics was closely associated with his perception of the need for applying the operational ideology in a flexible fashion. The connection is implied in his argument against a dogmatic approach to Marxist doctrine.[3]

Our doctrine—said Engels, referring to himself and his famous friend—is not a dogma, but a guide to action. This classical statement stresses with remarkable force and expressiveness that aspect of Marxism which is very often lost sight of. And by losing sight of it, we turn Marxism into something one-sided, distorted and lifeless; we deprive it of its life bood; we undermine its basic theoretical foundations—dialectics, the doctrine of historical development, all-embracing and full of contradictions; we undermine its connection with the definite practical tasks of the epoch, which may change with every new turn of history.

By the outbreak of World War I, Lenin's theory of revolutionary conflict had evolved to a point where it was more voluntaristic than it would have been had he stayed with the qualified determinism of classical Marxism. He was already probing beyond Marxism, seeking a rationale for his concept of political action in its philosophical—essentially metaphysical—underpinnings. Earlier, he had written a philosophical polemic, Materialism and Empirio-Criticism, *directed against the Russian Marxists who, in his view, had been overly influenced by Kantian idealism and the theories of scientific relativism that were beginning to emerge under the aegis of Ernst Mach and others. But this had been directed essentially to*

[3] From V. I. Lenin, "Certain Features of the Historical Development of Marxism" (1911), in *Marx, Engels, Marxism,* p. 241.

the needs of an obscure party dispute; Lenin himself seemed dis-satisfied with it in later years and turned to an intense analysis of the writings of Hegel. In his fragmentary notes on dialectics (1915 or 1916)—a summation of his notebooks on Hegelian and philo-sophical themes—Lenin delineates a view of the dialectic which could serve as a basis for his theory of conflict. His emphasis on the "break in continuity," the "transformation into the opposite," and the "destruction of the old and the emergence of the new" is associated with his increased preoccupation with the direct engineering of a political revolution and revolutionary transformation of society, a transformation that emphasized political voluntarism at the expense of historical determinism.[4]

Division of unity and cognition of its contradictory parts . . . are the *essence* (one of the "essentials," one of the principal, if not the principal, characteristics or features) of dialectics. This is precisely how Hegel too puts the matter. . . .

In mathematics: + and —. Differential and integral.

In mechanics: action and reaction.

In physics: positive and negative electricity.

In chemistry: the combination and dissociation of atoms.

In social science: the class struggle.

The identity of opposites (their "unity," perhaps, . . .) is the recognition . . . of the contradictory, *mutually exclusive,* opposite tendencies in *all* phenomena and processes of nature (*including* mind and society). The condition for the knowledge of all processes of the world in their *"self-movement,"* in their spontaneous development, in their real life, is the knowledge of them as a unity of opposites. Development is the "struggle" of opposites. The two basic (or two possible? or two histori-cally observable?) conceptions of development (evolution) are: develop-ment as decrease and increase, as repetition, *and* development as a unity of opposites (the division of a unity into mutually exclusive opposites and their reciprocal relation). In the first conception of motion, *self-movement,* its *driving* force, its source, its motive, remains in the shade (or this source is made *external*—God, subject, etc.). In the second con-ception it is to knowledge of the *source* of *"self"*-movement that attention is chiefly directed. The first conception is lifeless, pale and dry. The second is vital. The second *alone* furnishes the key to the "self-movement" of everything in existence; it alone furnishes the key to the "leaps," to the "break in continuity," to the "transformation into the opposite," to the destruction of the old and the emergence of the new.

The unity (coincidence, identity, resultant) of opposites is conditional, temporary, transitory, relative. The struggle of mutually exclusive opposites is absolute, just as development and motion are absolute.

LENIN ON IMPERIALISM

Lenin's theory of imperialism is the best known, and most influential, part of his writings. Although his main work on this subject, Imperialism: The Highest Stage of Capitalism, *was not completed until the beginning of 1916, Lenin had explored some of its basic themes as early as the 1890s. He was particularly concerned with the spread of capitalism into underdeveloped areas and its effect not only on the economies of such regions, but on the sociopolitical milieu. In first exploring this subject in connection with the controversies of the 1890s over Russia's development, he drew on detailed statistics of the spread of industry and a market economy in the Russian Empire, and was influenced by Russian socioeconomic thinkers who had earlier shown a radical opposition to both the organizational forms and the underlying ethos of modern capitalism.*

Only in the late 1890s, after his study, The Development of Capitalism in Russia, *was nearing completion, did he become acquainted with the work of such Western writers as J. A. Hobson. While in exile in Siberia, Lenin reviewed Hobson's* Evolution of Modern Capitalism, *based on an underconsumptionist analysis of economics that not only laid the basis for Hobson's later theory of imperialism but also influenced Keynes. Shortly after the publication of Hobson's* Imperialism *(1903), Lenin read it and considered preparing a Russian translation. In 1915, he was familiar enough with Hobson's views to assign the task of preparing detailed notes to his wife, Nadezhda Krupskaya.*

On close analysis, there is little to support the view that Lenin's Imperialism *was essentially cribbed from Hobson. The thrust of Lenin's argument is different. Hobson is concerned with problems of economic underconsumption in mature capitalist systems. He argues that imperial expansion, opening up new markets, is only one of the options available to cope with this problem and is an option that should not be chosen. For Lenin, the problem is only partially one of underconsumption. The heart of his argument deals with socio-organizational forms of concentration that he alleges are inevitable under conditions of advanced capitalism. Titanic organizational forms emerge for which expansion is virtually inevitable; conflict comes in the train of such expansion. Two things follow from this analysis: first, these organizational conflicts (both economic and political) weaken capitalist society globally and thus create crisis conditions necessary for revolution; second, it is Lenin's*

*view that, dialectically, these advanced forms of organization serve
as the foundation for advanced systemic evolution leading to socialism.*

*Lenin's theory lacks some of the fire of later writers who borrowed
from its analysis, but infused it with the rhetoric of revolutionary
nationalist movements (compare, for example, Franz Fanon). Lenin
stands somewhere between Marx and the contemporary critics of
imperialism. For Marx, imperialism was no special problem. His
main concern was the developed capitalism of Western Europe; the
European state, by expanding overseas, brought "progress" with it.
Even the British punitive expeditions in India and the French activities in North Africa were condoned, at one time or another, by
Marx and Engels. Lenin moved a considerable distance away from
this position. He was one of the first writers to recognize the need
to support peasant-based revolutionary nationalist movements. But
his criteria of progress and culture were still those of Western industrial society, as epitomized in classical Marxism. For Lenin, there
was no doubt as to which—the modern corporation or the peasant
commune—represented a more progressive, more "cultured," phase
of human activity. But if the corporate society represented a step-
ping-stone to the socialist future, it was also the prime enemy in the
immediate present; accordingly, Lenin was more than willing to
make common cause with revolutionary forces that Marx would
have dismissed as "primitive."*

In an article published shortly after the completion of Imperialism, *Lenin presents the most concise synopsis of his theory.*[5]

. . . Imperialism is a specific historical stage of capitalism. Its specific character is threefold: imperialism is (1) monopoly capitalism; (2)
parasitic, or decaying, capitalism; (3) moribund capitalism. The supplant-
ing of free competition by monopoly is the fundamental economic feature,
the *essence* of imperialism. Monopoly manifests itself in five principal
forms: 1) cartels, syndicates and trusts; the concentration of production
has reached the stage where it has given rise to these monopolist associations of capitalists; 2) the monopolist position of the big banks—3 to 5
gigantic banks manipulate the whole economic life of America, France,
Germany; 3) seizure of the sources of *raw material* by the trusts and the
financial oligarchy (finance capital is monopolist industrial capital
merged with bank capital); 4) the division (economic) of the world by

[5] From V. I. Lenin, "Imperialism and the Split in Socialism" (autumn, 1916), in
Marx, Engels, Marxism, pp. 288–90.

international cartels *has begun*. Such international cartels, which command the *entire* world market and divide it "amicably" among themselves —until war *redivides* it—already number over *a hundred*. The export of capital, a highly characteristic phenomenon distinct from the export of commodities under *non-monopoly* capitalism, is closely linked with the economic and territorial-political division of the world; 5) the territorial division of the world (colonies) is *finished*.

Imperialism, as the highest stage of capitalism in America and Europe, and later in Asia, fully developed in the period of 1898–1914. The Spanish-American War (1898), the Anglo-Boer War (1899–1902), the Russo–Japanese War (1904–05) and the economic crisis in Europe in 1900 are the chief historical landmarks in the new era of world history.

That imperialism is parasitic or decaying capitalism is manifested first of all in the tendency to decay characteristic of *all* monopoly where there is private ownership of the means of production. The difference between the democratic-republican and the reactionary-monarchist imperialist bourgeoisie is obliterated precisely because they are both rotting alive (which by no means precludes an extraordinarily rapid development of capitalism in individual industries, individual countries, and individual perods). Secondly, the decay of capitalism is manifested in the creation of a huge stratum of *rentiers,* capitalists who live by "clipping coupons."
. . . Thirdly, capital export is parasitism in the highest measure. Fourthly, "finance capital tends towards domination, not towards freedom." Political reaction *all along* the line is a characteristic feature of imperialism. Corruption, bribery on a huge scale, and gigantic frauds of all kinds. Fifthly, the exploitation of oppressed nations that is inseparably connected with annexations, and especially the exploitation of colonies by a handful of "great" powers, increasingly transforms the "civilised" world into a parasite on the body of hundreds of millions of uncivilised nations. The Roman proletarian lived at the expense of society. Contemporary society lives at the expense of the modern proletarian. . . . Imperialism somewhat changes the situation. A privileged upper stratum of the proletariat in the imperialist countries lives partly at the expense of hundreds of millions of members of uncivilised nations.

It is clear why imperialism is *moribund* capitalism, capitalism in *transition* to socialism: monopoly, which grows *out of* capitalism, is *already* capitalism dying out, the beginning of its transition to socialism. The tremendous *socialisation* of labour by imperialism (what the apologists— the bourgeois economists—call "interlocking") means the same thing.

In advancing this definition of imperialism, we come into complete contradiction with K. Kautsky, who refuses to regard imperialism as a "phase of capitalism" and defines imperialism as the *policy* "preferred" by finance capital, as the tendency of "industrial" countries to annex "agrarian" countries. Kautsky's definition is thoroughly false from the theoretical standpoint. What distinguishes imperialism is the domination *not* of industrial but of finance capital, the striving to annex *not* only agrarian countries, but *every kind* of country. Kautsky *divorces* the politics of imperialism from its economics, he divorces monopoly in politics from monopoly in economics, in order to pave the way for his vulgar bourgeois reformism, such as "disarmament," "ultra-imperialism" and similar nonsense. The aim and object of this theoretical falsity is to obscure the *most profound* contradictions of imperialism and thus to justify the theory of "unity" with the apologists of imperialism, the frank social-chauvinists and the opportunists.

> *Changes in economic organization under imperialism (the internal, or "monopoly capitalist," aspect of the phenomenon) are important not only for imperialism, but as the basis for the evolution of a new economic order.*[6]

. . . In its economic essence imperialism is monopoly capitalism. This in itself determines its place in history, for monopoly . . . is the transition from the capitalist system to a higher social economic order. We must take special note of the four . . . principal manifestations of monopoly capitalism, which are characteristic of the epoch we are examining.

Firstly, monopoly arose out of a very high stage of development of the concentration of production. This refers to the monopolist capitalist combines, cartels, syndicates and trusts. We have seen the important part these play in present-day economic life. At the beginning of the twentieth century, monopolies had acquired complete supremacy in the advanced countries. . . .

Secondly, monopolies have stimulated the seizure of the most important sources of raw materials, especially for the basic and most highly cartelized industries in capitalist society: the coal and iron industries. The monopoly of the most important sources of raw materials has enormously increased the power of big capital, and has sharpened the antagonism between cartelized and non-cartelized industry.

Thirdly, monopoly has sprung from the banks. The banks have developed from humble middlemen enterprises into the monopolists of finance capital. Some three to five of the biggest banks in each of the foremost capitalist countries have achieved the "personal union" of industrial and bank capital, and have concentrated in their hands the control of thousands upon thousands of millions which form the greater part of the capital and income of entire countries. A financial oligarchy, which throws

[6] From V. I. Lenin, *Imperialism: The Highest Stage of Capitalism* (Peking: Foreign Languages Press, 1965), pp. 148–51.

a close network of dependence relationships over all the economic and political institutions of present-day bourgeois society without exception— such is the most striking manifestation of this monopoly.

Fourthly, monopoly has grown out of colonial policy. To the numerous "old" motives of colonial policy, finance capital has added the struggle for the sources of raw materials, for the export of capital, for "spheres of influence," i.e., for spheres for profitable deals, concessions, monopolist profits and so on, and finally, for economic territory in general. . . .

The extent to which monopolist capital has intensified all the contradictions of capitalism is generally known. It is sufficient to mention the high cost of living and the tyranny of the cartels. This intensification of contradictions constitutes the most powerful driving force of the transitional period of history, which began from the time of the final victory of world finance capital. . . .

. . . It would be a mistake to believe that this tendency to decay precludes the rapid growth of capitalism. It does not. In the epoch of imperialism, certain branches of industry, certain strata of the bourgeoisie and certain countries betray, to a greater or lesser degree, now one and now another of these tendencies. On the whole, capitalism is growing far more rapidly than before; but this growth is not only becoming more and more uneven in general, its unevenness also manifests itself, in particular, in the decay of the countries which are richest in capital (England).

A new world politics is a concomitant of imperialism—and this, in turn, lays the basis (according to Lenin, see below, pp. 41–42) for the international conflict between imperialism in the phase of its decline and the emerging socialist system.[7]

. . . The capitalists divide the world, not out of any particular malice, but because the degree of concentration which has been reached forces them to adopt this method in order to obtain profits. And they divide it "in proportion to capital," "in proportion to strength," because there cannot be any other method of division under commodity production and capitalism. But strength varies with the degree of economic and political development. In order to understand what is taking place, it is necessary to know what questions are settled by the changes in strength. The question as to whether these changes are "purely" economic or *non*-economic (e.g., military) is a secondary one, which cannot in the least affect the fundamental views on the latest epoch of capitalism. To substitute the question of the form of the struggle and agreements (today peaceful, tomorrow warlike, the next day warlike again) for the question

[7] From V. I. Lenin, *Imperialism: The Highest Stage of Capitalism*, pp. 88–89.

of the *substance* of the struggle and agreements between capitalist combines is to sink to the role of a sophist.

The epoch of the latest stage of capitalism shows us that certain relations between capitalist combines grow up, *based on* the economic division
of the world; while parallel and in connection with it, certain relations
grow up between political combines, between states, on the basis of the
territorial division of the world, of the struggle for colonies, of the "struggle for economic territory."

> *Conflict among rival capitalist societies and rival imperialist*
> *states is seen as endemic to the system—and a source of weakness*
> *which can be exploited by its radical opponents. Lenin denies the*
> *feasibility of a genuine international organization that would arise*
> *under capitalism to control conflict within the system.*[8]

. . . From the standpoint of the economic conditions of imperialism
—i.e., export of capital and the fact that the world has been divided up
among the "advanced" and "civilised" colonial powers—a United States
of Europe, under capitalism, is either impossible or reactionary.

Capital has become international and monopolistic. The world has
been divided up among a handful of Great Powers, i.e., powers successful
in the great plunder and oppression of nations. . . .

A United States of Europe under capitalism is tantamount to an agreement to divide up the colonies. Under capitalism, however, no other basis,
no other principle of division is possible except force. A multimillionaire
cannot share the "national income" of a capitalist country with anyone
except "in proportion to the capital invested" (with an extra bonus
thrown in, so that the largest capital may receive more than its due).
Capitalism is private property in the means of production, and anarchy
in production. To preach a "just" division of income on such a basis is
Proudhonism, is stupid philistinism. Division cannot take place except
in "proportion to strength." And strength changes with the progress of
economic development. After 1871 Germany grew strong three or four
times faster than England and France; Japan, about ten times faster than
Russia. There is and there can be no other way of testing the real strength
of a capitalist state than that of war. War does not contradict the
principles of private property—on the contrary, it is a direct and inevitable outcome of these principles. Under capitalism the even economic
growth of individual enterprises, or individual states, is impossible. Under

[8] From V. I. Lenin, "On the Slogan for a United States of Europe" (August, 1915),
Marx, Engels, Marxism, pp. 268–70.

capitalism, there are no other means of restoring the periodically disturbed equilibrium than crises in industry and wars in politics.

Of course, *temporary* agreements between capitalists and between the powers are possible. In this sense a United States of Europe is possible as an agreement between the *European* capitalists . . . but what for? Only for the purpose of jointly suppressing socialism in Europe, of jointly protecting colonial booty *against* Japan and America, which feel badly done out of their share by the present division of colonies, and which, for the last half century, have grown strong infinitely faster than backward, monarchist Europe, which is beginning to decay with age. . . .

Increasing tension in the colonial world, and ultimately rebellion on the part of subject peoples, were seen as the dialectical antithesis of developing imperialism. Marx had based his concept of revolution on the notion of the "increasing misery" of the proletariat; Lenin, faced by the accommodation of the working class in advanced countries, to the system tended to transpose this approach to the national minorities and the colonial peoples. It now became the duty of the revolutionary to go beyond an appeal to the proletariat and to forge an alliance with revolutionary nationalism.[9]

The programme of Social-Democracy . . . must postulate the division of nations into oppressor and oppressed as basic, significant and inevitable under imperialism.

The proletariat of the oppressor nations must not confine themselves to general, stereotyped phrases against annexation and in favour of the equality of nations in general such as are repeated by any pacifist bourgeois. The proletariat cannot remain silent on the question of the *frontiers* of a state founded on national oppression, a question so "unpleasant" for the imperialist bourgeoisie. The proletariat must struggle against the enforced retention of oppressed nations within the bounds of the given state, which means that they must fight for the right to self-determination. The proletariat must demand freedom of political separation for the colonies and nations oppressed by "their own" nation. If the reverse were true, the internationalism of the proletariat would be nothing but empty words. . . .

On the other hand, the Socialists of the oppressed nation must, in par-

[9] From V. I. Lenin, "The Socialist Revolution and the Right of Nations to Self-Determination (Theses)" (first published April, 1916), *Questions of National Policy and Proletarian Internationalism* (Moscow: Foreign Languages Publishing House, n.d.), pp. 140–41, 144–45, 147, 149–50.

ticular, defend and implement the full and unconditional unity, including organizational unity, of the workers of the oppressed nation and those of the oppressor nation. Without this it is impossible to defend the independent policy of the proletariat and their class solidarity with the proletariat of other countries in face of all manner of intrigues, treachery and trickery on the part of the bourgeoisie. The bourgeoisie of the oppressed nations persistently utilize the slogans of national liberation to deceive the workers; in their internal policy they use these slogans for reactionary agreements with the bourgeoisie of the dominant nation (for example, the Poles in Austria and Russia who come to terms with reaction for the oppression of the Jews and Ukrainians); in their foreign policy they strive to come to terms with one of the rival imperialist powers for the sake of implementing their predatory plans (the policy of the small Balkan states, etc.).

The circumstance that the struggle for national liberation against one imperialist power may be, under certain conditions, utilized by another "great" power for its own, equally imperialist, aims, is as little likely to make the Social-Democrats refuse to recognize the right of nations to self-determination as are the numerous cases of bourgeois utilization of republican slogans for the purpose of political deception and financial plunder (as in the Romance countries for example), likely to make the Social-Democrats reject their republicanism. . . .

. . . Countries must be divided into three main types.

First, the advanced capitalist countries of Western Europe and the United States. In these countries the bourgeois-progressive national movements came to an end long ago. Every one of these "great" nations oppresses other nations both in the colonies and within its own country. The tasks of the proletariat of these ruling nations are the same as those of the proletariat in England in the nineteenth century in relation to Ireland.

Secondly, Eastern Europe: Austria, the Balkans and particularly Russia. Here it was the twentieth century that particularly developed the bourgeois-democratic national movements and intensified the national struggle. The tasks of the proletariat in these countries—as far as the consummation of their bourgeois-democratic reforms, and the rendering of assistance to the socialist revolution in other countries are concerned—cannot be carried out unless it champions the right of nations to self-determination. In this connection, the most difficult and most important task is to unite the class struggle of the workers of the oppressor nations with that of the workers of the oppressed nations.

Thirdly, the semi-colonial countries, such as China, Persia and Turkey, and all the colonies, which have a combined population amounting to 1,000 million. In these countries the bourgeois-democratic movements have either hardly begun, or are far from having been completed. Socialists must not only demand the unconditional and immediate liberation of the colonies without compensation—and this demand in its political expression signifies nothing else than the recognition of the right to self-determination—they must also render determined support to the more revolutionary elements in the bourgeois-democratic movements for national liberation in these countries and assist their uprising—or revolutionary war, if there be one—*against* the imperialist powers that oppress them.

WAR AND PEACE: SOME COROLLARIES
OF THE THEORY OF IMPERIALISM

Lenin's theory of war stemmed from his conception of imperialism and from the value judgments that lay behind the critique of capitalist expansion. As the following two selections indicate, his position, ultimately, can be boiled down to a basic proposition: wars waged by, and in the interests of, imperialist systems are bad; wars waged against such systems, from almost any quarter, no matter how "primitive" according to nineteenth-century Marxism, are good! The pacifism which some socialists had adopted as their position on the war-peace issue was scornfully rejected. Lenin had made up his mind that conflict was of the essence of the contemporary situation; what mattered was which side one supported.[10]

. . . Every war is the exercise of violence against nations, but that does not prevent socialists from being in *favour* of a revolutionary war. The class character of the war—that is the fundamental question which confronts a socialist (who is not a renegade). The imperialist war of 1914–1918 is a war between two coalitions of the imperialist bourgeoisie for the partition of the world, for the division of the booty, and for the plunder and strangulation of small and weak nations. . . . Whoever departs from this point of view ceases to be a socialist.

If a German, under Wilhelm, or a Frenchman, under Clemenceau, says: As a socialist, it is my right and duty to defend my country if it is invaded by an enemy, he argues not like a socialist, not like an internationalist, not like a revolutionary proletarian, but like a *petty-bourgeois nationalist.* Because this argument leaves out of account revolutionary class struggle of the workers against capital, it leaves out of account the appraisal of the war as a *whole* from the point of view of the world bourgeoisie and the world proletariat: that is, it leaves out internationalism, and all that remains is a miserable and narrow-minded nationalism. My country is being wronged, that is all I care about—this is what this argument reduces itself

---

[10] From V. I. Lenin, *The Proletarian Revolution and the Renegade Kautsky* (New York: International Publishers, 1934), pp. 65–67.

to, and that is why it is petty-bourgeois nationalist narrow-mindedness. . . .

The socialist, the revolutionary proletarian, the internationalist, argues differently. He says: The character of the war (whether reactionary or revolutionary) is not determined by who the aggressor was, or whose territory the "enemy" has occupied; it is *determined by the class* that is waging the war, and the politics of which this war is a continuation. If the war is a reactionary, imperialist war, that is, if it is being waged by two world coalitions of the imperialist, violent, predatory reactionary bourgeoisie, then every bourgeoisie (even of the smallest country) becomes a participant in the plunder, and my duty as a representative of the revolutionary proletariat is to prepare for the *world proletarian revolution* as the *only* escape from the horrors of a world war. I must argue, not from the point of view of "my" country (for this is the argument of a poor, stupid, nationalist philistine who does not realise that he is only a plaything in the hands of the imperialist bourgeoisie), but from the point of view of *my share* in the preparation, in the propaganda and in the accelerations of the world proletarian revolution.

This is what internationalism is, and this is the duty of the internationalist, of the revolutionary worker, of the genuine socialist.

The history of the twentieth century, this century of "unbridled imperialism," is replete with colonial wars. But what we Europeans, the imperialist oppressors of the majority of the peoples of the world, with our habitual, despicable, European chauvinism, call "colonial wars" are often national wars, or national rebellions of those oppressed peoples. One of the main features of imperialism is that it accelerates the development of capitalism in the most backward countries, and thereby widens and intensifies the struggle against national oppression. This is a fact. It inevitably follows from this that imperialism must often give rise to national wars. . . . And it would be simply ridiculous if we declared, for instance, that after the present war, if it ends in the extreme exhaustion of all the belligerents, "there can be no" national, progressive, revolutionary wars "whatever," waged, say, by China in alliance with India, Persia, Siam, etc., against the Great Powers.

To deny all possibility of national wars under imperialism is wrong in theory, obviously mistaken historically, and in practice is tantamount to European chauvinism: we who belong to nations that oppress hundreds of millions of people in Europe, Africa, Asia, etc., must tell the oppressed peoples that it is "impossible" for them to wage war against "our" nations! [11]

[11] From V. I. Lenin, "The Military Programme of the Proletarian Revolution" (autumn, 1916), in *Marx, Engels, Marxism*, pp. 304–305.

War was the "womb of revolution." And the course of the revolution, both in Russia, and as an anticipated international phenomenon, was consistently related by Lenin to the fortunes of the struggle against the continuation of the First World War.[12]

. . . The war is a product of half a century of development of world capital and of its billions of threads and connections. It is *impossible* to escape from the imperialist war at one jump, it is *impossible* to achieve a democratic, non-coercive peace without overthrowing the power of capital and transferring state power to *another* class, the proletariat.

The Russian revolution of February–March 1917 was the beginning of the transformation of the imperialist war into a civil war. This revolution took the *first* step towards ending the war; but it requires a *second* step, namely, the transfer of state power to the proletariat, to make the end of the war a *certainty*. This will be the beginning of a "breach in the front" on a world-wide scale, a breach in the front of the interests of capital; and only after having broken through *this* front *can* the proletariat save mankind from the horrors of war and endow it with the blessings of a durable peace.

World politics would continue to be dominated by conflict even after one or more states managed to break away from the existing capitalist-imperialist system. More or less endemic warfare between these states and the remaining capitalist countries could be expected, broken by mere intervals of "coexistence." [13]

. . . The victory of socialism in one country does not at one stroke eliminate all war in general. On the contrary, it presupposes such wars. The development of capitalism proceeds extremely unevenly in the various countries. It cannot be otherwise under the commodity production system. From this it follows irrefutably that socialism cannot achieve victory simultaneously *in all* countries. It will achieve victory first in one or several countries, while the others will remain bourgeois or prebourgeois for some time. This must not only create friction, but a direct striving on the part of the bourgeoisie of other countries to crush the victorious proletariat of the socialist state. In such cases a war on our part would be a legitimate and just war. It would be a war for socialism, for the liberation of other nations from the bourgeoisie. . . .

---

[12] From V. I. Lenin, "The Tasks of the Proletariat in Our Revolution" (September, 1917) in *Selected Works* (Moscow: Foreign Languages Publishing House, n.d.; trans. of Russian edition of 1960), II, 64.

[13] From V. I. Lenin, "The Military Programme of the Proletarian Revolution," in *Marx, Engels, Marxism*, pp. 306–307.

Only after we have overthrown, finally vanquished, and expropriated the bourgeoisie of the whole world, and not only of one country, will wars become impossible. . . .

Theoretically, it would be quite wrong to forget that every war is but the continuation of politics by other means; the present imperialist war is the continuation of the imperialist politics of two groups of Great Powers, and these politics are engendered and fostered by the sum total of the relationships of the imperialist epoch. But this very epoch must also necessarily engender and foster the politics of struggle against national oppression and of the proletarian struggle against the bourgeoisie, and therefore, also the possiblity and the inevitability, first, of revolutionary national rebellions and wars; second, of proletarian wars and rebellions *against* the bourgeoisie; and, third, of a combination of both kinds of revolutionary war, etc.

A United States of the World (not of Europe alone) is the state form of the union and freedom of nations which we associate with socialism—until the complete victory of communism brings about the total disappearance of the state, including the democratic state. As a separate slogan, however, the slogan of a United States of the World would hardly be a correct one, first, because it merges with socialism; second, because it may be wrongly interpreted to mean that the victory of socialism in a single country is impossible, and it may also create misconceptions as to the relations of such a country to the others.

Uneven economic and political development is an absolute law of capitalism. Hence, the victory of socialism is possible first in several or even in one capitalist country alone. The victorious proletariat of that country, having expropriated the capitalists and organised its own socialist production, would stand up *against* the rest of the world, the capitalist world, attracting to its cause the oppressed classes of other countries, raising revolts in those countries against the capitalists, and in the event of necessity coming out even with armed force against the exploiting classes and their states. The political form of society in which the proletariat is victorious by overthrowing the bourgeoisie will be a democratic republic, which will more and more centralise the forces of the proletariat of the given nation, or nations, in the struggle against the states that have not yet gone over to socialism. The abolition of classes is impossible without the dictatorship of the oppressed class, the proletariat. The free union of nations in socialism is impossible without a more or less prolonged and stubborn struggle of the socialist republics against the backward states.[14]

[14] From V. I. Lenin, "On the Slogan for a United States of Europe" (August, 1915), in *Marx, Engels, Marxism,* p. 270.

2

Lenin and Revolution: Theory and Practice

THE REVOLUTIONARY PARTY

To the theory and practice of modern revolution Lenin contributed his concept of the "party of a new type": an organization of revolutionary activists, subject to quasimilitary discipline, with a hierarchy that culminated in a leadership distinguished by the high level of its ideological "consciousness." In part, this conception derives from earlier European and Russian experience of conspiratorial revolutionary groups; yet too much can be made of this derivation. Lenin was highly sensitive to the emerging prospects for mass propaganda, made possible by the concentration of masses of workers in industrial centers and by the new technologies of communication. He insisted that conspiracy in small groups was not enough and could be harmful to the revolutionary cause. The task of the professional revolutionaries was to infuse consciousness (ideological and otherwise) into what already was a potentially revolutionary situation—to act, in other words, as a catalyst to upheaval. At the same time, the revolutionaries were to draw experience from their contacts with the masses in order to refine and strengthen their own approach.

Lenin's theory of the party is significant not only for contemporary Communism, in its numerous variants, but also for the movements that borrowed Leninist organization, if not his ideology. Yet it is important to keep Lenin's ideas in their historical context. His notion of the party stemmed from his image of the enemy; his emphasis on the hierarchical nature of revolutionary organization and discipline derives in large measure from his assessment of the difficulties posed by the Tsarist secret police—the Okhrana. After the revolution, his image of the enemy shifted, of course: the rationalization for a tightly disciplined party now depended on the fragility of the newly created Soviet state and the danger from external and internal enemies. Lenin insisted on applying his concept of the party to groups, even in democratic societies, that wished to adhere to the Third (Communist) International. Such insistence illustrates the dogmatic and antidemocratic side of Lenin's political character, a side that was often dominant. Yet, it is at odds with the fact that, although no believer in democracy in general, Lenin did admit, on a number of occasions both before and after the Revolution, that it was possible in milieus less oppressive than Tsarism for socialist parties to arise that were democratic in their internal functioning and used parliamentary means to enhance their influence.

It would also be erroneous to infer from the repeated statements about the monolithic discipline of the Bolshevik Party that, in fact, a party was *always a tightly disciplined and unified group. In the prerevolutionary period, at the same time that Lenin promoted Bolshevism and accentuated splits with rival socialisms, the Bolshevik group was itself riven by splits. At times, Lenin found himself in a minority in his own group. Again, on a number of occasions in 1917 and 1918 (the timing of the insurrection; peace with Germany) Lenin met serious opposition from his colleagues.*

In 1920, looking back to the early years of Bolshevism, Lenin stressed the need to combat anarchistic views.[1]

. . . Opportunism, which in 1914 definitely grew into social-chauvinism and definitely sided with the bourgeoisie against the proletariat, . . . was the principal enemy of Bolshevism. . . . This enemy has claimed, and still claims, most of the attention of the Bolsheviks. . . .

Something . . . must be said of the other enemy of Bolshevism. . . . Bolshevism grew, took shape, and became steeled in long years of struggle against *petty-bourgeois revolutionariness,* which smacks of, or borrows something from, anarchism, and which in all essentials falls short of the conditions and requirements of a sustained proletarian class struggle. . . . The small proprietor, the small master craftsman (a social type that is represented in many European countries on a wide, mass scale), who under capitalism suffers constant oppression and, very often, an incredibly acute and rapid deterioration in his conditions of life, ending in ruin, easily goes to revolutionary extremes, but is incapable of perseverance, organisation, discipline and steadfastness. The petty bourgeois, "driven to frenzy" by the horrors of capitalism, is a social phenomenon which, like anarchism, is characteristic of all capitalist countries. The instability of such revolutionariness, its barrenness, its liability to become swiftly transformed into submission, apathy, fantasy, and even a "frenzied" infatuation with one or another bourgeois "fad"—all that is a matter of common knowledge. . . .

At its inception in 1903, Bolshevism adopted the tradition of ruthless struggle against petty-bourgeois, semi-anarchist (or dilettante-anarchist)

[1] From V. I. Lenin, *"Left-Wing" Communism: An Infantile Disorder* (New York: International Publishers, 1940), pp. 17–18.

revolutionariness, the tradition which has always existed in revolutionary Social-Democracy, and which struck particularly deep root in Russia. . . . [The Socialist-Revolutionary Party] considered itself to be particularly "revolutionary," or "Left," on account of its recognition of individual terrorism, assassination—which we Marxists emphatically rejected. Of course, we rejected individual terrorism only on the grounds of expediency. . . .

Lenin's theory of the party was elaborated in What Is to Be Done? *(1902). His description of the historical situation out of which the "party of a new type" was emerging echoes the frustration of the revolutionary circles of Alexander Ulyanov's day and the lessons that Lenin had learned from his brother's experience and his own work in poorly organized revolutionary groups in the 1890s. In Lenin's view, the time for such "organizational primitivism" was past. What was now required was a party which, by its discipline, could survive against the forces of Tsarism and, by the very act of surviving, begin to gain the confidence of the Russian working class.*

At the same time, Lenin saw some dangers in the links that were being forged with the workers. There would be a temptation to be, not the head, but the "tail" (khvost) of the worker's movement, with the party following the demands of the newly industrialized masses rather than using these masses to carry out the revolution against Tsarism, which had long been the dream of the radical intelligentsia. While the worker was indeed important, it would be necessary to maintain the ideological purity ("consciousness") of the Marxist party against his too direct influence. An ambiguity, often resolved in favor of instrumentalism, characterized Lenin's balancing of the relationship between the "spontaneity" of the proletariat and the "consciousness" required for effective party leadership.[2]

Strikes occurred in Russia in the seventies, and in the sixties (and also in the first half of the nineteenth century), and these strikes were accompanied by the "spontaneous" destruction of machinery, etc. . . . The "spontaneous element," in essence, represents nothing more nor less than consciousness in an *embryonic form.* Even the primitive rebellions expressed the awakening of consciousness to a certain extent: The workers abandoned their age-long faith in the permanence of the system which oppressed them. . . . The strikes of the nineties revealed far greater flashes of consciousness: Definite demands were put forward, the time to

---

[2] From V. I. Lenin, *What Is to Be Done?* (New York: International Publishers, 1929), pp. 32–33 and pp. 95–97.

strike was carefully chosen, known cases and examples in other places were discussed, etc. While the revolts were simply uprisings of the oppressed, the systematic strikes represented the class struggle in embryo, but only in embryo. . . . They testified to the awakening antagonisms between workers and employers, but the workers were not and could not be conscious of the irreconcilable antagonism of their interests to the whole of the modern political and social system, *i.e.*, it was not yet Social-Democratic consciousness. . . .

We said that *there could not yet be* Social-Democratic consciousness among the workers. This consciousness could only be brought to them from without. The history of all countries shows that the working class exclusively by its own efforts is able to develop only trade union consciousness, *i.e.*, it may itself realise the necessity for combining in unions, to fight against the employers and to strive to compel the government to pass necessary labour legislation, etc.

The theory of Socialism, however, grew out of the philosophic, historical and economic theories that were elaborated by the educated representatives of the propertied classes, the intellectuals. The founders of modern scientific Socialism, Marx and Engels, themselves belonged to the bourgeois intelligentsia. Similarly, in Russia, the theoretical doctrine of Social-Democracy arose quite independently of the spontaneous growth of the labour movement; it arose as a natural and inevitable outcome of the development of ideas among the revolutionary Socialist intelligentsia. . . .

Hence, simultaneously we had both the spontaneous awakening of the masses of the workers—the awakening to conscious life and struggle, and the striving of the revolutionary youth, armed with the Social-Democratic theories, to reach the workers. . . .

A students' circle with no contacts with the old members of the movement, no contacts with circles in other districts, or even in other parts of the same city (or with other schools), without the various sections of the revolutionary work being in any way organised, having no systematic plan of activity covering any length of time, establishes contacts with the workers and sets to work. The circle gradually expands its propaganda and agitation; by its activities it wins the sympathies of a rather large circle of workers and of a certain section of the educated classes, which provides it with money and from which the "committee" recruits new groups of members. The fascination which the committee (or the League of Struggle) exercises on the youth increases, its sphere of activity becomes wider and its activities expand quite spontaneously: the very people who a year or a few months previously had spoken at the gatherings of the students' circle and discussed the question, "Whither?" who established and maintained contacts with the workers, wrote and published leaflets, established contacts with other groups of revolutionists and procured literature, now set to work to establish a local newspaper, begin to talk about organising demonstrations, and finally, commence open conflicts (these open conflicts may, according to circumstances, take the form of issuing the very first agitational leaflet, or the first newspaper, or of organising the first demonstration). And usually, the first action ends in immediate and complete defeat. Immediate and complete, precisely because these open conflicts were not the result of a systematic and carefully thought-out and gradually prepared plan for a prolonged and stubborn struggle, but simply the spontaneous growth of traditional circle work; because naturally, the police, almost in every case, knew the principal leaders of the local movement, for they had already "recommended" themselves to the police in their school-days, and the latter only waited for a convenient day to make their raid. . . .

. . . The government very soon adapted itself to the new conditions of the struggle and managed to place its perfectly equipped detachments of agent-provocateurs, spies, and gendarmes in the required places. Raids became so frequent, affected such a vast number of people, and cleared out the local circles so thoroughly, that the masses of the workers literally lost all their leaders, the movement assumed an incredibly sporadic character, and it became utterly impossible to established continuity and connectedness in the work. The fact that the local active workers were hopelessly scattered, the casual manner in which the membership of the circles were recruited, the lack of training in and narrow outlook on theoretical, political and organisational questions were all the inevitable result of the conditions described above. Things reached such a pass that in several places the workers, because of our lack of stamina and ability to maintain secrecy, began to lose faith in the intelligentsia and to avoid them: The intellectuals, they said, are much too careless and lay themselves open to police raids!

In contrast, Lenin advocated the kind of revolutionary party that later became identified with his own brand of Marxism—Bolshevism.[3]

Our movement . . . has hundreds and hundreds of thousands of roots deep down among the masses, but that is not the point. . . . As far as "roots in the depths" are concerned, we cannot be "caught" even now, in spite of all our primitiveness; but, we all complain, and cannot but complain, of the ease with which the *organisations* can be caught, with the result that it is impossible to maintain continuity in the move-

[3] From V. I. Lenin, *What Is to Be Done?*, pp. 116–18.

ment. I assert that it is far more difficult to catch ten wise men than it is to catch a hundred fools. And this premise I shall defend no matter how much you instigate the crowd against me for my "anti-democratic" views, etc. As I have already said, by "wise men," in connection with organisation, I mean *professional revolutionists,* irrespective of whether they are students or working men. I assert: 1. That no movement can be durable without a stable organisation of leaders to maintain continuity; 2. that the more widely the masses are drawn into the struggle and form the basis of the movement, the more necessary is it to have such an organisation and the more stable must it be (for it is much easier then for demagogues to side-track the more backward sections of the masses); 3. that the organisation must consist chiefly of persons engaged in revolution as a profession; 4. that in a country with a despotic government, the more we *restrict* the membership of this organisation to persons who are engaged in revolution as a profession and who have been professionally trained in the art of combating the political police, the more difficult will it be to catch the organisation; and 5. the *wider* will be the circle of men and women of the working class or of other classes of society able to join the movement and perform active work in it. . . .

The question as to whether it is easier to catch "a dozen wise men" or "a hundred fools," in the last analysis, amounts to . . . whether it is possible to have a mass *organisation* when the maintenance of strict secrecy is essential. We can never give a mass organisation that degree of secrecy which is essential for the persistent and continuous struggle against the government. But to concentrate all secret functions in the hands of as small a number of professional revolutionists as possible, does not mean that the latter will "do the thinking for all" and that the crowd will not take an active part in the movement. . . . The centralisation of the secret functions of the *organisation* does not mean the concentration of all the functions of the *movement.* The active participation of the greatest masses in the dissemination of illegal literature will not diminish because a dozen professional revolutionists concentrate in their hands the secret part of the work; on the contrary, it will *increase tenfold.* Only in this way will the reading of illegal literature, the contribution to illegal literature, and to some extent even the distribution of illegal literature *almost cease to be secret work,* for the police will soon come to realise the folly and futility of setting the whole judicial and administrative machine into motion to intercept every copy of a publication that is being broadcast in thousands. This applies not only to the press, but to every function of the movement, even to demonstrations. The active and widespread participation of the masses will not suffer; on the contrary, it will benefit by the fact that a "dozen" experienced revolutionists, no less professionally trained than the police, will concentrate all the secret side of the work in their hands—prepare leaflets, work out approximate plans and appoint bodies of leaders for each town district, for each factory district, and for each educational institution. . . .

. . . To serve the mass movement we must have people who will devote themselves exclusively to Social-Democratic activities, and . . . such people must *train* themselves patiently and steadfastly to be professional revolutionists. . . .

. . . The most grievous sin we have committed in regard to organisation is that *by our primitiveness we have lowered the prestige of revolutionists in Russia.* A man who is weak and vacillating on theoretical questions, who has a narrow outlook, who makes excuses for his own slackness on the ground that the masses are awakening spontaneously, who resembles a trade-union secretary more than a people's tribune, who is unable to conceive a broad and bold plan, who is incapable of inspiring even his enemies with respect for himself, and who is inexperienced and clumsy in his own professional art—the art of combating the political police—such a man is not a revolutionist but a hopeless amateur!

. . . We were proving ourselves to be amateurs at a moment in history when we might have been able to say: . . . "Give us an organisation of revolutionists, and we shall overturn the whole of Russia!" . . . Our task is not to degrade the revolutionist to the level of an amateur, but to *exalt* the amateur to the level of a revolutionist."

. . . [T]he significance of a party organisation and of party leaders worthy of the name lies precisely in the fact that they help . . . in the acquisition of the necessary knowledge, the necessary experience and—apart from knowledge and experience—the necessary political instinct for the speedy and correct solution of intricate political problems.[4]

. . . Every one will probably agree that "broad principles of democracy" presupposes the two following conditions: first, full publicity and second, election to all functions. It would be absurd to speak about democracy without publicity, that is a publicity that extends beyond the circle of the membership of the organisation. We call the German Socialist Party a democratic organisation because all it does is done publicly; even its party congresses are held in public. But no one would call an organisation that is hidden from every one but its members by a veil of secrecy, a democratic organisation.

. . . [W]ith regard to the second attribute of democracy, namely, the principle of election. . . . In politically free countries, this condition is taken for granted. "Membership of the party is open to those who accept the principles of the party programme, and render all the support they can to the party"—says paragraph 1 of the rules of the German Social-

[4] From V. I. Lenin, *"Left-Wing" Communism: An Infantile Disorder*, p. 51.

Democratic Party. And as the political arena is as open to the public view as is the stage in a theatre, this acceptance or non-acceptance, support or opposition is announced to all in the press and at public meetings. Every one knows that a certain political worker commenced in a certain way, passed through a certain evolution, behaved in difficult periods in a certain way; every one knows all his qualities, and consequently, knowing all the facts of the case, *every party member can decide for himself whether or not to elect this person for a certain party office.* . . .

Try to put this picture in the frame of our autocracy! Is it possible in Russia for all those "who accept the principles of the party programme and render it all the support they can," to control every action of the revolutionist working in secret? Is it possible for all the revolutionists to elect one of their number to any particular office when, in the very interests of the work, he *must conceal his identity* from nine out of ten of these "all"? Ponder a little over the real meaning of the high-sounding phrases . . . and you will realise that "broad democracy" in party organisation, amidst the gloom of autocracy and the domination of the gendarmes, is nothing more than a *useless and harmful toy.* It is a useless toy, because as a matter of fact, no revolutionary organisation has ever practiced *broad* democracy, nor could it, however much it desired to do so. It is a harmful toy, because any attempt to practice the "broad principles of democracy" will simply facilitate the work of the police in making big raids, it will perpetuate the prevailing primitiveness, divert the thoughts of the practical workers from the serious and imperative task of training themselves to become professional revolutionists to that of drawing up detailed "paper" rules for election systems. Only abroad, where very often people who have no opportunity of doing real live work gather together, can the "game of democracy" be played here and there, especially in small groups.[5]

> *Lenin was keenly aware of the importance of what may be termed the "psychology of revolution." A key role was to be played by the propagandists and agitators—the front-line troops of the organized revolutionary party.*[6]

. . . [A] propagandist, dealing with say the question of unemployment, must explain the capitalistic nature of crises, the reasons why crises are inevitable in modern society, must describe how present society must inevitably become transformed into Socialist society, etc. In a word, he must present "many ideas," so many indeed that they will be understood as a whole only by a (comparatively) few persons. An agitator,

[5] From V. I. Lenin, *What Is to Be Done?*, pp. 128–30.
[6] From V. I. Lenin, *What Is to Be Done?*, p. 65.

however, speaking on the same subject will take as an illustration a fact that is most widely known and outstanding among his audience—say the death from starvation of the family of an unemployed worker, the growing impoverishment, etc.—and utilising this illustration, will direct all his efforts to present *a single idea* to the "masses," *i.e.,* the idea of the senseless contradiction between the increase of wealth and increase of poverty; he will strive to *rouse* discontent and indignation among the masses against this crying injustice, and leave a more complete explanation of this contradiction to the propagandist. Consequently, the propagandist operates chiefly by means of the *printed* word; the agitator operates with the *living* word. The qualities that are required of an agitator are not the same as the qualities that are required of a propagandist. . . .

After the successful carrying out of the revolution, Lenin evolved new arguments in favor of the continuing hegemony of the party, and strengthening of its internal discipline. The party in this view was an island of order in a sea of chaos; a citadel for the defense of a country beseiged by enemies abroad and subject to the danger of subversion at home; and a directing brain in a society sadly lacking in the trained human resources needed for socioeconomic transformation. This view of things may, indeed, have been appropriate to the times. However, part of the tragedy of the Russian revolution is that Lenin formulated, in this way, the arguments that were to be used by Stalin and by more recent Soviet leaders to justify continuing superimposition on Russian society of a state and party apparatus more appropriate to the drastic conditions of revolution and civil war—to extreme emergency—than to the "normal" evolution of a modern society.[7]

We in Russia (in the third year since the overthrow of the bourgeoisie) are taking the first steps in the transition from capitalism to Socialism, or the lowest stage of Communism. Classes have remained, and will remain everywhere *for years after* the conquest of power by the proletariat. . . . The abolition of classes not only means driving out the landlords and capitalists—that we accomplished with comparative ease —it also means *abolishing the small commodity producers,* and they *cannot be driven out,* or crushed; we must live *in harmony* with them; they can (and must) be remoulded and re-educated only by very prolonged, slow, cautious organisational work. They encircle the proletariat on every side with a petty-bourgeois atmosphere, which permeates and corrupts the proletariat and causes constant relapses among the pro-

[7] From V. I. Lenin, *"Left-Wing" Communism: An Infantile Disorder,* pp. 28–29.

letariat into petty-bourgeois spinelessness, disunity, individualism, and alternate moods of exaltation and dejection. The strictest centralisation and discipline are required within the political party of the proletariat in order to counteract this, in order that the *organisational* role of the proletariat (and that is its *principal* role) may be exercised correctly, successfully, victoriously. The dictatorship of the proletariat is a persistent struggle—sanguinary and bloodless, violent and peaceful, military and economic, educational and administrative—against the forces and traditions of the old society. The force of habit of millions and tens of millions is a most terrible force. Without an iron party tempered in the struggle, without a party enjoying the confidence of all the honest elements in the given class, without a party capable of watching and influencing the mood of the masses, it is impossible to conduct such a struggle successfully. It is a thousand times easier to vanquish the centralised big bourgeoisie than to "vanquish" millions and millions of small proprietors, while they, by their ordinary, everyday, imperceptible, elusive, demoralising activity achieve the *very* results which the bourgeoisie need and which *restore* the bourgeoisie. Whoever weakens ever so little the iron discipline of the party of the proletariat (especially during the time of its dictatorship) actually aids the bourgeoisie against the proletariat.

STRATEGY AND TACTICS

At the operational level of ideology, Lenin developed not a set of "rules and regulations" for making a revolution, but rather a point of view for approaching the various strands that were combined in a revolutionary situation in order to disentangle and evaluate them.

In 1918, after the Bolshevik seizure of power, Lenin stressed that the "historical laws" out of which an operational analysis emerged only described an "ideal" situation. The revolutionary has to attune himself to what may be exceptional in a situation; victory may turn on the recognition and exploitation of the exceptional, rather than on what is "average, normal, typical." [8]

Are there historical laws governing revolution which know of no exception? . . . No, no such laws exist. These laws only apply to what is typical, to what Marx once termed the "ideal," in the sense of an average, normal, typical capitalism.

Further, was there in the seventies of last century anything which made England and America an exception in regard to what we *are now discuss-*

[8] From V. I. Lenin, *The Proletarian Revolution and the Renegade Kautsky*, p. 21.

ing? It will be obvious to any one familiar with the requirements of science in the domain of historical problems that such a question must be put. To fail to put it is tantamount to falsifying science, to engaging in sophistry. And the question having been put, there can be no doubt as to the reply: The revolutionary dictatorship of the proletariat is violence against the bourgeoisie; and the necessity for such violence is *particularly* created, as Marx and Engels have repeatedly explained in detail (particularly in *The Civil War in France* and in the preface to it), by the existence of militarism and bureaucracy. But it is precisely these institutions that were non-existent in England and America in the seventies of the nineteenth century when Marx made his observations (they *do* exist in England and in America *now*).

Historically, revolution is to be regarded as two-sided: it destroys the old order, and, at the same time, it provides the mould in which a new set of societal relationships can be fashioned. But, argues Lenin, it is here—partly because of the very factors that make the negative task of the revolution relatively easy to accomplish—that the revolutionary faces his most difficult challenge.[9]

One of the fundamental differences between bourgeois revolution and socialist revolution is that in the bourgeois revolution, which arises out of feudalism, the new economic organisations are gradually created in the womb of the old order, gradually changing all the aspects of feudal society. The bourgeois revolution faced only one task—to sweep away, to cast aside, to destroy all the fetters of the preceding social order. By fulfilling this task every bourgeois revolution fulfils all that is required of it; it accelerates the growth of capitalism.

The socialist revolution is in an altogether different position. The more backward the country, which, owing to the zigzags of history, has proved to be the one to start the socialist revolution, the more difficult is it for her to pass from the old capitalist relations to socialist relations. New incredibly difficult tasks, organisational tasks, are added to the tasks of destruction. . . .

"Revolution," Lenin wrote, "is impossible without a nationwide crisis." Such a crisis altered the balance of forces within a society: simultaneously, it made it impossible to continue governing

[9] From V. I. Lenin, "Report on War and Peace," 7th Congress, Russian Communist Party (Bolsheviks), March 7, 1918, in *Selected Works,* II, 625.

in the old way, while emboldening key segments of society to challenge the existing system. Elsewhere (see, for example, The Proletarian Revolution and the Renegade Kautsky, *pp. 35–36), Lenin warned that the shift which enabled the revolutionaries to seize power did not, in itself, provide them with the basis for immediately carrying out their revolutionary program. Because of the hostile international environment and the persistence of nonrevolutionized segments of the population, a revolution had to be a "protracted struggle." The moment of "victory" (in the political sense) was, indeed, significant; but it was an episode which had to be built upon, so as to complete and consolidate the gains by further revolutionary strategy and tactics.*[10]

The fundamental law of revolution, which has been confirmed by all revolutions, and particularly by all three Russian revolutions in the twentieth century, is as follows: it is not enough for revolution that the exploited and oppressed masses should understand the impossibility of living in the old way and demand changes; what is required for revolution is that the exploiters should not be able to live and rule in the old way. Only when the *"lower classes" do not want* the old way and when the "upper classes" *cannot carry on in the old way* can revolution win. This truth may be expressed in other words: revolution is impossible without a nationwide crisis (affecting both the exploited and the exploiters). It follows that revolution requires, firstly, that a majority of the workers (or at least a majority of the class-conscious, thinking and politically active workers) should fully understand that revolution is necessary and be ready to sacrifice their lives for it, secondly, that the ruling classes should be passing through a governmental crisis which would draw even the most backward masses into politics (a symptom of every real revolution is a rapid tenfold and even hundredfold increase in the number of representatives of the toiling and oppressed masses—who have hitherto been apathetic—capable of waging the political struggle), weaken the government and make it possible for the revolutionaries to overthrow it rapidly.

Doctrinaire approaches to revolution oversimplify an inherently complex situation. Lenin recognized that it was, in fact, the complexity of revolutionary crisis that gave the professional revolutionaries their chance. Reduction of the situation to "arithmetical" simplicities by either the "left" or the "right" wings of the radical movement could lead to adverse consequences. The

---

[10] From V. I. Lenin, *"Left-Wing" Communism: An Infantile Disorder,* pp. 66–67.

selection that follows is often referred to in the recent Soviet polemics against Maoism. Here, Lenin criticizes those who espouse only the more militant forms of struggle. The selections that follow it elaborate on the need to be flexible in determining revolutionary tactics.

. . . [P]olitics is more like algebra than arithmetic; it is more like higher mathematics than lower mathematics. In reality, all the old forms of the Socialist movement have acquired a new content, . . .

[Thus] . . . [i]t is not only Right doctrinairism that is a mistake; Left doctrinairism is also a mistake. Of course, the mistake of Left doctrinairism in Communism is at present a thousand times less dangerous and less significant than the mistake of Right doctrinairism (*i.e.,* social-chauvinism and Kautskyism); but, after all, that is only due to the fact that Left Communism is a very young trend, that it is only just coming into being. It is only for this reason that, under certain conditions, the disease can be easily cured; and we must set to work to cure it with the utmost energy.

The old forms have burst asunder, for it has turned out that their new content—an anti-proletarian and reactionary content—had attained inordinate development. We now have what from the standpoint of the development of international Communism is such a lasting, strong and powerful content of work (for the Soviet power, for the dictatorship of the proletariat) that it can *and must* manifest itself in every form, both new and old, it can and must regenerate, conquer and subjugate all forms, not only the new, but also the old—not for the purpose of reconciling itself with the old, but for the purpose of converting all and every form, new and old, into a weapon for the complete, final, decisive and irrevocable victory of Communism. . . .

. . . But it is enough to take one little step further—a step that might seem to be in the same direction—and truth is transformed into error! We have only to say, as the German and British "Left" Communists say, that we recognise only one road, only the straight road, that we do not agree with tacking, manoeuvring, compromising—and it will be a mistake which may cause, and in part has already caused, and is causing, very serious harm to Communism. Right doctrinairism persisted in recognising only the old forms, and became totally bankrupt, for it did not perceive the new content. Left doctrinairism persists in the unconditional repudiation of certain old forms and fails to see that the new content is forcing its way through all and sundry forms, that it is our duty as Communists to master all forms, to learn how with the maximum rapidity to supplement one form with another, to substitute one for another, and to adapt our tactics to every such change not called forth by our class, or by our efforts.[11]

. . . Where, in what books, have you read that such variations of the customary historical order of events are impermissible or impossible?

Napoleon, I think, wrote: *"On s'engage et puis . . . on voit."* Rendered freely this means: "First engage in a serious battle and then see what happens." Well, we did first engage in a serious battle in October 1917, and then saw such details of development (from the standpoint of world history they were certainly details) as the Brest Peace, the New Economic Policy, and so forth. And now there can be no doubt that in the main we have been victorious.

Our Sukhanovs, not to speak of Social-Democrats still farther to the right, never even dream that revolutions could be made otherwise. Our European philistines never even dream that the subsequent revolutions in Oriental countries, which possess much vaster populations and a much vaster diversity of social conditions, will undoubtedly display even greater peculiarities than the Russian revolution.

It need hardly be said that a textbook written on Kautskian lines was a very useful thing in its day. But it is time, for all that, to abandon the idea that it foresaw all the forms of development of subsequent world history. It would be timely to say that those who think so are simply fools.[12]

What are the fundamental demands which every Marxist should make of an examination of the question of forms of struggle? In the first place, Marxism differs from all primitive forms of socialism by not binding the movement to any one particular form of struggle. It recognises the most varied forms of struggle; and it does not "concoct" them, but only generalises, organises, gives conscious expression to those forms of struggle of the revolutionary classes which arise of themselves in the course of the movement. Absolutely hostile to all abstract formulas and to all doctrinaire recipes, Marxism demands an attentive attitude to the *mass* struggle in progress, which, as the movement develops, as the class-consciousness of the masses grows, as economic and political crises become acute, continually gives rise to new and more varied methods of defence and attack. Marxism, therefore, positively does not reject any form of struggle. Under no circumstances does Marxism confine itself to the forms of struggle possible and in existence at the given moment only, recognising as it does that new forms of struggle, unknown to the par-

[11] From V. I. Lenin, *"Left-Wing" Communism: An Infantile Disorder*, pp. 83–84.
[12] From V. I. Lenin, "Our Revolution: A Propos of N. Sukhanov's Notes" (January 16, 1923), in *Marx, Engels, Marxism*, p. 448.

ticipants of the given period, *inevitably* arise as the given social situation changes. In this respect Marxism *learns,* if we may so express it, from mass practice, and makes no claim whatever to *teach* the masses forms of struggle invented by "systematisers" in the seclusion of their studies. . . .

In the second place, Marxism demands an absolutely *historical* examination of the question of the forms of struggle. To treat this question apart from the concrete historical situation betrays a failure to understand the rudiments of dialectical materialism. At different stages of economic evolution, depending on differences in political, national-cultural, living and other conditions, different forms of struggle come to the fore and become the principal forms of struggle; and in connection with this, the secondary, auxiliary forms of struggle undergo change in their turn. To attempt to answer yes or no to the question whether any particular means of struggle should be used, without making a detailed examination of the concrete situation of the given movement at the given stage of its development, means completely to abandon the Marxist position.

These are the two principal theoretical propositions by which we must be guided. . . .[13]

A constant theme in Lenin's discussion of revolution was the need for the revolutionary to adopt a stance of ultimate political realism. An example occurs in Lenin's advocacy of the need to accept the onerous peace terms offered by Germany in 1918. Here, he expresses his disdain for those who prefer "beautiful fairy-tales" to a recognition of the need to adapt to reality. The revolutionary must be prepared "to crawl on [his] belly" if that is necessary to reach his objective.

If you are unable to adapt yourself, if you are not inclined to crawl on your belly in the mud, you are not a revolutionary but a chatterbox; and I propose this, not because I like it, but because we have no other road, because history has not turned out to be kind enough to bring the revolution to maturity everywhere simultaneously. . . .

Yes, we shall see the world revolution, but for the time being it is a very good fairy-tale, a very beautiful fairy-tale—I quite understand children liking beautiful fairy-tales. But I ask, is it proper for a serious revolutionary to believe in fairy-tales?[14]

[13] From V. I. Lenin, "Guerrilla Warfare" (1906), in *Marx, Engels, Marxism*, pp. 155–56.

[14] From V. I. Lenin, "Report on War and Peace," Seventh Congress, Russian Communist Party (Bolsheviks), March 7, 1918, in *Selected Works*, II, 636.

The strictest loyalty to the ideas of Communism must be combined
with the ability to make all the necessary practical compromises, to
manoeuvre, to make agreements, zigzags, retreats and so on, so as to
accelerate the coming to power and subsequent loss of political power of
the Hendersons (. . . the representatives of petty-bourgeois democracy
who call themselves Socialists); to accelerate their inevitable bankruptcy
in practice, which will enlighten the masses in the spirit of our ideas, in
the direction of Communism; to accelerate the inevitable friction, quar-
rels, conflicts and complete disintegration among the Hendersons, the
Lloyd Georges and Churchills . . . and to select the proper moment
when the disintegration among these "pillars of the sacred right of private property" is at its height, in order, by a determined attack of the
proletariat, to defeat them all and capture political power.

History generally, and the history of revolutions in particular, is always richer in content, more varied, more many-sided, more lively and
"subtle" than even the best parties and the most class-conscious vanguards
of the most advanced classes imagine. . . . From this follow two very
important practical conclusions: first, that in order to fulfill its tasks the
revolutionary class must be able to master *all* forms or sides of social
activity without exception (completing, after the capture of political
power, sometimes at great risk and very great danger, what it did not
complete before the capture of power); second, that the revolutionary
class must be ready to pass from one form to another in the quickest and
most unexpected manner.[15]

*A key to Bolshevik tactics was Lenin's keen sensitivity to
the requirements for alliance. Actually, this fell under two main
heads, both of which are illustrated in the selections that follow.
First, it is necessary to fragment one's opponents, to win over those
elements that can be attracted to one's cause, to neutralize others,
and, in general, to make use of conflicts inherent in the enemy's
position. Any enemy, therefore, was to be treated not as a unitary
whole, but rather as a whole made up of parts that could be identified, split, and dealt with in detail. "Split, split, and split yet again"
was the Leninist formulation of the old doctrine of "divide and
conquer," and it was as an adept at causing factional splits in the
effort to gain his objective that Lenin first became widely known
in socialist circles in Russia and abroad. At the same time, he realized both the value and the dangers of alliance when it could be
used to support one's own position. The straight alliance of people
of various views was not to be disdained (as long as it could be*

¹⁵ From V. I. Lenin, *"Left-Wing" Communism: An Infantile Disorder*, p. 76.

dominated by ideologically "conscious" professional revolutionaries).

Capitalism would not be capitalism if the "pure" proletariat were not surrounded by a large number of exceedingly mixed transitional types, from the proletarian to the semi-proletarian (who earns half of his livelihood by the sale of his labour power), from the semi-proletarian to the small peasant (and petty artisan, handicraft worker and small proprietor in general), from the small peasant to the middle peasant, and so on, and if the proletariat itself were not divided into more or less developed strata, if it were not divided according to territorial origin, trade, sometimes according to religion, and so on. . . .

The petty-bourgeois democrats (including the Mensheviks) inevitably vacillate between the bourgeoisie and the proletariat, between bourgeois democracy and the Soviet system, between reformism and revolutionariness, between love for the workers and fear of the proletarian dictatorship, etc. The proper tactics for the Communists to adopt is to *utilise* these vacillations and not to ignore them; and utilising them calls for concessions to those elements which are turning towards the proletariat, whenever and to the extent that they turn towards the proletariat, in addition to demanding a fight against those who turn towards the bourgeoisie. The result of the application of correct tactics in our country is that Menshevism has disintegrated and is disintegrating more and more, that the stubbornly opportunist leaders are becoming isolated, and that the best of the workers and the best elements among the petty-bourgeois democrats are being brought into our camp. This is a long process, and the hasty "decision"—"No compromise, no manoeuvres!"—can only hinder the work of strengthening the influence of the revolutionary proletariat and enlarging its forces.[16]

It is no secret that the brief appearance of Marxism on the surface of our literature was called forth by the alliance between people of extreme and of extremely moderate views. In point of fact, the latter were bourgeois democrats. . . .

That being the case, does not the responsibility for the subsequent "confusion" rest mainly upon the revolutionary Social-Democrats who entered into alliance with these future "critics"? This question, together with a reply in the affirmative, is sometimes heard from people with excessively rigid views. But these people are absolutely wrong. Only those who have no reliance in themselves can fear to enter into temporary

[16] From V. I. Lenin, *"Left-Wing" Communism: An Infantile Disorder*, pp. 56–57.

alliances with unreliable people. Besides, not a single political party
could exist without entering into such alliances. The combination with
the legal Marxists was in its way the first really political alliance con-
tracted by Russian Social-Democrats. Thanks to this alliance an astonish-
ingly rapid victory was obtained over Populism, and Marxian ideas (even
though in a vulgarised form) became very widespread. . . .

The rupture, of course, did not occur because the "allies" proved to
be bourgeois democrats. On the contrary, the representatives of the latter
tendency were the natural and desirable allies of the Social-Democrats
in so far as their democratic tasks that were brought to the front by the
prevailing situation in Russia were concerned. But an essential condition
for such an alliance must be complete liberty for Socialists to reveal to
the working class that its interests are diametrically opposed to the interests of the bourgeoisie. However, the Bernsteinist and "critical" tendency
to which the majority of the legal Marxists turned, deprived the Socialists
of this liberty and corrupted Socialist consciousness by vulgarising Marxism, by preaching the toning down of social antagonisms, by declaring
the idea of the social revolution and the dictatorship of the proletariat to
be absurd, by restricting the labour movement and the class struggle to
narrow trade unionism and to a "practical" struggle for petty, gradual
reforms. This was tantamount to the bourgeois democrat's denial of
Socialism's right to independence, and consequently, of its right to existence; in practice it meant a striving to convert the nascent labour movement into a tail of the liberals.[17]

*Lenin recommended that, where appropriate, the revolu-
tionaries not disdain to make full use of all available structures
for political activity, including parliamentary institutions. In 1920,
he castigated the ultraleft militants of the Western European Communist movement for the disdain which they showed for such institutions. He reminded them of his own struggle against the opponents of participation in the Duma. However, it is clear from
the context in which Lenin writes that his position was primarily
instrumental: parliaments were to be exploited as forums for propaganda, as centers for revolutionary organizational activity—as
means to an end rather than an end in their own right. Ultimately,
the revolutionary struggle would end in the insurrectionary application of armed violence to the solution of social problems. Parliaments and other legal vehicles for the mobilization and expression
of political opinion were useful in the interim, as the revolutionaries
gathered strength for the struggle that was to come.[18]*

[17] From V. I. Lenin, *What Is to Be Done?*, pp. 21–22.
[18] From V. I. Lenin, *"Left-Wing" Communism: An Infantile Disorder*, pp. 20–21.

In 1908 the "Left" Bolsheviks were expelled from our Party for stubbornly refusing to understand the necessity of participating in a most reactionary "parliament." The "Lefts" . . . based themselves particularly on the successful experiment of the boycott in 1905. When in August 1905 the tsar announced the convocation of an advisory "parliament," the Bolsheviks—unlike all the opposition parties and the Mensheviks—proclaimed a boycott of it, and it was actually swept away by the revolution of October 1905. At that time the boycott proved correct, not because non-participation in reactionary parliaments is correct in general, but because we correctly estimated the objective situation that was leading to the rapid transformation of the mass strikes into a political strike, then into a revolutionary strike, and then into insurrection. Moreover, the struggle at that time centred around the question whether to leave the convocation of the first representative assembly to the tsar, or to attempt to wrest its convocation from the hands of the old government. . . .

The Bolshevik boycott of "parliament" in 1905 . . . showed that when combining legal and illegal, parliamentary and non-parliamentary forms of struggle, it is sometimes useful, and even essential, to be able to reject parliamentary forms. But it is a very great mistake to apply this experience blindly, imitatively and uncritically to *other* conditions and to *other* circumstances. The boycott of the "Duma" by the Bolsheviks in 1906 was a mistake, although small and easily remediable. The boycott of the Duma in 1907, 1908 and subsequent years was a serious mistake and one difficult to remedy, because, on the one hand, a very rapid rise of the revolutionary tide and its transformation into an insurrection could not be expected, and, on the other hand, the whole historical situation of the renovated bourgeois monarchy called for the combining of legal and illegal work. . . . [T]he Bolsheviks *could not have* preserved (let alone strengthened, developed and reinforced) the sound core of the revolutionary party of the proletariat in 1908–14 had they not strenuously fought for the viewpoint that it is *obligatory* to combine legal and illegal forms of struggle, that it is *obligatory* to participate even in the most reactionary parliament and in a number of other institutions that were restricted by reactionary laws (benefit societies, etc.).

On many occasions, Lenin expressed his views on the requirements and modes of operation of revolutionary insurrection. The following sample of his writings is typical of his views in this regard.

. . . [A]rmed uprising is a *special* form of political struggle, one subject to special laws which must be attentively thought over. Karl

Marx expressed this truth with remarkable clarity when he wrote that *"insurrection is an art quite as much as war."* . . .

Of the principal rules of this art, Marx noted the following:

(1) Never *play* with insurrection, but when beginning it firmly realise that you must *go all the way.*

(2) Concentrate a *great superiority of forces* at the decisive point, at the decisive moment, otherwise the enemy, who has the advantage of better preparation and organisation, will destroy the insurgents.

(3) Once the insurrection has begun, you must act with the greatest *determination,* and by all means, without fail, take the *offensive.* "The defensive is the death of every armed rising."

(4) You must try to take the enemy by surprise and seize the moment when his forces are scattered.

(5) You must strive for *daily* successes, however small (one might say hourly, if it is the case of one town), and at all costs retain the *"moral superiority."*

Marx summed up the lessons of all revolutions in respect to armed uprising in the words of "Danton, the greatest master of revolutionary policy yet known: de l'audace, de l'audace, encore de l'audace." [19]

. . . [T]he historically effective forces of all classes—positively of all the classes of the given society without exception—are aligned in such a way that . . . (1) all the class forces hostile to us have become sufficiently entangled, sufficiently at loggerheads with each other, have sufficiently weakened themselves in a struggle which is beyond their strength; (2) all the vacillating, wavering, unstable, intermediate elements—the petty bourgeoisie and the petty-bourgeois democrats, as distinct from the bourgeoisie—have sufficiently exposed themselves in the eyes of the people, and have sufficiently disgraced themselves through their practical bankruptcy; and (3) among the proletariat a mass sentiment in favour of supporting the most determined, supremely bold revolutionary action against the bourgeoisie has arisen and begun vigorously to grow. Then revolution is indeed ripe; then, indeed, if we have correctly gauged all the conditions indicated, briefly outlined above, and if we have chosen the moment rightly, our victory is assured.[20]

THE ROAD TO POWER, 1917

"The outbreak of the Russian Revolution had, as its initial consequence, the abolition of the tsarist regime and, as its ultimate

---

[19] From V. I. Lenin, "Advice of an Onlooker" (October 8/21, 1917), in *Selected Works,* II, 468–69.

[20] From V. I. Lenin, *"Left-Wing" Communism: An Infantile Disorder,* p. 75.

result, the complete breakdown of all forms of organized life throughout Russia." [21] *Chronologically, the revolution had two peaks: the February-March overthrow of Tsarism, and the October-November Bolshevik coup. But it was a dual revolution in another sense as well: a* political *revolution (a wave of crises, culminating in the Bolshevik victory) was superimposed on a more basic conflict in which the peasant ("the real autocrat of Russia," as Victor Chernov once called him) took advantage of the breakdown of the system in order to stake his claim to the land.*

In our Introduction, we have already discussed Lenin's role in 1917. The selections that follow illustrate his reaction to the various phases of the Revolution. Here, again, we see the characteristic mixture of Lenin's consistency of ultimate purpose and his day-to-day flexibility in analyzing events and framing policy.

Prior to Lenin's arrival in Petrograd, the Bolshevik leaders on the scene—Stalin and Kamenev, set free from Siberian exile by the fall of Tsarism—had adopted a position of relative accommodation with the Provisional Government. Paradoxically, the "practical" underground leaders who had spent the war years in Russia were less radical than Lenin, perhaps because the latter had spent the war years in Switzerland in an intense effort to create a revolutionary International that was dedicated to exploiting the war and to converting wartime unrest into revolution.

But the fall of Tsarism had caught Lenin by surprise. In January, 1917, he told a Swiss audience that it was possible that the revolution (the European revolution, in which the Russian was encompassed) would not break out in his lifetime. News of the fall of Tsarism unleashed frenzied excitement in Lenin, who conjured up the wildest schemes—including an airplane flight across the German lines—for an immediate return to Russia. The Swiss socialists relieved him of the need to consider such dangerous expedients. At the initial instigation of the Menshevik, Martov, they negotiated for the return of Lenin and other emigrés by special train across Germany and thence via Sweden to Russia. Lenin brought with him a more radical conception of the requirements of the revolution, the famous "April Theses." [22]

1) In our attitude towards the war, which also under the new government of Lvov and Co. unquestionably remains on Russia's part a

[21] Richard Pipes, *The Formation of the Soviet Union: Communism and Nationalism, 1917–1923* (Cambridge, Mass.: Harvard University Press, 1957), p. 50.

[22] V. I. Lenin, "The April Theses," in "The Tasks of the Proletariat in the Present Revolution," *Pravda* (April 7/April 20, 1917), in Lenin, *Selected Works*, II, 45–48.

predatory imperialist war owing to the capitalist nature of that government, not the slightest concession to "revolutionary defencism" is permissible.

The class-conscious proletariat can give its consent to a revolutionary war, which would really justify revolutionary defencism, only on condition: (a) that the power pass to the proletariat and the poorest sections of the peasants bordering on the proletariat; (b) that all annexations be renounced in deed and not in word; (c) that a complete break be effected in actual fact with all capitalist interests.

In view of the undoubted honesty of the broad sections of the mass believers in revolutionary defencism, who accept the war only as a necessity, and not as a means of conquest, in view of the fact that they are being deceived by the bourgeoisie, it is necessary with particular thoroughness, persistence and patience to explain their error to them, to explain the inseparable connection existing between capital and the imperialist war, and to prove that without overthrowing capital *it is impossible* to end the war by a truly democratic peace, a peace not imposed by violence.

The most widespread campaign for this view must be organised in the army at the front.

2) It is a specific feature of the present situation in Russia that it represents a *transition* from the first stage of the revolution—which, owing to the insufficient class-consciousness and organisation of the proletariat, placed power in the hands of the bourgeoisie—to its *second* stage, which must place power in the hands of the proletariat and the poorest sections of the peasants.

This transition is characterised, on the one hand, by a maximum of legally recognised rights (Russia is *now* the freest of all the belligerent countries in the world); on the other, by the absence of violence in relation to the people, and, finally, by the unreasoning confidence of the people in the government of capitalists, the worst enemies of peace and socialism.

This peculiar situation demands of us an ability to adapt ourselves to the *special* conditions of Party work among unprecedentedly large masses of proletarians who have just awakened to political life.

3) No support for the Provisional Government; the utter falsity of all its promises should be explained, particularly those relating to the renunciation of annexations. . . .

4) Recognition of the fact that in most of the Soviets of Workers' Deputies our Party is in . . . [a] small minority, as against *a bloc of all* the petty-bourgeois opportunists, who have yielded to the influence of the bourgeoisie and convey its influence to the proletariat. . . .

It must be explained to the people that the Soviets of Workers' Deputies are the *only possible* form of revolutionary government, and that therefore our task is, as long as *this* government yields to the influence of the bourgeoisie, to present a patient, systematic, and persistent *explanation* of the errors of their tactics, an explanation especially adapted to the practical needs of the people.

As long as we are in the minority we carry on the work of criticising and exposing errors and at the same time we preach the necessity of transferring the entire state power to the Soviets of Workers' Deputies, so that the people may overcome their mistakes by experience.

5) Not a parliamentary republic—to return to a parliamentary republic from the Soviets of Workers' Deputies would be a retrograde step—but a republic of Soviets of Workers', Agricultural Labourers' and Peasants' Deputies throughout the country, from top to bottom.

Abolition of the police, the army and the bureaucracy.

The salaries of all officials, all of whom are to be elected and to be subject to recall at any time, not to exceed the average wage of a competent worker.

6) In the agrarian programme the most important part to be assigned to the Soviets of Agricultural Labourers' Deputies.

Confiscation of all landed estates.

Nationalisation of *all* lands in the country, the disposal of the land to be put in the charge of the local Soviets of Agricultural Labourers' and Peasants' Deputies. The organisation of separate Soviets of Deputies of Poor Peasants. The creation of model farms on each of the large estates . . . under the control of the Soviets of Agricultural Labourers' Deputies and for the public account.

7) The immediate amalgamation of all banks in the country into a single national bank, and the institution of control over it by the Soviets of Workers' Deputies.

8) It is not our *immediate* task to "introduce socialism," but only to bring social production and distribution of products at once under the *control* of the Soviets of Workers' Deputies.

9) Party tasks:
   (a) Immediate convocation of a Party congress;
   (b) Alteration of the Party Programme, mainly:
      (1) On the question of imperialism and the imperialist war;
      (2) On our attitude towards the state and *our* demand for a "commune state";[23]
      (3) Amendment of our out-of-date minimum programme.
   (c) Change of the Party's name.[24]

10) We must take the initiative in creating a revolutionary International, an International against the *social-chauvinists* and against the "Centre."

[23] I.e., a state of which the Paris Commune was the prototype. [Lenin.]

[24] Instead of "Social-Democracy," whose official leaders *throughout* the world have betrayed socialism and deserted to the bourgeoisie (the "defencists" and the vacillating "Kautskyites"), we must call ourselves the Communist Party. [Lenin.]

Lenin's "Letters on Tactics" amplify certain points made in the theses about the initial phases of the revolutionary situation.[25]

What, then, are the precisely established objective *facts* by which the party of the revolutionary proletariat must be guided at present in defining the tasks and forms of its activity? . . .

Before the February-March Revolution of 1917, state power in Russia was in the hands of one old class, namely, the feudal landed nobility, headed by Nicholas Romanov.

Now, after that revolution, the power is in the hands of *another* class, a new class, namely, the *bourgeoisie.*

The transfer of state power from one *class* to another *class* is the first, the principal, the basic sign of a *revolution*, both in the strictly scientific and in the practical political meaning of the term.

To this extent, the bourgeois, or the bourgeois-democratic, revolution in Russia *has been completed.* . . .

A new and different task now faces us: to effect a split between the proletarian elements (the anti-defencist, internationalist, "communist" elements, who stand for a transition to the commune) *within* this dictatorship and the *small-proprietor* or *petty-bourgeois* elements (Chkheidze, Tsereteli, Steklov, the Socialist-Revolutionaries and the other revolutionary defencists, who are opposed to moving towards the commune and who are in favour of "supporting" the bourgeoisie and the bourgeois government).

In July, 1917, the Provisional Government faced a major crisis from the left. The crisis was compounded of a number of elements: primary social unrest—mobs in the cities and increasing land seizure by the peasantry; growing rivalry between the Soviets, or workers' councils (still dominated by non-Bolsheviks), and the government—a split epitomized by the slogan "All power to the Soviets!"; and, perhaps most important as catalyst, the strains imposed by a desperate final offensive against the Austrians—an offensive which initially seemed successful, but which, by mid-July, had given way to a vigorous Austrian-German counteroffensive. The final stage in the collapse of the Russian armies was now starting, and desertions became virtually uncontrollable.

On July 16 and 17 (July 3–4, old style), demonstrations in Petrograd reached a peak. The Bolsheviks came to play a leading role— but a role that many felt was imposed by events, rather than in-

[25] From V. I. Lenin, "Letters on Tactics. First Letter: Assessment of the Present Situation" (April, 1917), in *Marx, Engels, Marxism*, pp. 313–15.

tended at the time. The rising may, indeed, have been as spontaneous as the ire of one demonstrator who assaulted the Socialist-Revolutionary leader Victor Chernov and demanded: "Take the power, you son of a bitch, when they offer it to you!" [26] *But the tide turned, for the moment. The Provisional Government managed to reassert a precarious control over the situation; and Bolshevik leaders, including Lenin, were forced into hiding.*

In the immediate sense, the July days were a setback for the Bolsheviks. Moreover, they offered powerful evidence for those of Lenin's associates who argued, up to the eve of the November rising, that an effort to seize power was "adventurism" of the wildest sort, and that it could only jeopardize the interests of the workers and peasants, as well as the Bolshevik party. But in a sense, the July days turned the tide against the Provisional Government. Its victory had been only marginal. Splits within the regime were exacerbated. Right-wing opponents of Premier Kerensky were emboldened to prepare a coup of their own on the pretext of guarding against a "softness" that would open the way to further disorder. Finally, the potential for a left-wing uprising, the success of which would depend on improved organization, better timing, and more explicit leadership, had been shown.

Lenin assessed the significance of these events on a number of occasions. The first example stems from the period immediately following the suppression of the July unrest. [27]

The counter-revolution has . . . taken state power into its hands. . . . (1) [T]he Constitutional-Democratic Party, i.e., the real leader of the organised bourgeoisie, by withdrawing from the Cabinet, confronted it with an ultimatum, thus clearing the way for the Cabinet's overthrow by the counter-revolution. (2) The General Staff and the high ranking officers, with the deliberate or semi-deliberate assistance of Kerensky, . . . have seized actual state power and proceeded to shoot down revolutionary units at the front, disarm the revolutionary regiments and workers in Petrograd and Moscow, suppress unrest in Nizhni-Novgorod, arrest the Bolsheviks and ban their papers, not only without trial, but even without a governmental order. At present basic state power in Russia is in fact a military dictatorship. This fact is still obscured by a number of institutions, revolutionary in words, but powerless in deeds. . . . (3) The Black-Hundred monarchist and bourgeois press that have switched from furi-

[26] Donald W. Treadgold, *Twentieth Century Russia*, 2nd ed. (Chicago: Rand McNally, 1964), p. 133. A recent, detailed study of the July days and their aftermath is Alexander Rabinowitch, *Prelude to Revolution* (Bloomington: Indiana University Press, 1968).

[27] From V. I. Lenin, "The Political Situation" (July 10/23, 1917; originally published July 20/August 2, 1917), in *Selected Works*, II, 202–204.

ously hounding the Bolsheviks to hounding the Soviets, the "incendiary" Chernov, etc., has indicated with the utmost clarity that the real essence of the present policy of military dictatorship, which is supported by the Cadets and monarchists, is preparations for breaking up the Soviets. . . .

All hopes for a peaceful development of the Russian revolution have finally vanished. This is the objective situation: either complete victory for the military dictatorship, or victory for the workers' insurrection; the latter victory is only possible when the insurrection coincides with a deep, mass upheaval against the government and the bourgeoisie caused by economic disruption and the prolongation of the war.

The slogan "All Power to the Soviets" was a slogan for peaceful development of the revolution which was possible in April, May, June, and up to July 5–9, i.e., up to the time when actual power passed into the hands of the military dictatorship. This slogan is no longer correct for it does not take into account that power has been transferred and that the revolution has in fact been completely betrayed by the S.R.s and Mensheviks. The situation cannot be saved by impetuous actions, revolts, partial resistance, or hopeless hit-and-run attempts to oppose reaction. The only assistance is a clear understanding of the situation, the endurance and determination of the workers' vanguard, preparation of forces for the insurrection, for the victory of which conditions at present are tremendously difficult, but still possible if the facts and trends mentioned above coincide. Let us have no constitutional or republican illusions of any kind, no more illusions about a peaceful path, no sporadic actions, no yielding *now* to provocation on the part of the Black Hundreds and Cossacks. Let us gather forces, reorganise them, and resolutely prepare for the insurrection, if the course of the crisis permits it on a really mass, national scale. Transfer of land to the peasants is impossible at present without insurrection, since the counter-revolution, having taken power, has completely united with the landlords as a class. . . .

The party of the working class, not abandoning legal activity, but never for a moment exaggerating its importance, must *combine* legal with illegal work, as it did in 1912–14.

Don't let slip a single hour of legal work. But don't cherish any constitutional or "peaceful" illusions. Form illegal organisations or cells everywhere and at once for the publication of leaflets, etc. Reorganise immediately, consistently, resolutely, all along the line.

Act as we did in 1912–14 when we could speak about overthrowing tsarism by a revolution and an armed uprising, without at the same time losing our legal base in the Duma, in the insurance societies and in the trade unions, etc.

In September, in the aftermath of the Kornilov putsch, Lenin
looked back on the events of July and assessed the reasons why

the Bolsheviks would have been unable to gain power at that time.[28]

On July 3–4 . . . the objective conditions for the victory of the insurrection did not exist.

1) We still lacked the support of the class which is the vanguard of the revolution. . . .

2) There was no country-wide revolutionary upsurge at that time. . . .

3) At that time there was no *vacillation* on any serious political scale among our enemies and among the irresolute petty bourgeoisie. . . .

4) Therefore, an insurrection on July 3–4 would have been a mistake: we could not have retained power either physically or politically. We could not have retained it physically in spite of the fact that at certain moments Petrograd was in our hands, because at that time our workers and soldiers would not have *fought and died* for Petrograd. There was not at that time that "savageness," or fierce hatred *both of* the Kerenskys *and of* the Tseretelis and Chernovs. Our people had still not been tempered by the experience of the persecution of the Bolsheviks in which the Socialist-Revolutionaries and Mensheviks participated.

We could not have retained power politically on July 3–4 because, *before the Kornilov affair,* the army and the provinces might and would have marched against Petrograd. Now the picture is entirely different.

Another turning point occurred at the beginning of September (August 25–30, old style). In a rather confused affair (in which Prime Minister Kerensky may have been an accomplice), General Kornilov, the commander-in-chief of the Russian Army, sent a cavalry corps to Petrograd. Originally, this may have stemmed from a request to buttress the government against possible renewed unrest from the left; inevitably, the move of the troops was seen as the opening gambit in a military coup. Whatever was intended backfired. There was further disaffection among the troops; partly for this reason, partly because of noncooperation by railway and other workers, Kornilov's adventure was abortive.

The Bolsheviks reemerged in the guise of "defenders of the revolution" and gained prestige among both civilians and soldiers. Their growing strength became visible as Bolshevik motions began to carry in the meetings of the Petrograd Soviet. Relations between Kerensky's government and the Soviet were exacerbated. The Socialist Revolutionaries—vital holders of the balance in the politics

---

[28] From V. I. Lenin, "Marxism and Insurrection: A Letter to the Central Committee . . . " (September, 1917), in *Selected Works,* II, 405–406.

of 1917—were increasingly alienated from the Provisional Govern-
ment. A cabinet crisis ensued, and it took Kerensky over a month to
patch together a new coalition. As his writings of the period indicate,
Lenin was increasingly impatient to make his bid for power.

The Kornilov revolt is an extremely unexpected (unexpected at such a moment and in such a form) and downright unbelievably sharp turn in events.

Like every sharp turn, it calls for revision and change of tactics. And, as is the case with every revision, we must be supercautious not to lose sight of principles. . . .

Even now we must not support Kerensky's government. This is unprincipled. If you ask whether we must fight against Kornilov the answer is: Of course we must! But this is not the same thing; there is a dividing line here, which is being stepped over by some Bolsheviks who fall into "conciliation," and allow themselves to be *carried away* by the course of events.

We shall fight, we are fighting against Kornilov, just *as Kerensky's troops do,* but we do not support Kerensky. *On the contrary,* we expose his weakness. There is the difference. It is rather a subtle difference, but it is highly essential and must not be forgotten.

What, then, constitutes our change of tactics after the Kornilov revolt? We are changing the *form* of our struggle against Kerensky. Without in the least relaxing our hostility towards him, without taking back a single word said against him, without renouncing the task of overthrowing Kerensky, we say: we must *take into account* the present situation. We shall not overthrow Kerensky right now. We shall approach the task of fighting against him *in a different way,* namely, we shall point out to the people (who are fighting against Kornilov) Kerensky's *weakness* and *vacillation.* That has *also* been done before. Now, however, it has become the *main* thing. This constitutes the change.

The change, further, is that the *main* thing now has become the intensification of our campaign for some kind of "partial demands" to be presented to Kerensky—arrest Milyukov, arm the Petrograd workers, summon the Kronstadt, Vyborg and Helsingfors troops to Petrograd, disperse the State Duma, arrest Rodzyanko, legalise the transfer of the landed estates to the peasants, introduce workers' control over grain and factories, etc. We must present these demands not only *to* Kerensky, and *not so much* to Kerensky, but to the workers, soldiers and peasants who have been *carried away* by the course of the struggle against Kornilov. Keep up their enthusiasm, encourage them to beat up the generals and officers who have expressed support for Kornilov, urge *them* to demand the immediate transfer of the land to the peasants, convince *them* of the necessity for arresting Rodzyanko and Milyukov, dispersing the Duma, closing down *Rech* and other bourgeois papers, and instituting investigations against them. The "Left" S.R.s must be especially pushed on in this direction.

It would be wrong to think that we have moved *away* from the task of the proletariat winning power. No. We have come tremendously nearer to it, *not directly*, but from the side. *This very minute* we must campaign not so much directly against Kerensky, as *indirectly* against him, namely, by demanding an active and most active, truly revolutionary war against Kornilov. The developments of this war alone can lead *us* to power, but we must *speak* of this as little as possible in our propaganda. . . .

We must relentlessly fight against phrases about the defence of the country, about a united front of revolutionary democracy, about supporting the Provisional Government, etc., etc., since they are just empty *phrases*. . . . Now is the time for *action;* the war against Kornilov must be conducted in a revolutionary way by drawing in the people, by arousing them, by inflaming them (Kerensky is *afraid* of the masses, *afraid* of the people). In the war against the Germans *action* is required right now; *immediate* and *unconditional* *peace must be offered* on *precise* terms. If we do this either a speedy peace *can* be attained or the war can be turned into a revolutionary war, otherwise all the Mensheviks and Socialist-Revolutionaries remain lackeys of imperialism.[29]

In a peasant country, and under a revolutionary, republican government, which enjoys the support of the Socialist-Revolutionary and Menshevik parties, parties that only yesterday dominated the petty-bourgeois democracy, a *peasant revolt* is developing.

It is incredible, but it is a factor. . . .

[The] leaders of the official Socialist-Revolutionary Party in an editorial of their official organ, *Dyelo Naroda,* of September 29, wrote as follows:

. . . Practically nothing has been done up to the present to put an end to the shackling relations that still prevail in the villages of Central Russia. . . . Are we not right in asserting that our republican government is still a long way from having rid itself of the old habits of the tsarist administration, and that the dead hand of Stolypin is still strongly felt in the methods of the revolutionary ministers?

. . . Just think: the supporters of the coalition are *forced* to admit that in a peasant country, after seven months of revolution, "practically

[29] From V. I. Lenin, Letter to the Bolshevik Central Committee (August 30/September 12, 1917), in *Selected Works,* II, 233–34, 237.

nothing has been done to put an end to the servitude" of the peasants, to their enslavement by the landlords! These Socialist-Revolutionaries are forced to call their colleague, Kerensky, and his gang of ministers *"Stolypinists."*

Can we find coming from the camp of our opponents more eloquent testimony not only that the coalition has collapsed and that the official Socialist-Revolutionaries who tolerate Kerensky have become *an anti-popular, anti-peasant and counter-revolutionary* party, but also that the whole Russian revolution has reached a turning-point? . . .

In the face of such facts, can one remain a conscientious partisan of the proletariat and yet deny that a crisis has matured, that the revolution is passing through an extremely critical moment, that the government's victory over the peasant *revolt* would now sound the death knell of the revolution, would be the final triumph of the Kornilov affair? [30]

Applied to Russia and to October 1917, [armed uprising] means: a simultaneous offensive to Petrograd, as sudden and as rapid as possible, which must without fail be carried out from within and from without, from the working-class quarters and from Finland, from Revel and from Kronstadt, an offensive of the *entire* navy, the concentration of a *gigantic superiority* of forces over the 15,000 or 20,000 (perhaps more) of our "bourgeois guard" (the officers' schools), our "Vendée troops" (part of the Cossacks), etc.

Our *three* main forces—the navy, the workers, and the army units—must be so combined as to occupy without fail and to hold *at any cost:* (a) the telephone exchange; (b) the telegraph office; (c) the railway stations; (d) and above all, the bridges.

The *most determined* elements (our "shock forces" and *young workers, as well as the best of the sailors) must be formed into small detachments to occupy all the more important points and to *take part* everywhere in all important operations, for example:

To encircle and cut off Petrograd; to seize it by a combined attack of the navy, the workers, and the troops—a task which requires *art and triple audacity.*

To form detachments from the best workers, armed with rifles and bombs, for the purpose of attacking and surrounding the enemy's "centres" (the officers' schools, the telegraph office, the telephone exchange, etc.). Their watchword must be: *"Better die to a man than let the enemy pass!"*

Let us hope that if action is decided on, the leaders will successfully apply the great precepts of Danton and Marx.

---

[30] From V. I. Lenin, "The Crisis Has Matured" (September 29/October 12, 1917), in *Selected Works,* II, 411–12.

The success of both the Russian and the world revolution depends on two or three days fighting.[31]

On the evening of October 24/November 6 Lenin sent the Central Committee his final written instructions for the insurrection; he then departed from his hiding place in order to personally participate in the decisive events of the next few days.[32]

Comrades,

I am writing these lines on the evening of the 24th. The situation is critical in the extreme. It is absolutely clear that now, in fact, to delay the uprising would be fatal.

I urge comrades with all my strength to realise that everything now hangs by a thread; that we are confronted by problems which are not solved by conferences or congresses (even congresses of Soviets), but exclusively by peoples, by the masses, by the struggle of the armed people.

. . . We must at all costs, this very evening, this very night, arrest the government, having first disarmed the military cadets (defeating them, if they resist), and so on.

We must not wait!! We may lose everything!!

The value of the seizure of power immediately will be the defence of the *people* (not of the congress, but of the people, the army and the peasants in the first place) from the . . . government, which . . . has hatched a second Kornilov plot.

Who must take power?

That is not important at present. Let the Revolutionary Military Committee take it, or "another institution" which will declare that it will relinquish the power only to the true representatives of the interests of the people, the interests of the army (the immediate proposal of peace), the interests of the peasants (the land to be taken immediately and private property abolished), the interests of the starving.

All districts, all regiments, all forces must mobilise themselves at once and immediately send their delegations to the Revolutionary Military Committee and to the Central Committee of the Bolsheviks with the insistent demand that under no circumstances should power be left in the hands of Kerensky and Co. until the 25th—not under any circumstances; the matter must be decided without fail this very evening, or this very night.

[31] From V. I. Lenin, "Advice of an Onlooker" (October 8/21, 1917), in *Selected Works*, II, 469–70.

[32] From V. I. Lenin, Letter to the Central Committee (October 24/November 6–7, 1917), in *Selected Works*, II, 493–94.

History will not forgive revolutionaries for procrastinating when they could be victorious today (and will certainly be victorious today), while they risk losing much tomorrow, in fact, risk losing everything.

If we seize power today, we seize it not in opposition to the Soviets but on their behalf.

The seizure of power is the business of the uprising; its political purpose will become clear after the seizure.

It would be a disaster, or a sheer formality, to await the wavering vote of October 25. The people have the right and are in duty bound to decide such questions not by a vote, but by force; in critical moments of revolution, the people have the right and are in duty bound to direct their representatives, even their best representatives, and not to wait for them.

This is proved by the history of all revolutions; and it would be an infinite crime on the part of the revolutionaries were they to let the chance slip, knowing that upon them depends the *salvation of the revolution,* the offer of peace, the salvation of Petrograd, salvation from famine, the transfer of the land to the peasants.

The government is tottering. It must be *given the death-blow* at all costs.

To delay action is fatal.

In 1920, Lenin summarized the reasons which—in his opinion— made it possible to carry out the revolution in Russia.[33]

. . . [I]t was easy for Russia in the specific, historically very unique situation of 1917 to *start* a Socialist revolution, but it will be more difficult for Russia than for the European countries to *continue* it and consummate it. . . . Certain specific conditions, viz., (1) the possibility of linking up the Soviet revolution with the ending (as a consequence of this revolution) of the imperialist war, which had exhausted the workers and peasants to an incredible degree; (2) the possibility of taking advantage for a certain time of the mortal conflict between two world-powerful groups of imperialist robbers, who were unable to unite against their Soviet enemy; (3) the possibility of enduring a comparatively lengthy civil war, partly owing to the enormous size of the country and to the poor means of communication; (4) the existence of such a profound bourgeois-democratic revolutionary movement among the peasantry that the party of the proletariat was able to adopt the revolutionary demands of the peasant party (the Socialist-

[33] From V. I. Lenin, *"Left-Wing" Communism: An Infantile Disorder,* p. 47.

Revolutionary Party, the majority of the members of which were definitely hostile to Bolshevism) and to realise them at once, thanks to the conquest of political power by the proletariat—these specific conditions do not exist in Western Europe at present; and a repetition of such or similar conditions will not come about easily. That is why, apart from a number of other causes, it will be more difficult to *start* a Socialist revolution in Western Europe than it was for us.

PROBLEMS OF REVOLUTIONARY CONSOLIDATION (1917–1918)

Lenin and the Bolsheviks had come to power, but Lenin himself was unsure how long they could maintain their position (see Trotsky below, p. 163). At times in the days following the coup, he noted that he would consider it a revolutionary advance if the Soviet Republic could outlast the short-lived Paris Commune of 1871. Nevertheless, he proceeded to issue decrees and to govern as if assured of power for a long period to come. "The will to govern" was as much a factor in consolidating the Bolshevik victory as the "will to power" had been in bringing Lenin to the pinnacle of revolutionary success in the first place (see Louis Fischer, below, pp. 187–88). As Lenin himself recognized, exceptional factors combined to prolong the life of the Bolshevik regime, even in the absence of complementary revolutionary successes in the West.

The months up to the Brest-Litovsk peace in March, 1918, may be seen as an extension of the immediate revolutionary period. Lenin's policies are reflected in the decrees which he drafted and which were proclaimed in the early days of the Soviet experiment. These were responses to the most immediate problems of revolutionary consolidation: peace, land seizures, and the outlining of a new system of government. In many cases, the positions adopted in the effort to rally support were to be repudiated within a few years (contrast the decree on workers' control with the later policy on trade unions, pp. 81–82 and 109, below).

The day after the coup, the following proclamation was issued.[34]

To Workers, Soldiers and Peasants:

The Second All-Russian Congress of Soviets of Workers' and Soldiers' Deputies has opened. . . . Backed by the will of the vast majority of the workers, soldiers and peasants, backed by the victorious uprising of the workers and the garrison which has taken place in Petrograd, the Congress takes power into its own hands.

The Provisional Government has been overthrown. . . .

[34] From V. I. Lenin, *Selected Works,* II, 501–502.

The Soviet government will propose an immediate democratic peace to all the nations and an immediate armistice on all fronts. It will secure the transfer of the land of the landlords, of the crown and monasteries to the peasants' committees without compensation; it will protect the rights of the soldiers by introducing complete democracy in the army; it will establish workers' control over production; it will ensure the convocation of the Constituent Assembly at the time appointed; it will see to it that bread is supplied to the cities and prime necessities to the villages; it will guarantee all the nations inhabiting Russia the genuine right of self-determination.

The Congress decrees: all power in the localities shall pass to the Soviets of Workers', Soldiers' and Peasants' Deputies, which must guarantee genuine revolutionary order.

The Congress calls upon the soldiers in the trenches to be vigilant and firm. The Congress of Soviets is convinced that the revolutionary army will be able to defend the revolution against all attacks of imperialism until such time as the new government succeeds in concluding a democratic peace, which it will propose directly to all peoples. The new government will do everything to fully supply the revolutionary army by means of a determined policy of requisitions and taxation of the propertied classes, and also will improve the condition of soldiers' families. . . .

Soldiers, workers and employees, the fate of the revolution and the fate of the democratic peace is in your hands!

Long live the Revolution!

The All-Russian Congress of Soviets of Workers' and Soldiers' Deputies

The Delegates from the Peasants' Soviets

Lenin presented the Congress of Soviets with his proposals for peace with Germany: they were vital to the survival of the regime and, so he thought, the spread of revolution westward. What follows are the major clauses of the draft Decree on Peace (as presented to the Congress by Lenin on October 28/November 10, 1917), as well as a portion of his explanatory comments which followed the reading of the Decree (see below, p. 78).[35]

The workers' and peasants' government . . . calls upon all the belligerent peoples and their governments to start immediate negotiations for a just, democratic peace. . . .

[35] From V. I. Lenin, *Selected Works*, II, 503–505, 506.

[B]y such a peace the government means an immediate peace without annexations (i.e., without the seizure of foreign lands, without the forcible incorporation of foreign nations) and without reparations.

The government of Russia proposes this kind of peace be immediately concluded by all the belligerent nations, and expresses its readiness to take all the resolute measures now, without the least delay, pending the final ratification of all the terms of such a peace by authoritative assemblies of the people's representatives of all countries and all nations.

In accordance with the sense of justice of democrats in general, and of the working people in particular, the government conceives the annexation or seizure of foreign lands to mean every incorporation of a small or weak nation into a large or powerful state without the precisely, clearly and voluntarily expressed consent and wish of that nation, irrespective of the time when such forcible incorporation took place, irrespective also of the degree of development or backwardness of the nation forcibly annexed to the given state, or forcibly retained within its borders, and irrespective, finally, of whether this nation is in Europe or in distant, overseas countries. . . .

At the same time the government declares that it does not regard the above-mentioned peace terms as an ultimatum; in other words, it is prepared to consider any other peace terms, and insists only that they be advanced by any of the belligerent countries as speedily as possible, and that in the peace proposals there should be absolute clarity and the complete absence of all ambiguity and secrecy.

The government abolishes secret diplomacy, and, for its part, announces its firm intention to conduct all negotiations quite openly in full view of the whole people. It will proceed immediately with the full publication of the secret treaties endorsed or concluded by the government of landlords and capitalists from February to October 25, 1917. The government proclaims the unconditional and immediate annulment of everything contained in these secret treaties insofar as it is aimed, as is mostly the case, at securing advantages and privileges for the Russian landlords and capitalists and at the retention, or extension, of the annexations made by the Great Russians. . . .

The government proposes an immediate armistice to the governments and peoples of all the belligerent countries, and, for its part, considers it desirable that this armistice should be concluded for a period of not less than three months, i.e., a period long enough to permit the completion of negotiations for peace. . . .

While addressing this proposal for peace to the governments and peoples of all the belligerent countries, the Provisional Workers' and Peasants' Government of Russia appeals in particular also to the class-conscious workers of the three most advanced nations of mankind and the largest states participating in the present war, namely, Great Britain, France and Germany. . . . [T]he workers of the countries mentioned

will understand the duty that now faces them of saving mankind from
the horrors of war and its consequences; . . . these workers, by comprehensive, determined, and supremely vigorous action, will help us to
conclude peace successfully, and at the same time emancipate the
labouring and exploited masses of our population from all forms of
slavery and all forms of exploitation.

Lenin's Comments on the Decree on Peace:

. . . Our appeal must be addressed both to the governments and to
the peoples. We cannot ignore the governments, for that would delay the
possibility of concluding peace, and the people's government dare not
do that; but we have no right not to appeal to the peoples at the same
time. Everywhere there are differences between the governments and the
peoples, and we must therefore help the peoples to intervene in questions of war and peace. We will, of course, insist upon the whole of our
programme for a peace without annexations and reparations. We shall
not retreat from it; but we must not give our enemies an opportunity
to say that their conditions are different from ours and that therefore it
is useless to start negotiations with us. No, we must deprive them of
that advantageous position and not present our terms in the form of an
ultimatum. Therefore the point is included that we are willing to
consider any peace terms and all proposals. We shall consider them, but
that does not necessarily mean that we shall accept them.

> *Lenin's draft Decree on Land was presented to the Con-
> gress of Soviets as the internal corollary to the peace program. It
> was based on demands of the peasant spokesmen, nominally sup-
> porters of the Socialist Revolutionaries (see below, pp. 159, 161).*[36]

Lenin's Introductory Comments:

We maintain that the revolution has proved and demonstrated how
important it is that the land question should be put clearly. The outbreak of the armed uprising, the second, the October Revolution, clearly
proves that the land must be turned over to the peasants. The government that has been overthrown and the compromising parties of the
Mensheviks and Socialist-Revolutionaries committed a crime when they
kept postponing the settlement of the land question on various pretexts
and thereby brought the country to economic dislocation and a peasant
revolt. . . . If the government had acted wisely, and if their measures

[36] From V. I. Lenin, "Report on the Land," *Izvestia* and *Pravda* (October 28/Novem-
ber 10, 1917), in *Selected Works*, II, 511–15. In Lenin's text, the "Peasant Mandate on
Land" is given in full; abridgements in the text as presented here are made by the editor.

had met the needs of the poor peasants, would there have been unrest among the peasant masses? But all the measures of the government . . . went counter to the interests of the peasants and compelled them to revolt.

. . . The first duty of the government of the workers' and peasants' revolution must be to settle the land question, which can pacify and satisfy the vast masses of poor peasants. I shall read to you the clauses of a decree your Soviet Government must issue. In one of the clauses of this decree is embodied the Mandate to the Land Committees, compiled from 242 mandates from local Soviets of Peasants' Deputies.

Decree on Land

1) Landlord ownership of land is abolished forthwith without any compensation.

2) The landed estates, as also all crown, monastery, and church lands, with all their livestock, implements, buildings and everything pertaining thereto, shall be placed at the disposal of the volost land committees and the uyezd Soviets of Peasants' Deputies pending the convocation of the Constituent Assembly.

3) All damage to confiscated property, which henceforth belongs to the whole people, is proclaimed a grave crime to be punished by the revolutionary courts. The uyezd Soviets of Peasants' Deputies shall take all necessary measures to assure the observance of the strictest order during the confiscation of the landed estates, to determine the size of estates, and the particular estates subject to confiscation, to draw up exact inventories of all property confiscated and to protect in the strictest revolutionary way all agricultural enterprises transferred to the people, with all buildings, implements, livestock, food stocks, etc.

4) The following peasant Mandate, compiled by the newspaper *Izvestia of the All-Russian Soviet of Peasants' Deputies* from 242 local peasant mandates and published in . . . *Izvestia* (. . . August 19, 1917), shall serve everywhere to guide the implementation of the great land reforms until a final decision on the latter is taken by the Constituent Assembly.

5) The land of ordinary peasants and ordinary Cossacks shall not be confiscated.

Peasant Mandate on the Land

The land question in its full scope can be settled only by the popular Constituent Assembly.

The most equitable settlement of the land question is to be as follows:

1) *Private ownership of land shall be abolished for ever;* land shall not be sold, purchased, leased, mortgaged, or otherwise alienated.

All land, whether *state, crown, monastery, church, factory, entailed, private, public, peasant, etc., shall be alienated without compensation* and become the property of the whole people, and pass into the use of all those who cultivate it.

Persons who suffer by this property revolution shall be deemed to be entitled to public support only for the period necessary for adaptation to the new conditions of life.

2) All mineral wealth, e.g., ore, oil, coal, salt, etc., as well as all forests and waters of state importance, shall pass into the exclusive use of the state. All the small streams, lakes, woods, etc., shall pass into the use of the communes, to be administered by the local self-government bodies.

3) Lands on which *high-level scientific* farming is practised, e.g., orchards, plantations, seed plots, nurseries, hothouses, etc., *shall not be divided up, but shall be converted into model farms,* to be turned over for exclusive use *to the state or to the communes,* depending on the size and importance of such lands.

Household land in towns and villages, with orchards and vegetable gardens, shall be reserved for the use of their present owners, the size of the holdings, and the size of tax levied for the use thereof, to be determined by law. . . .

6) The right to use the land shall be accorded to all citizens of the Russian state (without distinction of sex) desiring to cultivate it by their own labour, with the help of their families, or in partnership, but only as long as they are able to cultivate it. The employment of hired labour is not permitted. . . .

7) Land tenure shall be on an equality basis, i.e., the land shall be distributed among the toilers in conformity with a labour standard or a consumption standard, depending on local conditions.

There shall be absolutely no restriction on the forms of land tenure: household, farm, communal, or co-operative, as shall be decided in each individual village and settlement. . . .

From Lenin's Concluding Comments:

Voices are being raised here that the decree itself and the Mandate were drawn up by the Socialist-Revolutionaries. What of it? Does it matter who drew them up? As a democratic government, we cannot ignore the decision of the masses of the people, even though we may disagree with it. In the fire of experience, applying the decree in practice, and carrying it out locally, the peasants will themselves realise where the truth lies. . . . The old government, which was overthrown by armed uprising, wanted to settle the land question with the help of the old, unchanged tsarist bureaucracy. But instead of solving the question, the bureaucracy only fought the peasants. The peasants have learnt something during the eight months of our revolution; they want to settle all land questions themselves. We are therefore opposed to all amendments to this draft law. We want no details in it, for we are writing a decree, not a programme of action. Russia is vast, and local conditions vary. We trust that the peasants themselves will be able to solve the problem correctly, properly, better than we could do it. Whether they do it in our spirit or in the .spirit of the programme of the Socialist-Revolutionaries is not the point. The point is that the peasants should be firmly assured that there are no more landlords in the countryside, that they themselves must decide all questions, and that they themselves must arrange their own lives.

The following "Draft Regulations on Workers' Control" (written between October 26 and 31/November 8–13), reflect the euphoria of the early phase of the Revolution; at the same time, an underlying theme is Lenin's calculated use of workers' power as a means of intimidating those who might be tempted to obstruct the operations of the new regime.[37]

1. *Workers' control* over the production, storage, purchase and sale of all products and raw materials shall be introduced in all industrial, commercial, banking, agricultural and other enterprises employing not less than five workers and employees (together), or with an annual turnover of not less than 10,000 rubles.

2. Workers' control shall be exercised by all the workers and employees of an enterprise, either directly, if the enterprise is small enough to permit it, or through their elected representatives, who shall be elected *immediately* at general meetings, at which minutes of the elections shall be taken and the names of those elected communicated to the government and to the local Soviets of Workers', Soldiers' and Peasants' Deputies.

3. Unless permission is given by the elected representatives of the workers and employees, the suspension of work of an enterprise or an industrial establishment of state importance (see §7), or any change in its operation is absolutely prohibited.

4. The elected representatives shall be given access to *all* books and documents and *all* warehouses and stocks of materials, instruments and products, without exception.

5. The decisions of the elected representatives of the workers and employees are binding upon the owners of enterprises and may be annulled only by trade unions and their congresses.

6. In all enterprises of state importance *all* owners and *all* representatives of the workers and employees elected for the purpose of exercising workers' control shall be answerable to the state for the maintenance of the strictest order and discipline and for the protection of property.

[37] From V. I. Lenin, *Selected Works,* II, pp. 519–20.

Persons guilty of neglect of duty, concealment of stocks, accounts, etc., shall be punished by the confiscation of the whole of their property and by imprisonment for a term of up to five years.

7. By enterprises of state importance are meant all enterprises working for defence, or in any way connected with the manufacture of articles necessary for the existence of the masses of the population.

8. More detailed rules on workers' control shall be drawn up by the local Soviets of Workers' Deputies and by conferences of factory trade union committees, and also by committees of employees at general meetings of their representatives.

Lenin had to surmount two major obstacles before he could consider the first phase of postrevolutionary consolidation complete. The first was the problem of the Constituent Assembly. Initially, plans to convene such a body had been developed under the Provisional Government; the Bolsheviks had pushed for it and had accused the government of undue delay. In the immediate aftermath of the seizure of power, Lenin still seemed to believe that such an assembly could be tolerated (see above, p. 76). But the elections of November 25 (new style) gave the Bolsheviks only a quarter of the votes and only 168 seats of a total of 703 (the Socialist Revolutionaries had 380). On January 18, the delegates to the Assembly attempted to meet. Their meeting lasted only one day, and they spoke amidst heckling from a crowd of Bolshevik sailors and soldiers; when dark came, the electricity was cut off, and finally the delegates were dispersed. The suppression of the Assembly, the ending of Russia's "one day of democracy," was not in itself a decisive act in more than a symbolic sense; it reflected the power situation that had existed since November. Lenin, in eliminating what in his view was simply a relic of the period of Provisional Government, made clear that he would brook no challenge to the undivided authority of his regime.[38]

At its very inception, the Russian revolution gave rise to Soviets of Workers', Soldiers' and Peasants' Deputies as the only mass organisation of all the toiling and exploited classes capable of leading the struggle of these classes for their complete political and economic emancipation. . . .

The Constituent Assembly, elected on the basis of electoral lists drawn up prior to the October Revolution, was an expression of the old relation

[38] From V. I. Lenin, "Draft Decree on the Dissolution of the Constituent Assembly" (January 6/19, 1918), in *Selected Works*, II, 573–74.

of political forces which existed when power was held by the compromisers and the Cadets. When the people at that time voted for the candidates of the Socialist-Revolutionary Party, they were not in a position to choose between the Right Socialist-Revolutionaries, the supporters of the bourgeoisie, and the Left Socialist-Revolutionaries, the supporters of socialism. The Constituent Assembly, therefore, which was to have crowned the bourgeois parliamentary republic, was bound to become an obstacle in the path of the October Revolution and Soviet power.

The October Revolution, by giving power to the Soviets, and through the Soviets to the toiling and exploited classes, aroused the desperate resistance of the exploiters. . . . The toiling classes learned by experience that the old bourgeois parliamentary system had outlived its purpose and was absolutely incompatible with the aim of achieving socialism, and that not national institutions, but only class institutions (such as the Soviets) were capable of overcoming the resistance of the propertied classes and of laying the foundations of socialist society. To relinquish the sovereign power of the Soviets, to relinquish the Soviet Republic won by the people, for the sake of the bourgeois parliamentary system and the Constituent Assembly, would now be a step backwards and would cause the collapse of the October workers' and peasants' revolution.

Owing to the above-mentioned circumstances, the majority in the Constituent Assembly which met on January 5 was secured by the party of the Right Socialist-Revolutionaries, the party of Kerensky, Avksentyev and Chernov. Naturally this party refused . . . to recognise the programme of Soviet power. . . . By this action the Constituent Assembly severed all ties with the Soviet Republic of Russia. The withdrawal from such a Constituent Assembly of the Bolshevik group and the Left Socialist-Revolutionary group, who now patently constitute the overwhelming majority in the Soviets and enjoy the confidence of the workers and the majority of the peasants, was inevitable.

The Right Socialist-Revolutionary and Menshevik parties are in fact carrying on outside the walls of the Constituent Assembly a most desperate struggle against Soviet power. . . . It is obvious that under such circumstances the remaining part of the Constituent Assembly could only serve as a screen for the struggle of the counterrevolutionaries to overthrow Soviet power.

Accordingly, the Central Executive Committee resolves:

The Constituent Assembly is hereby dissolved.

Lenin's most difficult task during the revolutionary period, and one which illustrates his qualities as a political realist of exceptional skill, was to persuade his colleagues to negotiate and sign a humiliating peace treaty with the Germans. The war-peace issue ran like a thread throughout the whole period leading up to and through the Bolshevik seizure of power. Lenin realized that it was the disastrous continuation of the war, more than any other single factor, that had contributed to the failure of the Provisional Government; the new regime's own political future would depend on how it dealt with the question of war and peace. The German terms for peace were exceedingly harsh—ultimately, Russia lost 1.3 million square miles of some of its best territory and a quarter of its population, besides paying a heavy indemnity in both gold and raw materials. But Lenin felt the price had to be met; he said, in connection with this Treaty of Brest-Litovsk, that, if necessary, a revolutionary had to learn to put pride aside and to crawl on his belly.

Many who otherwise supported Lenin did not share his views on acceptance of the German peace terms. The left-wing Socialist Revolutionaries, who had joined Lenin's government in November and who provided a link to the peasantry, withdrew from the Council of People's Commissars. Trotsky, who had been the chief negotiator with the Germans, balked at signing a peace treaty; he advanced the doctrine of "neither war nor peace," counting, apparently, on such factors as spontaneous resistance and the vastness of the Russian territory to cushion a further German advance. Others, like Bukharin, advocated continued resistance, but under the banner of "revolutionary war," the aim of which would be to spark dissent among the enemy's own soldiers and subjects and to promote revolution in the West by example and propaganda.

Throughout this period, Lenin was intransigent. Almost his only concession to his opponents was to toy with the Allied Powers (with whom Russia was still technically linked) to find out what they could do in the event of a further German advance. But, in the main, he staked the Bolshevik regime on his ability to take Russia out of the war. His arguments were twofold. He began with a realistic assessment of Russia's position: she did not possess the organized power to offer serious resistance to the Germans; survival of the Bolshevik revolution within Russia was more important than anything else—land, population, pride, or international revolutionary reputation.

The revolutionary state needed a breathing space to organize itself, mobilize its forces for the civil war that was erupting, and develop its strength to survive and carry out basic social reconstruction. Beyond this basic argument, Lenin made a secondary appeal, an appeal to opportunism. He suggested that, in the long run, any peace treaty negotiated with Germany would be a "Tilsit Peace." (At Tilsit, in 1807, Prussia had surrendered to Napoleon, making peace at the expense of heavy territorial losses and a large indemnity. Less than a decade later, the balance of forces had shifted against Napoleon, and Prussia was a member of a coalition that was victorious against France.) Lenin was confident that new factors would come into play to cancel Russia's losses; in fact, Germany's own defeat seven months after the Treaty of Brest-Litovsk moderated the significance of many of the concessions that had been made by Russia.

But the arguments were not decisive in themselves. It took a breakdown in negotiations, a rapid German advance almost to the gates of Petrograd, and, in the end, Lenin's own threat to resign, to win a narrow margin of support for the peace treaty that Lenin believed essential to the survival of the revolution.

2. . . . [T]he Civil War . . . has not yet reached its climax. . . . [A] certain period of acute economic dislocation and chaos, which accompany all wars, and civil war in particular, is inevitable, before the resistance of the bourgeoisie is crushed. . . .

5. . . . [F]or the success of socialism in Russia a certain amount of time, several months at least, will be necessary, during which the hands of the socialist government must be absolutely free for achieving victory over the bourgeoisie in our own country first, and for launching on a wide scale far-reaching mass organisational work.

6. This position of the socialist revolution in Russia must form the basis of any definition of the international tasks of our Soviet power, for the international situation in the fourth year of the war is such that it is quite impossible to predict the probable moment of outbreak of revolution and overthrow of any of the European imperialist governments (including the German). That the socialist revolution in Europe must come, and will come, is beyond doubt. All our hopes for the *final* victory of socialism are founded on this certainty and on this scientific prognosis. . . . It would be a mistake, however, to base the tactics of the Russian socialist Government on attempts to determine whether the European, and especially the German, socialist revolution will take place in the next six months (or some such brief period), or not. Inasmuch as it is quite impossible to determine this, all such attempts, objectively speaking, would be nothing but a blind gamble.

7. The peace negotiations in Brest-Litovsk have by now—January 7, 1918—made it perfectly clear that the war party has undoubtedly gained the upper hand in the German Government . . . and has virtually already presented Russia with an ultimatum: . . . either the continuation of the war, or a peace with annexations . . .

8. The socialist Government of Russia is faced with the question—a

question whose solution brooks no delay—of whether to accept this peace with annexations now, or to immediately wage a revolutionary war. In fact, no middle course is possible. . . . [T]he underlying principle of our tactics must . . . be, . . . how can the socialist revolution be most firmly and reliably ensured the possibility of consolidating itself, or, at least, of maintaining itself in one country until it is joined by other countries. . . .

12. It is said that in a number of Party statements we actually "promised" a revolutionary war, and that by concluding a separate peace we would be going back on our word.

That is not true. We said that in the era of imperialism a socialist government *had* to *"prepare for and carry on"* a revolutionary war; we said this in order to combat abstract pacifism . . . but we never gave any pledge to start a revolutionary war without considering how far it is possible to wage it at a given moment. . . .

13. Summing up the arguments in favour of an immediate revolutionary war, we have to conclude that such a policy might perhaps answer the human yearning for the beautiful, dramatic and striking, but that it would totally disregard the objective balance of class forces and material factors at the present stage of the socialist revolution now under way.

14. There can be no doubt that our army is absolutely in no condition . . . , and will not be for the next few weeks (and probably for the next few months), to beat back a German offensive successfully; . . .

16. The poor peasants in Russia are capable of supporting the socialist revolution led by the working class, but they are not capable of agreeing to fight a serious revolutionary war immediately, at the present juncture. To ignore this objective balance of class forces on this issue would be a fatal error.

17. . . . If . . . the German revolution does not occur in the next few months, the course of events, if the war is continued, will inevitably be such that grave defeats will compel Russia to conclude an even more disadvantageous separate peace; . . . the peasant army, which is unbearably exhausted by the war, will after the very first defeats . . . overthrow the socialist workers' government.

18. This being the state of affairs, it would be absolutely impermissible tactics to stake the fate of the socialist revolution, which has already begun in Russia, merely on the chance that the German revolution may begin . . . within a matter of weeks. Such tactics would be a reckless gamble. We have no right to take such risks. . . .

20. In concluding a separate peace we free ourselves as *much as is possible at the present moment* from both hostile imperialist groups, we take advantage of their mutual enmity and warfare which hamper concerted action on their part against us, and for a certain period have our hands free to advance and to consolidate the socialist revolution. The

reorganisation of Russia on the basis of the dictatorship of the proletariat, and the nationalisation of the banks and large-scale industry, coupled with *exchange of products* in kind between the towns and the small peasants' consumers' societies, is economically quite feasible, provided we are assured a few months in which to work in peace. And such a reorganisation will render socialism invincible both in Russia and all over the world, and at the same time will create a solid economic basis for a mighty workers' and peasants' Red Army.[39]

. . . [O]ne must know how to retreat. We cannot hide the incredibly bitter, deplorable reality from ourselves with empty phrases; we must say: God grant that we retreat in what is halfway good order. We cannot retreat in good order, but God grant that our retreat is halfway good order, that we gain a little time in which the sick part of our organism can be absorbed at least to some extent. On the whole the organism is sound, it will overcome its sickness. But you cannot expect it to overcome it all at once, instantaneously, you cannot stop an army in flight. . . . We are now signing a peace treaty, we have a respite, we are taking advantage of it the better to defend our fatherland—because had we been at war we should have had an army fleeing in panic which would have had to be stopped, and which our comrades cannot and could not stop, because war is more powerful than sermons, more powerful than ten thousand arguments. . . . [W]e shall take advantage of this respite to persuade the people to unite, to fight, to say to the Russian workers and peasants: "Organise self-discipline, strict discipline, otherwise you will have to remain lying under the German jackboot as you are lying now, as you will inevitably have to lie until the people learn to fight and to create an army capable, not of flight, but of bearing untold suffering." It is inevitable, because the German revolution has not yet begun, and we cannot guarantee that it will come tomorrow. . . .

We do not know how long the respite will last—we will try to take advantage of the situation. . . . [A] disgraceful peace is proper, because it is in the interests of the proletarian revolution and the regeneration of Russia, because it will help to get rid of the sick organ. As every sensible man understands, by signing this peace treaty we do not put a stop to our workers' revolution; . . .

Grasp even an hour's respite if it is given you, in order to maintain contact with the remote rear and there create new armies. Abandon illusions for which real events have punished you and will punish you more severely in the future. An epoch of most grievous defeats is ahead

---

[39] From V. I. Lenin, "Theses on the Question of Immediate Conclusion of a Separate and Annexationist Peace" (January 8/21, 1918), in *Selected Works*, II, 575–81.

of us, it has set in, we must be able to reckon with it, we must be prepared for persistent work in conditions of illegality, in conditions of
downright slavery to the Germans; it is no use painting it in bright
colours, it is a real Peace of Tilsit. If we are able to act in this way,
then, in spite of defeats, we shall be able to say with absolute certainty—
victory will be ours.[40]

[40] From V. I. Lenin, "Report on War and Peace," Seventh Congress of the Russian
Communist Party (Bolsheviks) (March 7, 1918), in *Selected Works*, II, 629–31, 635, 637–
38, 641.

3

Lenin in Power: Theory, Practice, and Policy

THEORY OF THE STATE

In the midst of the revolution of 1917, Lenin showed great concern for what is, on the surface, his least directly applicable work: State and Revolution. *In April, on his way to Petrograd, he took care to leave a notebook of extracts and comments on the state for safekeeping in Stockholm. He considered this to be a vital part of his intellectual legacy, and a short time later cautioned Zinoviev to undertake, in the event of his death, the publication of these notes. In hiding, after July, 1917, Lenin—the notebook once more in his possession—began to convert these notes into a book;* State and Revolution *was only partially completed, however, by the time the successful Bolshevik rising was launched.*

Why was this book so important, psychologically, to Lenin? The answer must be sought at the esoteric level, in what is implicit in the incomplete manuscript, and in the context of other writings of the period from the completion of Imperialism *onwards. The theoretical analysis of class dictatorship had practical implications. Direct popular administration, using techniques taken over from advanced capitalism, and combined with a continued emphasis on party control, underlay Lenin's confidence in his ability to impart some degree of order to a crumbling social structure. Thus, the theory of the state that emerged on the eve of the revolution reflected, and at the same time provided an intellectual rationale for, Lenin's will to power. It was his answer to those who maintained that the odds against creation of a viable post-revolutionary order were so great that a seizure of power would be an exercise in futility. And, perhaps, it was a way of stilling occasional doubts that arose in his own mind, of rationalizing the revolution to himself.*

Lenin's emphasis on dictatorship requires some comment. State and Revolution—*together with* The Proletarian Revolution and the Renegade Kautsky, *which is, in some respects, its sequel—marks Lenin's final break with the "two-stage" theory of revolution. Lenin had prepared for this break in his writings on the party and had made a significant step in this direction in the aftermath of 1905: the party of the proletariat would make its revolution not in parallel to the bourgeoisie, but by alliance with disaffected sections of*

*the peasantry, the bourgeoisie, and the nationalities; afterwards, it
would continue to direct the postrevolutionary state. But taken
to this point, the rejection of a two-phase concept of revolution
has more to do with strategy; it leaves unanswered the question of
whether one can establish a viable political order after the revolution, in the military and political sense, has been made. According
to his earlier conception, a country as "backward" as Russia would
have to go through a period of bourgeois-democratic development
before it could begin the transition to socialism.*

*Lenin could no longer accept this. In 1917, looking at the im-
mediate situation—the collapse of the armies and civil order—he
could see not only the prospect for a Bolshevik-directed seizure of
power, but also two dangerous alternatives: either a slide into
anarchy or a victory by the right-wing contenders for power. The
growing support for the Soviets, if tapped by the Bolsheviks, could
provide the practical base for striking for power; the analysis of
emerging forms of organization in Lenin's study of the state provided a theoretical rationale for asserting that this power could be
exercised to create a socialist state.*

*Thus, the notion of mass participation in the operations of the
state should be associated not, as is commonly the case, with the
anarchistic overtones that some have detected in* State and Revolution, *but rather, as we shall see, with the concept of a dictatorship
using mass participation and integrating the techniques of administration that Lenin saw emerging under modern capitalism. These
had first been noted in his work on imperialism; they were elaborated on, and their possible transmutation to serve socialist revolution was discussed, in* State and Revolution; *and the theory of a
new type of dictatorship on a mass base was elaborated in* The
Proletarian Revolution and the Renegade Kautsky. *The selections
that follow illustrate the various aspects of this analysis.*

*The first two selections illustrate Lenin's continuing repudiation
of anarchy and assert the notion of class dictatorship against Kautsky's democratic socialism.*

Marxism differs from anarchism in that it recognises the *need* for
a state and for state power in the period of revolution in general, and
in the period of transition from capitalism to socialism in particular.[1]

"Literally," [Kautsky] writes, "the word 'dictatorship' means the abolition of democracy."

[1] From V. I. Lenin, "The Task of the Proletariat in Our Revolution" (c. April 10,
1917; first published September, 1917) in *Selected Works*, II, 65. This was from Lenin's
draft of a new party program.

In the first place this is not a definition. . . .

Secondly, it is obviously wrong. A liberal naturally speaks of "democracy" in general; but a Marxist will never forget to ask: for what class? Everybody knows, for instance (and Kautsky the "historian" also knows it), that the rebellions of and even the strong ferment among the slaves in antiquity immediately revealed the fact that in essence the state of antiquity was the *dictatorship of the slave-owners.* Did this dictatorship abolish democracy *among* and *for* the *slave-owners?* Everybody knows that it did not. . . .

. . . [D]ictatorship does not necessarily mean the abolition of democracy for the class that exercises dictatorship over other classes; but it certainly does mean the abolition (or very material restriction, which is also a form of abolition) of democracy for that class over which, or against which, the dictatorship is exercised. But however true this assertion may be, it does not give a definition of dictatorship. . . .

Dictatorship is power, based directly upon force, and unrestricted by any laws.

The revolutionary dictatorship of the proletariat is power won and maintained by the violence of the proletariat against the bourgeoisie, power that is unrestricted by any laws.[2]

Lenin emphasizes class dominance as the distinctive characteristic of state power and elaborates a dialectical formulation of the way in which one type of state gives way to the next. Thus, "capitalist democracy," seen as the dictatorship of the bourgeoisie, may be regarded as the thesis *in a classical Marxist-Hegelian triad. In Lenin's words, "progress marches onward," not "directly" but dialectically—through the* antithesis *of "capitalist democracy": the "dictatorship of the proletariat," which is seen as the only form of state organization in which it becomes possible "to* break the resistance *of capitalist exploiters." The* synthesis—*the end product of this dialectical opposition of proletarian dictatorship to the earlier dictatorship of the bourgeoisie—is the creation of Communist society. Then, Lenin writes, "the state ceases to exist" and "it becomes possible to speak of freedom"; in more abstract terms, only then has the "negation of the negation" occurred.[3]*

. . . [F]rom capitalist democracy—inevitably narrow, subtly rejecting the poor, and therefore hypocritical and false to the core—

[2] From V. I. Lenin, *The Proletarian Revolution and the Renegade Kautsky,* pp. 18–19.

[3] From V. I. Lenin, *State and Revolution,* completed 1917 (New York: International Publishers, 1932), pp. 73–75.

progress does not march onward, simply, smoothly and directly, to "greater and greater democracy," as the liberal professors and petty-bourgeois opportunists would have us believe. No, progress marches onward, *i.e.*, towards Communism, through the dictatorship of the proletariat; it cannot do otherwise, for there is no one else and no other way to *break the resistance* of the capitalist exploiters.

But the dictatorship of the proletariat—*i.e.*, the organisation of the vanguard of the oppressed as the ruling class for the purpose of crushing the oppressors—cannot produce merely an expansion of democracy. *Together* with an immense expansion of democracy which *for the first time* becomes democracy for the poor, democracy for the people, and not democracy for the rich folk, the dictatorship of the proletariat produces a series of restrictions of liberty in the case of the oppressors, the exploiters, the capitalists. We must crush them in order to free humanity from wage-slavery; their resistance must be broken by force; it is clear that where there is suppression there is also violence, there is no liberty, no democracy. . . .

Democracy for the vast majority of the people, and suppression by force, *i.e.*, exclusion from democracy, of the exploiters and oppressors of the people—this is the modification of democracy during the *transition* from capitalism to Communism.

Only in Communist society, when the resistance of the capitalists has been completely broken, when the capitalists have disappeared, when there are no classes (*i.e.*, there is no difference between the members of society in their relation to the social means of production), *only then* "the state ceases to exist" and "*it becomes possible to speak of freedom.*" Only then a really full democracy, a democracy without any exceptions, will be possible and will be realised. And only then will democracy itself begin to *wither away* due to the simple fact that, freed from capitalist slavery, from the untold horrors, savagery, absurdities and infamies of capitalist exploitation, people will gradually *become accustomed* to the observance of the elementary rules of social life that have been known for centuries and repeated for thousands of years in all school books; they will become accustomed to observing them without force, without compulsion, without subordination, without the *special apparatus* for compulsion which is called the state. . . .

In other words: under capitalism we have a state in the proper sense of the word, that is, special machinery for the suppression of one class by another, and of the majority by the minority at that. Naturally, for the successful discharge of such a task as the systematic suppression by the exploiting minority of the exploited majority, the greatest ferocity and savagery of suppression are required, seas of blood are required, through which mankind is marching in slavery, serfdom, and wage-labour.

Again, during the *transition* from capitalism to Communism, suppression is *still* necessary; but it is the suppression of the minority of exploiters by the majority of exploited. A special apparatus, special machinery for suppression, the "state," is *still* necessary, but this is now a transitional state, no longer a state in the usual sense, for the suppression of the minority of exploiters, by the majority of the wage slaves *of yesterday*, is a matter comparatively so easy, simple and natural that it will cost far less bloodshed than the suppression of the risings of slaves, serfs or wage labourers, and will cost mankind far less. This is compatible with the diffusion of democracy among such an overwhelming majority of the population, that the need for *special machinery* of suppression will begin to disappear. The exploiters are, naturally, unable to suppress the people without a most complex machinery for performing this task; but *the people* can suppress the exploiters even with very simple "machinery," almost without any "machinery," without any special apparatus, by the simple *organisation of the armed masses* (such as the Soviets of Workers' and Soldiers' Deputies, we may remark, anticipating a little).

Finally, only Communism renders the state absolutely unnecessary, for there is *no one* to be suppressed—"no one" in the sense of a *class*, in the sense of a systematic struggle with a definite section of the population. We are not Utopians, and we do not in the least deny the possibility and inevitability of excesses on the part of *individual persons*, nor the need to suppress *such* excesses. But, in the first place, no special machinery, no special apparatus of repression is needed for this; this will be done by the armed people itself, as simply and as readily as any crowd of civilised people, even in modern society, parts a pair of combatants or does not allow a woman to be outraged. And, secondly, we know that the fundamental social cause of excesses which consist in violating the rules of social life is the exploitation of the masses, their want and their poverty. With the removal of this chief cause, excesses will inevitably begin to *"wither away."* We do not know how quickly and in what succession, but we know that they will wither away. With their withering away, the state will also *wither away.* . . .

In order to flesh out this somewhat abstract schema, it is necessary to turn back to Lenin's analysis of imperialism. Lenin saw the final subphase of capitalism not only as imperialism per se (its external, global manifestation), but as characterized by changes within the capitalist state and society. These changes laid the foundations for the transformation to socialism; in dialectical terms, advanced capitalism was, in its organizational dimension, a "nodal point," the womb of the old in which the new society was gestating. The expansion of large-scale socioeconomic organization that

would burst the bounds of capitalism was discussed in Imperialism;
this theme was picked up and elaborated more specifically in re-
lation to the state a few months prior to the Bolshevik seizure of
power.

Competition becomes transformed into monopoly. The result is
immense progress in the socialization of production. In particular, the
process of technical invention and improvement becomes socialized.

This is something quite different from the old free competition between manufacturers, scattered and out of touch with one another, and
producing for an unknown market. Concentration has reached the point
at which it is possible to make an approximate estimate of all sources
of raw materials (for example, the iron ore deposits) of a country and
even, as we shall see, of several countries, or of the whole world. Not
only are such estimates made, but these sources are captured by gigantic
monopolist combines. An approximate estimate of the capacity of
markets is also made, and the combines "divide" them up amongst themselves by agreement. Skilled labour is monopolized, the best engineers
are engaged; the means of transport are captured: railways in America,
shipping companies in Europe and America. Capitalism in its imperialist stage leads right up to the most comprehensive socialization of production; it, so to speak, drags the capitalists, against their will and
consciousness, into some sort of a new social order, a transitional one
from complete free competition to complete socialization.

Production becomes social, but appropriation remains private. The
social means of production remain the private property of a few. The
general framework of formally recognized free competition remains, but
the yoke of a few monopolists on the rest of the population becomes a
hundred times heavier, more burdensome and intolerable.[4]

. . . [W]hat is the state? It is an organisation of the ruling class—in
Germany, for instance, of the Junkers and capitalists. And therefore
what the German Plekhanovs (Scheidemann, Lensch and others) call
"war-time socialism" is in fact war-time state-monopoly capitalism or,
to put it more simply and clearly, war-time penal servitude for the
workers and war-time protection for the profits of the capitalists.

Now, try to *substitute* for the Junker-capitalist state, for the landlord-
capitalist state, a *revolutionary-democratic* state, i.e., a state which in a
revolutionary way destroys *all* privileges and does not fear to introduce
the fullest democracy in a revolutionary way, and you will find that,
given a really revolutionary-democratic state, state-monopoly capitalism

[4] From V. I. Lenin, *Imperialism*, pp. 24–25.

inevitably and unavoidably implies a step, and more than one step, towards socialism!

For if a huge capitalist enterprise becomes a monopoly, it means that it serves the whole nation. If it has become a state monopoly, it means that the state (i.e., the armed organisation of the population, the workers and peasants in the first place, provided there is *revolutionary* democracy) directs the whole enterprise. In whose interest?

Either in the interest of the landlords and capitalists, in which case what we have is not a revolutionary-democratic, but a reactionary-bureaucratic state, an imperialist republic.

Or in the interest of the revolutionary democracy—and then *it will be a step towards socialism.*

For socialism is nothing but the next step forward from state-capitalist monopoly. Or, in other words, socialism is nothing but state-capitalist monopoly *which is made to serve the interests of the whole people* and has to that extent *ceased* to be capitalist monopoly.

There is no middle course here. The objective process of development is such that it is *impossible* to advance from *monopolies* (and the war has magnified their number, role and importance tenfold) without advancing towards socialism. . . .

Imperialist war is the eve of socialist revolution. And this not only because the horrors of the war give rise to proletarian revolt—no revolt can bring about socialism if the economic conditions for it have not ripened—but because state monopoly capitalism is a complete *material* preparation for socialism, the *threshold* of socialism, a rung in the ladder of history between which and the rung called socialism *there are no intermediate rungs.* . . .

. . . [S]ocialism is now gazing at us from all the windows of modern capitalism; socialism is outlined directly, *practically,* by every important measure that constitutes a forward step on the basis of this modern capitalism.

What is universal labour conscription?

It is a step forward on the basis of modern monopoly capitalism, a step towards the regulation of economic life as a whole in accordance with a certain general plan, a step towards the economy of national labour and towards the prevention of its senseless wastage by capitalism.

In Germany it is the Junkers (landowners) and capitalists who are introducing universal labour conscription, and therefore it inevitably becomes war-time penal servitude for the workers.

But take the same institution and ponder over its significance in a revolutionary-democratic state. Universal labour conscription, introduced, regulated and directed by the Soviets of Workers', Soldiers' and Peasants' Deputies, will *still not* be socialism, but it will *no longer* be capitalism. It will be a tremendous *step towards* socialism, a step from which, if complete democracy is preserved, there can no longer be any

retreat back to capitalism, without unparalleled violence being committed against the masses.[5]

The following key sections of Lenin's State and Revolution
*elaborate his view of state and governmental organization under
"socialism"; they are more easily understandable in the light of the
selections from other works that we have already presented. About
the time he was working on* State and Revolution, *Lenin also wrote
an article on whether the Bolsheviks would be able to retain power
once they had made a successful armed uprising. Here, the formulation of the tasks and means of governing a complex society is
both more detailed in certain respects and somewhat at variance
with what is presented in the major work. The two, accordingly,
may be profitably considered together.*

Capitalism simplifies the functions of "state" administration; it
makes it possible to throw off "commanding" methods and to reduce
everything to a matter of the organisation of the proletarians (as the
ruling class), hiring "workmen and managers" in the name of the whole
of society.

We are not Utopians, we do not indulge in "dreams" of how best
to do away *immediately* with all administration, with all subordination;
these Anarchist dreams, based upon a lack of understanding of the
task of proletarian dictatorship, are basically foreign to Marxism, and,
as a matter of fact, they serve but to put off the Socialist revolution
until human nature is different. No, we want the Socialist revolution
with human nature as it is now, with human nature that cannot do
without subordination, control, and "managers."

But if there be subordination, it must be to the armed vanguard of
all the exploited and the labouring—to the proletariat. The specific
"commanding" methods of the state officials can and must begin to be
replaced—immediately, within twenty-four hours—by the simple functions of "managers" and bookkeepers, functions which are now already
within the capacity of the average city dweller and can well be performed for "workingmen's wages."

We organise large-scale production, starting from what capitalism has
already created; we workers *ourselves,* relying on our own experience as
workers, establishing a strict, an iron discipline, supported by the state
power of the armed workers, shall reduce the rôle of the state officials
to that of simply carrying out our instructions as responsible, moderately
paid "managers" (of course, with technical knowledge of all sorts, types

[5] From V. I. Lenin, "The Impending Catastrophe and How to Combat It" (September 10–14/23–27, 1917), in *Selected Works,* II, 286–88.

and degrees). This is *our* proletarian task, with this we can and must *begin* when carrying through a proletarian revolution. Such a beginning, on the basis of large-scale production, of itself leads to the gradual "withering away" of all bureaucracy, to the gradual creation of a new order, an order without quotation marks, an order which has nothing to do with wage slavery, an order in which the more and more simplified functions of control and accounting will be performed by each in turn, will then become a habit, and will finally die out as *special* functions of a special stratum of the population.

A witty German Social-Democrat of the 'seventies of the last century called the *post-office* an example of the socialist system. This is very true. At present the post-office is a business organised on the lines of a state *capitalist* monopoly. Imperialism is gradually transforming all trusts into organisations of a similar type. Above the "common" workers, who are overloaded with work and starving, there stands here the same bourgeois bureaucracy. But the mechanism of social management is here already to hand. Overthrow the capitalists, crush with the iron hand of the armed workers the resistance of these exploiters, break the bureaucratic machine of the modern state—and you have before you a mechanism of the highest technical equipment, freed of "parasites," capable of being set into motion by the united workers themselves who hire their own technicians, managers, bookkeepers, and pay them *all*, as, indeed, every "state" official, with the usual workers' wage. Here is a concrete, practicable task, immediately realisable in relation to all trusts, a task that frees the workers of exploitation and makes use of the experience (especially in the realm of the construction of the state) which the Commune began to reveal in practice.

To organise the *whole* national economy like the postal system, in such a way that the technicians, managers, bookkeepers as well as all officials, should receive no higher wages than "workingmen's wages," all under the control and leadership of the armed proletariat—this is our immediate aim. This is the kind of state and economic basis we need. This is what will produce the destruction of parliamentarism, while retaining representative institutions. This is what will free the labouring classes from the prostitution of these institutions by the bourgeoisie. . . .

Democracy is a form of the state—one of its varieties. Consequently, like every state, it consists in organised, systematic application of force against human beings. This on the one hand. On the other hand, however, it signifies the formal recognition of the equality of all citizens, the equal right of all to determine the structure and administration of the state. This, in turn, is connected with the fact that, at a certain stage in the development of democracy, it first rallies the proletariat as a revolutionary class against capitalism, and gives it an opportunity to crush, to smash to bits, to wipe off the face of the earth the bourgeois state machinery—even its republican variety: the standing army, the police, and bureaucracy; then it substitutes for all this a *more* democratic, but still a state machinery in the shape of armed masses of workers, which becomes transformed into universal participation of the people in the militia.

Here "quantity turns into quality": *such* a degree of democracy is bound up with the abandonment of the framework of bourgeois society, and the beginning of its Socialist reconstruction. If *every one* really takes part in the administration of the state, capitalism cannot retain its hold. In its turn, capitalism as it develops, itself creates *prerequisites* for "every one" *to be able* really to take part in the administration of the state. Among such prerequisites are: universal literacy, already realised in most of the advanced capitalist countries, then the "training and disciplining" of millions of workers by the huge, complex, and socialised apparatus of the post-office, the railways, the big factories, large-scale commerce, banking, etc., etc.

With such *economic* prerequisites it is perfectly possible, immediately, within twenty-four hours after the overthrow of the capitalists and bureaucrats, to replace them, in the control of production and distribution, in the business of *control* of labour and products, by the armed workers, by the whole people in arms. (The question of control and accounting must not be confused with the question of the scientifically educated staff of engineers, agronomists and so on. These gentlemen work today, obeying the capitalists; they will work even better tomorrow, obeying the armed workers.)

Accounting and control—these are the *chief* things necessary for the organising and correct functioning of the *first phase* of Communist society. *All* citizens are here transformed into hired employees of the state, which is made up of the armed workers. *All* citizens become employees and workers of *one* national state "syndicate." All that is required is that they should work equally, should regularly do their share of work, and should receive equal pay. The accounting and control necessary for this have been *simplified* by capitalism to the utmost, till they have become the extraordinarily simple operations of watching, recording and issuing receipts, within the reach of anybody who can read and write and knows the first four rules of arithmetic.

When the *majority* of the people begin everywhere to keep such accounts and maintain such control over the capitalists (now converted into employees) and over the intellectual gentry, who still retain capitalist habits, this control will really become universal, general, national; and there will be no way of getting away from it, there will be "nowhere to go."

The whole of society will have become one office and one factory, with equal work and equal pay.

But this "factory" discipline, which the proletariat will extend to the whole of society after the defeat of the capitalists and the overthrow of the exploiters, is by no means our ideal, or our final aim. It is but a *foothold* necessary for the radical cleansing of society of all the hideousness and foulness of capitalist exploitation, *in order to advance further*.

From the moment when all members of society, or even only the overwhelming majority, have learned how to govern the state *themselves*, have taken this business into their own hands, have "established" control over the insignificant minority of capitalists, over the gentry with capitalist leanings, and the workers thoroughly demoralised by capitalism— from this moment the need for any government begins to disappear. The more complete the democracy, the nearer the moment when it begins to be unnecessary. The more democratic the "state" consisting of armed workers, which is "no longer a state in the proper sense of the word," the more rapidly does *every* state begin to wither away.

For when *all* have learned to manage, and independently are actually managing by themselves social production, keeping accounts, controlling the idlers, the gentlefolk, the swindlers and similar "guardians of capitalist traditions," then the escape from this national accounting and control will inevitably become so increasingly difficult, such a rare exception, and will probably be accompanied by such swift and severe punishment (for the armed workers are men of practical life, not sentimental intellectuals, and they will scarcely allow any one to trifle with them), that very soon the *necessity* of observing the simple, fundamental rules of every-day social life in common will have become a *habit*.

The door will then be wide open for the transition from the first phase of Communist society to its higher phase, and along with it to the complete withering away of the state.[6]

. . . In addition to the chiefly "oppressive" apparatus—the standing army, the police and the bureaucracy—the modern state possesses an apparatus which has extremely close connections with the banks and syndicates, an apparatus which performs an enormous amount of accounting and registration work, if it may be expressed this way. This apparatus must not, and should not, be smashed. It must be wrested from the control of the capitalists; the capitalists and the wires they pull must be *cut off, lopped off, chopped away from* this apparatus; it must be *subordinated* to the proletarian Soviets; it must be expanded, made more comprehensive, and country-wide. And this *can* be done by utilising the achievements already made by large-scale capitalism (as, in general, the proletarian revolution can reach its goal only by utilising these achievements).

Capitalism has created an accounting *apparatus* in the shape of the

[6] From V. I. Lenin, *State and Revolution*, pp. 42–44, 82–85.

banks, syndicates, postal service, consumers' societies, and office employees' unions. *Without big banks socialism would be impossible.*

The big banks *are* the "state apparatus" which we *need* for bringing about socialism, and which we *take ready-made* from capitalism; our task here is merely to *lop off* what *capitalistically mutilates* this excellent apparatus, to make it *even bigger,* even more democratic, even more comprehensive. Quantity will be transformed into quality. A single State Bank, the biggest of the big, with branches in every rural district, in every factory, will constitute as much as nine-tenths of the *socialist* apparatus. This will be country-wide *book-keeping,* country-wide *accounting* of the production and distribution of goods, this will be, so to speak, something in the nature of the *skeleton* of socialist society.

We can "lay hold of" and "set in motion" this "state aparatus" (which is not fully a state apparatus under capitalism, but which will be so with us, under socialism) at one stroke, by a single decree, because the actual work of book-keeping, control, registering, accounting and counting is performed by *employees,* the majority of whom are themselves proletarians or semi-proletarians.

By a single decree of the proletarian government these employees can and must be transferred to the status of state employees. . . . We shall need many more state employees of this kind, and more *can* be obtained, because capitalism has simplified the work of accounting and control, has reduced it to a comparatively simple system of making *entries,* which any literate person can do.

The conversion of the rank-and-file bank, syndicate, commercial, etc., etc., employees into state employees is quite feasible both technically (thanks to the preliminary work performed for us by capitalism and finance capitalism) and politically, provided the *Soviets* exercise control and supervision.

As for the higher officials, of whom there are very few, but who gravitate towards the capitalists, they will have to be dealt with in the same way as the capitalists, i.e., "severely." Like the capitalists, they will offer *resistance.* This resistance will have to be *broken.* . . .

We can do this, for it is merely a question of breaking the resistance of an insignificant minority of the population, literally a handful of people, over each of whom the employees' unions, the trade unions, the consumers' societies and the Soviets will institute such *supervision* that every [one] will be *surrounded.* . . . We know these . . . by name: we only have to consult the lists of directors, board members, large shareholders, etc. There are several hundred, at most several thousand of them in the *whole* of Russia, and over each of them the proletarian state, with the apparatus of the Soviets, of the employees' unions, etc., will be able to appoint ten or even a hundred supervisers, so that instead of "breaking resistance" it may even be possible, by means of *workers' control* (over the capitalists), to make all resistance *impossible.*

Not even the confiscation of the capitalists' property will be the essence of the matter; the essence will be country-wide, all-embracing workers' control over the capitalists and their possible supporters. Confiscation alone leads nowhere, as it does not contain the element of organisation, accounting of proper distribution. . . .

Compulsory syndication, i.e., compulsory amalgamation in associations under state control—this is what capitalism has prepared the way for, this is what has been carried out in Germany by the Junkers' state, this is what can be easily carried out in Russia by the Soviets, by the proletarian dictatorship, and this is what will *provide us with* a *"state apparatus"* that will be universal, up-to-date, and non-bureaucratic.[7]

DILEMMAS OF POWER

"It was easy," Lenin wrote in 1920, "for Russia in the specific, historically very unique situation of 1917 to start a Socialist revolution, but . . . it will be more difficult for Russia than for the European countries to continue it and consummate it."

The most immediate problems that Lenin faced arose from three circumstances: the fiercely fought civil war that ranged the length and breadth of the territory of the former Russian Empire; the devastation of the economy (it is estimated that, in 1920, Russian industrial output had declined to twenty percent of the 1913 level); and, finally, Russia's isolation during these years from the mainstream of the international economy.

Lenin's pronouncements on military and political strategy of the civil war are omitted from this section (see Louis Fischer's summary of the problems he had to deal with, pp. 182–88). Rather, we have chosen the selections that follow with an eye to the problems that were to have long-range and recurrent significance for the evolution of the Soviet system: the role of the peasants and industrial workers, the problems of bureaucracy and party organization, planning and economic policy, and the thorny question of national minorities.

One of Lenin's clearest presentations of the general problems of the transition to the revolutionary state is contained in his 1919 pamphlet, "Economics and Politics in the Era of the Dictatorship of the Proletariat." [8]

In Russia, the dictatorship of the proletariat must inevitably differ in certain particulars from what it would be in the advanced countries,

---

[7] From V. I. Lenin, "Can the Bolsheviks Retain State Power?" (c. end of September–October 1/14, 1917), in *Selected Works,* II, 438–40.

[8] From V. I. Lenin, "Economics and Politics in the Era of the Dictatorship of the Proletariat" (October 30, 1919), in *Marx, Engels, Marxism,* pp. 417, 418, 419.

owing to the very great backwardness and petty-bourgeois character of our country. But the basic forces—and the basic forms of social economy —are the same in Russia as in any capitalist country, so that these peculiarities can apply only to what is of lesser importance. . . .

We speak of "the first steps" of communism in Russia . . . because all these conditions have been only partially achieved in our country, . . . the achievement of these conditions is only in its early stages. . . . [O]n the first day of the dictatorship of the proletariat, October 26 (November 8), 1917, the private ownership of land was abolished without compensation to the big landowners; the big landowners were expropriated. Within the space of a few months practically all the big capitalists, owners of mills and factories, joint-stock companies, banks, railways, and so forth, were also expropriated without compensation. The state organisation of large-scale production in industry and the transition from "workers' control" to "workers' administration" of factories and railways—this has, by and large, already been accomplished; but in relation to agriculture it has only just begun ("state farms," i.e., large farms organised by the workers' state on state-owned land). Similarly, we have only just begun the organisation of various forms of co-operative societies of small farmers as a transition from petty commodity agriculture to communist agriculture. The same must be said of the state-organised distribution of products in place of private trade, i.e., the state procurement and delivery of grain to the cities and of industrial products to the countryside. . . .

Peasant farming continues to be petty commodity production. Here we have an extremely broad and very sound, deep-rooted basis for capitalism. On this basis capitalism persists and arises anew in a bitter struggle against communism. The forms of this struggle are private speculation and profiteering, as against state procurement of grain (and other products) and state distribution of products in general.

> In 1918 and 1919, Lenin surveyed the question of how management and increased labor productivity could serve to speed up the transition. Here, already, one can see—for example, in the survey of resources in the first selection, and also in the emphasis on the scientific management of labor—the germ of the Soviet planned economy.[9]

In every socialist revolution, after the proletariat has solved the problem of capturing power, and to the extent that the task of expropriating the expropriators and suppressing their resistance has been carried

[9] From V. I. Lenin, "The Immediate Tasks of the Soviet Government" (April 30-May 3, 1918), in *Selected Works*, II, 714–17.

out in the main, there necessarily comes to the forefront the fundamental task of creating a social system superior to capitalism, namely, raising the productivity of labour, and in this connection (and for this purpose) securing better organisation of labour. . . . [W]hile it is possible to capture the central government in a few days, . . . solution of the problem of raising the productivity of labour requires, at all events (particularly after a most terrible and devastating war), several years. . . .

The raising of the productivity of labour first of all requires that the material basis of large-scale industry shall be assured, namely, the development of the production of fuel, iron, the engineering and chemical industries. The Russian Soviet Republic enjoys the favourable position of having at its command, even after the Brest Peace, enormous reserves of ore (in the Urals), fuel in Western Siberia (coal), in the Caucasus and the South-East (oil), in Central Russia (peat), enormous timber reserves, water power, raw materials for the chemical industry (Karabugaz), etc. The development of these natural resources by methods of modern technology will lay the basis for the unprecedented progress of the productive forces.

Another condition for raising the productivity of labour is, firstly, the raising of the educational and cultural level of the mass of the population. This is now taking place extremely rapidly. . . . Secondly, a condition for economic revival is the raising of the working people's discipline, their skill, their dexterity, increasing the intensity of labour and improving its organisation. . . .

The more class-conscious vanguard of the Russian proletariat has already set itself the task of raising labour discipline. . . . This work must be supported and pushed ahead with all speed. We must raise the question of piece-work and apply and test it in practice; we must raise the question of applying much of what is scientific and progressive in the Taylor system[10] we must make wages correspond to the total amount of goods turned out, or to the amount of work done by the railways, the water transport system, etc., etc.

The Russian is a bad worker compared with people in advanced countries. It could not be otherwise under the tsarist regime and in view of the tenacity of the remnants of serfdom. The task that the Soviet government must set the people in all its scope is—learn to work. The Taylor system, the last word of capitalism in this respect, like all capitalist progress, is a combination of the refined brutality of bourgeois exploitation and a number of the greatest scientific achievements in the field of analysing mechanical motions during work, the elimination of superfluous and awkward motions, the elaboration of correct methods of work, the introduction of the best system of accounting and control, etc. The Soviet Republic must at all costs adopt all that is valuable in the achievements

[10] [Of "scientific management" based on time and motion studies—ED.]

of science and technology in this field. The possibility of building socialism depends exactly upon our success in combining the Soviet power and the Soviet organisation of administration with the up-to-date achievements of capitalism. We must organise in Russia the study and teaching of the Taylor system and systematically try it out and adapt it to our own ends. At the same time, in working to raise the productivity of labour, we must take into account the specific features of the transition period from capitalism to socialism, which, on the one hand, require that the foundations be laid of the socialist organisation of emulation, and, on the other hand, the use of compulsion, so that the slogan of the dictatorship of the proletariat shall not be desecrated by the practice of a lily-livered proletarian government.

In the last analysis, productivity of labour is the most important, the principal thing for the victory of the new social system. Capitalism created a productivity of labour unknown under serfdom. Capitalism can be utterly vanquished, and will be utterly vanquished by the fact that socialism creates a new and much higher productivity of labour. This is a very difficult matter and must take a long time; but *it has been started,* and that is the main thing. . . .

In *Capital,* Karl Marx ridicules the pompous and grandiloquent bourgeois-democratic great charter of liberty and the rights of man, ridicules all this phrase-mongering about liberty, equality and fraternity *in general,* which dazzles the petty bourgeois and philistines of all countries, . . . The "formulas" of genuine communism differ from the pompous, intricate, and solemn phraseology of the Kautskys, the Mensheviks and the Socialist-Revolutionaries. . . . Less chatter about "labor democracy," about "liberty, equality and fraternity," about "government by the people," and all such stuff; the class-conscious workers and peasants of our day see the trickery of the bourgeois intellectual through these pompous phrases. . . .

Fewer pompous phrases, more plain, *everyday* work, concern for the pood of grain and the pood of coal! More concern for supplying this pood of grain and pood of coal needed by the hungry workers and ragged and barefoot peasants, *not* by means of *haggling,* not in a capitalist manner, but by means of the conscious, voluntary, boundlessly heroic labour of plain working men like the unskilled labourers and railwaymen of the Moscow-Kazan line.[11]

Shortly after the conclusion of the Brest-Litovsk peace and, perhaps, because of his acute awareness of the loss of Russian resources

[11] From V. I. Lenin, "A Great Beginning" (June 28, 1919), in *Selected Works,* III, 253–54.

and older industrial centers to the Germans, Lenin wrote the following memorandum, which ranks as the founding document of the Soviet economic plans.[12]

The Supreme Economic Council should immediately give its instructions to the Academy of Sciences that has begun the systematic study and investigation of the natural productive forces of Russia, to set up a number of expert commissions for the speediest possible compilation of a plan for the reorganisation of industry and the economic progress of Russia.

The plan should include:

the rational *distribution* of industry in Russia from the standpoint of closeness to raw materials and the lowest consumption of labour-power in the transition from the processing of the raw materials to all subsequent stages in the processing of semi-manufactured goods, up to and including the output of the finished product;

the rational merging and concentration of industry in a few big enterprises from the standpoint of the most up-to-date large-scale industry, especially trusts;

the fullest possible *independent* supply of the present Russian Soviet Republic (without the Ukraine and the regions occupied by the Germans) with *all* the chief items of raw materials; the organisation of the main branches of industry;

special attention to the electrification of industry and transport and the application of electricity to farming, and the use of lower grades of fuel (peat, low-grade coal) for the production of electricity, with the lowest possible expenditure on extraction and transport;

water power and wind motors in general and in their application to farming.

Some of the persistent bureaucratic problems inherent in "planning to plan" are touched on in Lenin's critique of the Communist economic administration, dated just before the start of the New Economic Policy.[13]

. . . It is essential particularly to link the scientific electrification plan with current practical plans and their actual implementation. This,

[12] From V. I. Lenin, "Draft Plan of Scientific and Technical Work" (April, 1918), in *Selected Works*, II, 736.

[13] From V. I. Lenin, "The Single Economic Plan" (February 21, 1921), in *Selected Works*, III, 603–605.

of course, is quite beyond dispute. How is this link to be made? To know
this requires that the economists, literati and statisticians should stop
chattering about a plan in general, but should study in detail the fulfilment of our plans, our mistakes in this practical matter, and the methods
of correcting these mistakes. Without such a study we are blind. With
such a study and alongside it, provided the practical experience is studied,
there remains the quite small question of administrative technique. . . .

The weak spot lies in the . . . relation of the Communists to the specialists. . . . The task of the Communists within GOELRO [The State
Committee for the Electrification of Russia, established in February,
1920] is to issue fewer commands, or rather not to command at all, but
to approach the scientific and technological specialists ("in most cases
they are inevitably imbued with a bourgeois world outlook and habits,"
as the Programme of the R.C.P. states) extremely cautiously and skilfully, learning from them and helping them to widen their horizon,
proceeding from the achievements and data of the science concerned,
remembering that an engineer comes to recognise communism *not in the
same way* as an illegally working propagandist or writer, but *through
the data of his own science,* that an agronomist comes to recognise communism *by his own path,* and similarly a forestry expert, etc. A Communist who has not proved his ability to unite and modestly direct the
work of the specialists, getting to the heart of the matter and studying
it in detail—such a Communist is often harmful. We have many such
Communists; and I would give dozens of them for a single well-qualified
bourgeois specialist who conscientiously studies his job. . . .

. . . [I]f a Communist is an administrator, his first duty is to beware
of a fondness of giving orders, to be able from the beginning to take account of what has already been worked out by science, from the beginning to enquire whether the facts have been checked, from the beginning
to study (in reports, in the press, at meetings, and so on) where exactly
we had made a mistake and only on this basis to correct what has been
done. Let us have less of the methods of Tit Titych[14] ("I am able to
endorse, I am able not to endorse"), and more study of our practical
errors.

*The revolution meant something different to the mass of Rus-
sian peasants than it did to Lenin or to the Communist economic
planners. The "dark people," who still made up the overwhelming
proportion of the Russian population, saw the revolution—as Lenin
recognized—essentially as a chance to gain something immediate*

[14] A rich merchant in the play *Shouldering Another's Troubles* by A. N. Ostrovsky
(1823–86). Tit Titych is characterized by greed and *samodurstvo,* an obduracy carried
to such an extreme as to lead to one's own downfall.

for themselves: land of their own with which they could better their lot. How to fit the peasant into the evolving Soviet system, how to retain him as an ally and yet not surrender completely to the "primitivism" of the countryside: these were the problems that Lenin was to face throughout his period in power, problems that were to contribute significantly to the retreat which was initiated in 1921 under the title "New Economic Policy."

Lenin adopted a cautious attitude towards forced communization of the countryside. Yet, though Lenin might have been opposed to the kind of collectivization carried out by Stalin, we should not forget that until 1921 the dominant Soviet economic policy was that of "War Communism," which amounted, in the rural areas, to the violent expropriation of agricultural products in the desperate effort to sustain the cities, the citadels of Communist power.[15]

When we were taking power, we relied on the support of the peasants as a whole. At that time the aim of all the peasants was the same—to fight the landlords. But their prejudice against large-scale farming has remained to this day. The peasant thinks: "A large farm, that means I shall again be a farm-hand." That, of course, is a mistake. But the peasant's idea of large-scale farming is associated with a feeling of hatred and the memory of how the landlords used to oppress the people. That feeling still remains, it has not yet died.

We must particularly stress the truth that here, by the very nature of the case, coercive methods can accomplish nothing. The economic task here is an entirely different one. Here there is no upper layer that can be cut off, leaving the foundation and the building intact. That upper layer which in the cities was represented by the capitalists does not exist here. *Here coercion would ruin the whole cause.* What is required here is prolonged educational work. We have to give the peasant, who not only in our country but all over the world is a practical man and a realist, concrete examples to prove that the "communia" is the best possible thing. Of course, nothing will come of it if hasty individuals flit down to a village from a city, come there, chat about, stir up a number of intellectual-like and at times unintellectual-like squabbles, and then quarrel with everyone and go their way. That sometimes happens. Instead of evoking respect, they evoke ridicule, and deservedly so.

On this question we must say that we do encourage communes, but they must be so organised *as to gain the confidence of the peasants.* And

[15] From V. I. Lenin, "Report on the Party Programme" delivered at the Eighth Congress of the Russian Communist Party (Bolsheviks) (March 19, 1919), in *Selected Works*, III, 219–20.

until then we are pupils of the peasants and not their teachers. Nothing is more stupid than when people who know nothing about agriculture and its specific features, people who rush to the village only because they have heard of the advantages of socialised farming, are tired of urban life and desire to work in rural districts—when such people regard themselves as teachers of the peasants in every respect. *Nothing is more stupid than the very idea of applying coercion in economic relations with the middle peasant.*

The aim here is not to expropriate the middle peasant but to bear in mind the specific conditions in which the peasant lives, to learn from the peasant methods of transition to a better system, *and not to dare to give orders!* That is the rule we have set ourselves. . . .

Our decrees on peasant farming are in the main correct. We have no grounds for renouncing a single one of them, or for regretting a single one of them. But if the decrees are right, it *is wrong to impose them on the peasants by force.* . . .

By the end of 1920 and the beginning of 1921, though the Soviet system had managed to survive the Civil War, a fundamental economic crisis with social and political implications had developed to haunt the Communist leadership. The effort to push through militant policies in the economic field ("War Communism") in a country ravaged and exhausted by revolution and civil war had backfired. Segments of society on which the Bolsheviks depended for continued hegemony were alienated from the regime. Industrial and agricultural production had almost completely broken down; transport was in ruins; there was a severe famine and associated epidemics (particularly in Lenin's own Volga area); and peasant revolts had broken out in various regions. The international socialist revolution had failed to materialize, and "Soviet Republics," which had appeared in Hungary and Bavaria in the aftermath of World War I, had long been suppressed. Both the leadership and rank and file of the Communist Party were divided on many issues of policy. The climax came in March, 1921, at the time of the Tenth Congress of the Communist Party, when the sailors of "Red Kronstadt"—the great naval base on the Baltic whose support had been crucial for Lenin in 1917—raised the standard of revolt and appealed to the workers in Petrograd to join them in establishing "non-Bolshevik" Soviets and in securing for themselves and their families a better standard of living than was possible under the decaying Soviet system.

Kronstadt's rebellion was brutally suppressed; and the Soviet leadership initiated the retreat into neocapitalist economics known

*as the "New Economic Policy" (NEP). The NEP period, which lasted
until the beginning of the Stalinist plans at the end of the 1920s, is
generally regarded as the most "liberal" period in Soviet history. Yet,
together with NEP, Lenin decided on severe political and administrative measures. These were intended to give the party sufficient
strength to survive the dangers of relaxation in substantive policy
matters; their effect was to establish the base for the future Stalinist
dictatorship.*

*Before turning to the NEP, we should consider the two most im-
portant documents on the "hard-line" in Lenin's policy dialectic.
The first is his trade-union policy, which formalized what had already been developing: the retreat from worker's comanagement
and the subordination of the unions to Party and state economic
administration (compare this with the document on worker's management, above, pp. 81–82). The second, the Tenth Congress's "Resolution on Party Unity" (which we present here in Lenin's draft) was
the basis for the later suppression of free discussion within the Party.*

The Trade Unions and the Management of Industry

Following its capture of political power, the principal and fundamental interest of the proletariat lies in securing an enormous increase
in the productive forces of society and in the output of manufactured
goods. This task, which is clearly formulated in the Programme of the
Russian Communist Party, is particularly urgent in our country today
owing to post-war ruin, starvation and devastation. Hence, the speediest
and most enduring success in restoring large-scale industry is a condition
without which no success can be achieved in the general cause of emanci-
pating labour from the yoke of capital and securing the victory of
socialism. To achieve this success in Russia, in her present state, it is
absolutely essential that all authority in the factories should be concentrated in the hands of the management. The factory management,
usually built up on the principle of one-man responsibility, must have
authority independently to fix wages and distribute money wages, rations,
working clothes, and all other supplies on the basis and within the limits
of collective agreements concluded with the trade unions; it must enjoy
the utmost freedom to manoeuvre, exercise strict control of the actual
successes achieved in increasing production, in making the factory pay
its way and in increasing profits, and carefully select the most talented and
capable administrative personnel, etc.

Under these circumstances, all direct interference by the trade unions
in the management of factories must be regarded as positively harmful
and impermissible. . . .[16]

[16] From V. I. Lenin, "The Role and Function of the Trade Unions" (January 17,
1922), from *Selected Works*, III, 709–13 (headings in the original).

. . . [E]ven before the general Party discussion on the trade unions, certain signs of factionalism had been apparent in the Party—the formation of groups with separate platforms, striving to a certain degree to segregate and create their own group discipline. . . .

All class-conscious workers must clearly realise that factionalism of any kind is pernicious and impermissible, for no matter how members of individual groups may desire to safeguard Party unity, in practice factionalism inevitably leads to the weakening of team-work and to intensified and repeated attempts by the enemies of the Party, who have wormed their way into it because it is the governing Party, to widen the cleavage and to use it for counter-revolutionary purposes.

The way the enemies of the proletariat take advantage of every deviation from a thoroughly consistent communist line was perhaps most strikingly shown in the case of the Kronstadt mutiny. . . . [T]he Socialist-Revolutionaries and the bourgeois counter-revolutionaries in general resorted in Kronstadt to slogans calling for an insurrection against the Soviet Government of Russia ostensibly in the interest of Soviet power. These facts fully prove that the whiteguards strive, and are able, to disguise themselves as Communists, and even as the most Left Communists, solely for the purpose of weakening and destroying the bulwark of the proletarian revolution in Russia. . . .

In the practical struggle against factionalism, every organisation of the Party must take strict measures to prevent any factional actions whatsoever. Criticism of the Party's shortcomings, which is absolutely necessary, must be conducted in such a way that every practical proposal shall be submitted immediately, without any delay, in the most precise form possible for consideration and decision to the leading local and central bodies of the Party. Moreover, everyone who criticises must see to it that the form of his criticism takes into account the position of the Party, surrounded as it is by a ring of enemies, and that the content of his criticism is such that, by directly participating in Soviet and Party work, he can test the rectification of the errors of the Party or of individual Party members in practice. The analysis of the general line of the Party, the estimate of its practical experience, the verification of the fulfilment of its decisions, the study of methods of rectifying errors, etc., must under no circumstances be submitted for preliminary discussion to groups formed on the basis of "platforms," etc., but must in all cases be submitted for discussion directly to all the members of the Party. . . .

Rejecting in principle the deviation towards syndicalism and anarchism, . . . the Congress at the same time declares that every practical proposal concerning questions to which the so-called Workers' Opposition group, for example, has devoted special attention, such as purging the Party of non-proletarian and unreliable elements, combating bureaucracy, developing democracy and the initiative of the workers, etc., must be examined with the greatest care and tried out in practical work. . . .

The Congress, therefore, hereby declares dissolved and orders the immediate dissolution of all groups without exception that have been formed on the basis of one platform or another (such as the Workers' Opposition group, the Democratic Centralism group, etc.). Non-observance of this decision of the Congress shall incur absolute and immediate expulsion from the Party.

In order to ensure strict discipline within the Party and in all Soviet work and to secure the maximum unanimity in eliminating all factionalism, the Congress authorises the Central Committee, in cases of breach of discipline or of a revival or toleration of factionalism, to apply all Party penalties, including expulsion. . . .[17]

The more positive aspect of Lenin's New Economic Policy was actually a complex of adjustments to the desperate reality of Soviet economics at the beginning of the 1920s. Views on the economy and on the social implications of policy changes were diverse and often antagonistic; see, for instance, the selections from Liberman and Balabanoff in Part II (pp. 168–72). Concessions to capitalists both at home and abroad (the "concessions" proper of mining leases, rights to establish factories, etc.) constituted a bitter pill for the Bolshevik leaders. In the countryside, the peasant seemed to have triumphed: the government had been forced not only to recognize the peasant's own rights, but also to refashion the whole economic program of Bolshevism in order to establish a basis for exchanging manufactured goods for food and other rural products. For Lenin, the situation was analogous to the one at the time of Brest-Litovsk, and called for cool realism and biding one's time in the hope that, sooner or later, another offensive could be launched in pursuit of the goal of a truly socialist economy.

The basic arguments for the NEP were delineated at length in April, 1921, in Lenin's speech explaining the new basis for taxation in the rural areas.[18]

The essence of this peculiar War Communism was that we actually took from the peasant all surpluses—and sometimes even not only surpluses, but part of what the peasant needed for food—to meet the re-

---

[17] From V. I. Lenin, preliminary draft of the "Resolution on Party Unity," Tenth Congress of the Russian Communist Party (Bolsheviks) (March, 1921), in *Selected Works*, III, 626–29.

[18] From V. I. Lenin, "The Tax in Kind" (April 21, 1921), in *Selected Works*, III, 646–51.

quirements of the army and sustain the workers. Most of it we took on loan, for paper money. Had we not done that we would have been unable to vanquish the landowners and capitalists in a ruined small-peasant country. . . .

. . . We were forced to resort to War Communism by war and ruin. It was not, nor could it be, a policy that corresponded to the economic tasks of the proletariat. It was a temporary measure. The correct policy of the proletariat which is exercising its dictatorship in a small-peasant country is to obtain grain in exchange for the manufactured goods the peasant needs. . . . [O]nly such a policy can strengthen the foundations of socialism and lead to its complete victory.

. . . We are still so ruined, so crushed by the burden of war (the war of yesterday and the war which, owing to the rapacity and malice of the capitalists, may break out tomorrow) that we cannot give the peasant manufactured goods for *all* the grain we need. Knowing this, we are introducing the tax in kind, i.e., we shall take the minimum of grain we require (for the army and the workers) in the form of a tax and will obtain the rest in exchange for manufactured goods.

Moreover, we must not forget the following. Our poverty and ruin are so great that we cannot *at one stroke* restore socialist large-scale state factory production. This can be done if we have large stocks of grain and fuel in the big industrial centres, replace the worn-out machines with new ones, and so on. Experience has convinced us that this cannot be done at one stroke, and we know that after the ruinous imperialist war even the wealthiest and most advanced countries will be able to solve this problem only in the course of a fairly long period of years. Hence, it is necessary, to a certain extent, to help to restore *small* industry, which does not need machines, does not demand large stocks of raw material, fuel and food from the state, and which can immediately render some assistance to peasant farming and increase its productive forces.

What will be the effect of this?

The effect will be the revival of the petty bourgeoisie and of capitalism on the basis of a certain amount of free trade (if only local). This is beyond doubt. It would be ridiculous to shut our eyes to it.

The questions arise: Is it necessary? Can it be justified? Is it not dangerous?

. . . Since there is exchange, the development of small economy is petty-bourgeois development, it is capitalist development—this is an incontrovertible truth, an elementary truth of political economy, confirmed, moreover, by the everyday experience and observation of even the ordinary man in the street.

What policy can the socialist proletariat pursue in the face of this economic reality? To give the small peasant *all* he needs of the goods produced by large-scale socialist industries in exchange for his grain and raw materials? This would be the most desirable and the most "correct" policy—and we have started on it. But we cannot give *all* the goods, very far from it; nor shall we be able to do so very soon—at all events not until we complete the first stage of the electrification of the whole country. What is to be done? One way is to try to prohibit entirely, to put the lock on all development of private, non-state exchange, i.e., trade, i.e., capitalism, which is inevitable when there are millions of small producers. But such a policy would be foolish and suicidal for the party that tried to apply it. It would be foolish because such a policy is economically impossible. It would be suicidal because the party that tried to apply such a policy would meet with inevitable disaster. . . .

The alternative (and this is the last *possible* and the only sensible policy) is not to try to prohibit or put the lock on the development of capitalism, but to try to direct it into the channels of *state capitalism*. This is economically possible, for state capitalism—in one form or another, to some degree or other—exists wherever the elements of free trade and capitalism in general exist. . . .

The simplest case, or example, of how the Soviet government directs the development of capitalism into the channels of state capitalism, of how it "implants" state capitalism, is concessions. We all now agree that concessions are necessary; but not all of us have given thought to what concessions mean. . . . They are an agreement, a bloc, an alliance between the Soviet, i.e., proletarian, state power and state capitalism against the small-proprietor (patriarchal and petty-bourgeois) element. The concessionaire is a capitalist. He conducts his business on capitalist lines, for profit. He is willing to enter into an agreement with the proletarian government in order to obtain extra profits, over and above ordinary profits; or in order to obtain raw materials which he cannot otherwise obtain, or can obtain only with great difficulty. Soviet power gains by the development of the productive forces, by securing an increased quantity of goods immediately, or within a very short period. . . . By "implanting" state capitalism in the form of concessions, the Soviet government strengthens large-scale production as against petty production, advanced production as against backward production, machine production as against hand production. And it obtains a larger quantity of the products of large-scale industry (percentage deduction), and strengthens state-regulated economic relations as against petty-bourgeois anarchical relations. The moderate and cautious application of the concessions policy will undoubtedly help us quickly (to a certain, not very large, degree) to improve the state of industry and the conditions of the workers and peasants—of course, at the cost of certain sacrifices, the surrender to the capitalist of many million poods of very valuable products. The degree and the conditions that will make concessions advantageous and not dangerous to us are determined by the relation of forces, they are decided by struggle; for concessions are also a form of struggle, they are the continuation of the class struggle in another form, and under no circumstances are they the substitution of class peace for class war. Practice will determine the methods of struggle.

Compared with other forms of state capitalism within the Soviet system, state capitalism in the form of concessions is, perhaps, the simplest, most distinct, clearest and most precisely defined. Here we have a formal, written agreement with the most cultured, advanced, West-European capitalism. We know exactly our gains and our losses, our rights and obligations. . . . We pay a certain "tribute" to world capitalism; we "ransom" ourselves from it by such-and-such arrangements and obtain immediately the more stable position of Soviet power, and better conditions for our economy. The whole difficulty with concessions is the proper consideration and appraisal of all the circumstances when concluding a concession agreement, and then the ability to supervise its fulfilment. Undoubtedly, there are difficulties; and in all probability mistakes will be inevitable at first. But these difficulties are minor ones compared with the other problems of the social revolution and, in particular, compared with the difficulties involved in other forms of developing, permitting and implanting state capitalism.

Lenin became increasingly frustrated by the overly bureaucratic functioning of the Soviet system (see also his writings on economic planning, above pp. 105–6). Here, in his last published article, he suggests that what is needed is a really thoroughgoing supervision and uprooting of the state—and even the Party—machine.[19]

We have so far been able to devote so little thought and attention to the quality of our state apparatus that it would now be quite legitimate if we took special care to secure its thorough organisation. . . . [O]ur experience of the first five years has fairly crammed our heads with mistrust and scepticism. These qualities assert themselves involuntarily when, for example, we hear people dilating at too great length and too flippantly on "proletarian culture." For a start, we should be satisfied with real bourgeois culture, for a start, we should be glad to dispense with the cruder types of pre-bourgeois culture, i.e., bureaucratic culture or serf culture, etc. In matters of culture, haste and sweeping measures are most harmful. Many of our young writers and Communists should get this well into their heads.

Thus, in the matter of our state apparatus we should now draw the conclusion from our past experience that it would be better to proceed more slowly.

[19] From V. I. Lenin, "Better Fewer, But Better" (March 2, 1923), in *Selected Works*, III, 829, 835–36.

Our state apparatus is so deplorable, not to say disgusting, that we must first think very carefully how to combat its defects, bearing in mind that these defects are rooted in the past, which, although it has been overthrown, has not yet been overcome, has not yet reached the stage of a culture that has receded into the distant past. I say culture deliberately, because in these matters we can only regard as achieved what has become part and parcel of our culture, of our social life. . . .

. . . Under the guidance of their presidium, the members of the Central Control Commission should systematically examine all the papers and documents of the Political Bureau. At the same time they should divide their time correctly between various jobs in investigating the routine in our institutions, from the very small and privately-owned offices to the highest state institutions. And lastly, their functions should include the study of theory, i.e., the theory of organisation of the work they intend to devote themselves to, and practical work under the guidance either of older comrades or of teachers in the higher institutes for the organisation of labour.

I do not think, however, that they will be able to confine themselves to this sort of academic work. In addition, they will have to prepare themselves for work which I would not hesitate to call training to catch —I will not say rogues, but something like that—and working out special ruses to screen their movements, their approach, etc.

If such proposals were made in West-European government institutions they would rouse frightful resentment, a feeling of moral indignation, etc.; but I trust that we have not become so bureaucratic as to be capable of that. NEP has not yet succeeded in gaining such respect as to cause any of us to be shocked at the idea that somebody may be caught. Our Soviet Republic is of such recent construction, and there are such heaps of the old lumber still lying around that it would hardly occur to anyone to be shocked at the idea that we should delve into them by means of ruses, by means of investigations sometimes directed to rather remote sources or in a roundabout way. And even if it did occur to anyone to be shocked by this, we may be sure that such a person would make himself a laughing-stock.

Let us hope that our new Workers' and Peasants' Inspection will abandon what the French call *pruderie,* which we may call ridiculous primness, or ridiculous swank, and which plays entirely into the hands of our Soviet and Party bureaucracy. Let it be said in parentheses that we have bureaucrats in our Party offices as well as in Soviet offices.

One area where Party bureaucratism (and worse) cropped up was in the mishandling of the minority nationalities, an area that had always been one of great interest and sensitivity for Lenin. The growing rancor of his relations with Stalin (then Commissar of Nationalities, as well as General Secretary of the Party) can be seen in these notes—part of Lenin's "Testament"—which he dictated in the immediate aftermath of his second stroke.[20]

[20] From V. I. Lenin, "Letter to the Congress" (December 30–31, 1922), in *Selected Works*, III, 802–804. Headings in the original.

The Question of Nationalities or "Autonomisation"

I suppose I have been very remiss with respect to the workers of Russia for not having intervened energetically and decisively enough in the notorious question of autonomisation, which, it appears, is officially called the question of the Union of Soviet Socialist Republics.

When this question arose last summer, I was ill. . . .

It is said that a united apparatus was needed. Where did that assurance come from? Did it not come from that same Russian apparatus which, as I pointed out in one of the preceding sections of my diary, we took over from tsarism and tarred a little with the Soviet brush?

The apparatus we call ours is, in fact, still quite alien to us; it is a bourgeois and tsarist hotch-potch and there has been no possibility of getting rid of it in the course of the past five years without the help of other countries and because we have been "busy" most of the time with military engagements and the fight against famine.

It is quite natural that in such circumstances the "freedom to withdraw from the union" by which we justify ourselves will be a mere scrap of paper, unable to defend the non-Russians from the onslaught of that really Russian man, the Great-Russian chauvinist, in substance a rascal and lover of violence, such as the typical Russian bureaucrat is. There is no doubt that the infinitesimal percentage of Soviet and sovietised workers will drown in that sea of chauvinistic Great-Russian riff-raff like a fly in milk. . . .

. . . [W]ere we careful enough to give the people of other nationalities a real defence against the genuine Russian Derzhimordas? I do not think we took such measures although we could and should have done so.

I think that Stalin's haste and his infatuation with pure administration, together with his spite against the notorious "nationalist-socialism," played a fatal role here. In politics spite generally plays the basest of roles.

I also fear that Comrade Dzerzhinsky, who went to the Caucasus to investigate the "crime" of those "nationalist-socialists," distinguished himself there by his "genuine" Russian frame of mind (it is common knowledge that people of other nationalities who have become Russified overdo this Russian frame of mind). . . .

Here we have an important question of principle: how is internationalism to be understood? [21]

December 30, 1922

Continuation of the notes.
December 31, 1922
In my writings on the national question I have already said that an abstract presentation of the question of nationalism is of no use at all. A distinction must necessarily be made between the nationalism of an oppressor nation and that of an oppressed nation, the nationalism of a big nation and that of a small nation.

In respect of the second kind of nationalism we, nationals of a big nation, have nearly always been guilty, in historic practice, of an infinite number of cases of violence; furthermore, we commit violence and insult an infinite number of times without noticing it. It is sufficient to recall my Volga reminiscences of how non-Russians are treated; how the Poles are not called by any other name than Polyachishka [Polacks]. . . .

In 1920, in a speech to the Congress of the Young Communist League, Lenin put forward ideas about the task of the youth that may, properly, be regarded as his "testament" to the rising generation. This selection stresses the link between the cultural heritage of the past and the transformative tasks of the future.[22]

. . . Marx based his work on the firm foundation of the human knowledge acquired under capitalism. Marx studied the laws of development of human society and realised the inevitability of the development of capitalism towards communism. And the principal thing is that he proved this precisely on the basis of the most exact, most detailed and most profound study of this capitalist society, by fully assimilating all that earlier science had produced. He critically reshaped everything that had been created by human society, not ignoring a single point. Everything that had been created by human thought he reshaped, criticised, tested on the working-class movement, and drew conclusions which people restricted by bourgeois limits or bound by bourgeois prejudices could not draw.

[21] After this the following phrase was crossed out in the shorthand text: "It seems to me that our comrades have not studied this important question of principle sufficiently." [ED. Russian edition.]

[22] From V. I. Lenin, "The Tasks of the Youth Leagues" (October 2, 1920), in *Selected Works*, III, 506–507.

We must bear this in mind when, for example, we talk about proletarian culture. Unless we clearly understand that only by an exact knowledge of the culture created by the whole development of mankind and only by reshaping this culture can we build proletarian culture—unless we understand that, we shall not be able to solve this problem. Proletarian culture is not something that has sprung nobody knows whence, it is not an invention of people who call themselves experts in proletarian culture. That is all nonsense. Proletarian culture must be the result of the natural development of the stores of knowledge which mankind has accumulated under the yoke of capitalist society, landowner society, bureaucratic society. . . .

When we so often hear representatives of the youth and certain advocates of a new system of education attacking the old school and saying that it was a school of cramming, we say to them that we must take what was good from the old school. We must not take from the old school the system of loading young people's minds with an immense amount of knowledge, nine-tenths of which was useless and one-tenth distorted. But this does not mean that we can confine ourselves to communist conclusions and learn only communist slogans. You will not create communism that way. You can become a Communist only when you enrich your mind with the knowledge of all the treasures created by mankind. . . .

You must not only assimilate this knowledge, you must assimilate it critically, so as not to cram your mind with useless lumber, but enrich it with all those facts that are indispensable to the modern man of education. If a Communist took it into his head to boast about his communism because of the ready-made conclusions he had acquired, without putting in a great deal of serious and hard work, without understanding the facts which he must examine critically, he would be a very deplorable Communist. Such superficiality would be decidedly fatal. If I know that I know little, I shall strive to learn more; but if a man says that he is a Communist and that he need know nothing thoroughly, he will never be anything like a Communist. . . .

THE SUCCESSION

Immediately after his second stroke, Lenin turned his mind to the problem of succession within the political leadership. What has come to be known in the West as Lenin's "Testament" was actually a series of notes dictated in December, 1922, and January, 1923, as part of a planned "Letter to the Congress," i.e., a statement of his views to be read to the next regular Congress of the Soviet Communist Party. By the time the Congress met, in May, 1924, Lenin was dead; Stalin's influence, which was to culminate in the late 1920s in his complete control of the Soviet Communist Party and state, was on the rise.

Due, primarily, to the insistence of Lenin's wife, Nadezhda Krupskaya, the letter was, in fact, read to delegates. But it was only presented at selective caucuses of various deputations, rather than being openly debated at a full plenary session. Stalin, as General Secretary, was able to exert sufficient control to persuade the Congress delegates that it would not be in the interest of the Party either to debate the letter or to allow it to be published. Though a few, less controversial sections were published in 1927, it was not till 1956—after Khrushchev's "secret speech" denouncing Stalin— that the text of the "Testament" was published in the Soviet Union.

A few points must be made if we wish to place the following selections—the most controversial parts of the document—in perspective. First, the "Testament" did not deal in its entirety with leadership; other, less emotional, portions were concerned with such substantive issues as economics and the role of nationalities in the Soviet federation. Also, though Lenin's strictures against Stalin are clearly the key to this part of the "Testament," one should guard against the somewhat one-sided view of it that was promoted by Trotskyite circles when the document first became available in the West in the late 1920s. Trotsky's supporters stressed Lenin's attack on Stalin. But while the attack on Stalin was, indeed, most important, Lenin's real concern was that not only Stalin but also the other potential heirs were lacking in those qualities he regarded as needed for leadership of the Soviet system; thus his appraisal of Trotsky is an excellent example of damning with faint praise.

We can mention three factors that evidently contributed to the breach between Stalin and Lenin. The first was that while Stalin and Lenin had probably been able to get along with each other during the period of revolutionary struggle and civil war, when Stalin's ruthlessness served the tactical needs of Lenin's long-range revolutionary program, Stalin's reluctance to display "sufficient caution" in using his authority became an irritant once Lenin had decided on a policy of qualified retreat (as in the case of the NEP). At issue was Stalin's nationalities policy in the Caucasus (q.v. above, p. 116). Lenin desired to placate the nationalities and was particularly irritated by Stalin's propensity to demonstrate a chauvinism that Lenin considered to be worthy of the worst kind of Tsarist authoritarianism. Other factors in the break were more personal in nature. Thus, the immediate occasion for Lenin's informing Stalin that personal relations between them were at an end came about as a result of Stalin's rudeness to (and, apparently, his intimidation of) Lenin's wife, Krupskaya. Finally, we cannot doubt that Stalin's apparent inability to restrain himself, even prior to Lenin's death, in

*building a base on which to make a bid for supreme power had
come to Lenin's attention as he wrestled on his sickbed with the
problem of the future of the system he had brought into being.*

*Lenin did not merely deal with the succession problem in terms
of the personalities of protagonists; rather, he discussed the defects
and possible evolution of Soviet administrative machinery. One may
be tempted to ask why Lenin had not realized these defects earlier,
when he was still able to exercise power and carry out a fundamental reshaping of the Soviet system. His strictures had little effect:
the phenomena he analyzed are reflected in Soviet politics even in
our own day.*[23]

Continuation of the notes.
December 24, 1922

By stability of the Central Committee, . . . I mean measures against
a split, as far as such measures can at all be taken. For, of course, the
whiteguard . . . was right when, first, he banked on a split in our Party,
. . . and when, secondly, he banked on grave differences in our Party
to cause that split.

Our Party relies on two classes and therefore its instability would be
possible and its downfall inevitable if there were no agreement between
those two classes. In that event this or that measure, and generally all
talk about the stability of our C.C., would be futile. No measures of any
kind would be able to prevent a split in such a case. But I hope that
this is too remote a future and too improbable an event to talk about it.

I have in mind stability as a guarantee against a split in the immediate future, and I intend to deal here with a few ideas concerning
personal qualities.

I think that from this standpoint the prime factors in the question of
stability are such members of the C.C. as Stalin and Trotsky. I think
relations between them make up the greater half of the danger of a split,
which could be avoided, and the avoidance of which, in my opinion,
would be served, among other things, by increasing the number of C.C.
members to 50 or 100.

Comrade Stalin, having become General Secretary, has unlimited authority concentrated in his hands, and I am not sure whether he will
always be capable of using that authority with sufficient caution. Comrade
Trotsky, on the other hand, as his struggle against the C.C. on the question
of the People's Commissariat for Railways has already proved, is distinguished not only by outstanding ability. He is personally perhaps the
most capable man in the present C.C., but he takes things with exces-

---

[23] V. I. Lenin, excerpts from "Letter to the Congress" (dictated at various times in
December, 1922, and January, 1923) in *Selected Works*, III, 792–94.

sive self-assurance and shows excessive enthusiasm for the purely administrative side of the work.

These two qualities of the two outstanding leaders of the present C.C. can unconsciously lead to a split, and if our Party does not take steps to avert this, the split may come unexpectedly.

I shall not give any further appraisals of the personal qualities of other members of the C.C. I shall just recall that the October episode with Zinoviev and Kamenev was, of course, no accident,[24] but neither can the blame for it be laid upon him[25] personally, any more than non-Bolshevism can upon Trotsky.

Speaking of the young C.C. members, I wish to say a few words about Bukharin and Pyatakov. They are, in my opinion, the most outstanding figures (among the youngest ones), and the following must be borne in mind about them: Bukharin is not only a most valuable and major theorist of the Party. He is also rightly considered the favourite of the whole Party, but his theoretical views can be classified only with great reserve as fully Marxist, for there is something scholastic about him (he never learned, and, I think, never fully understood dialectics).

December 25. As for Pyatakov, he is unquestionably a man of outstanding will and outstanding ability, but shows too much enthusiasm for administrating and the administrative side of the work to be relied on in a serious political matter.

Both of these remarks, of course, are made only for the present, on the assumption that both these outstanding and devoted Party workers do not find an occasion to enhance their knowledge and amend their one-sidedness.

Lenin

December 25, 1922
Taken down by M. V.

Addition to the Letter of December 24, 1922

Stalin is too rude and this defect, although quite tolerable in our midst and in dealings among us Communists, becomes intolerable in a General Secretary. That is why I suggest that the comrades think about a way of removing Stalin from that post and appointing somebody else differing in all other respects from Comrade Stalin solely in the degree of being more tolerant, more loyal, more polite and more considerate to the comrades, less capricious, etc. This circumstance may appear to be a

---

[24] [Their opposition at the time of the seizure of power. Trotsky's "non-Bolshevism" refers to the pre–1917 period—ED.]

[25] Apparently a slip of the pen: the context suggests "them" for "him." [ED. Soviet text.]

negligible detail. But I think that from the standpoint of safeguards against a split and from the standpoint of what I wrote above about the mutual relations between Stalin and Trotsky it is not a detail, or it is a detail which can assume decisive importance.

Lenin

Taken down by L. F.
January 4, 1923

Continuation of the notes.
December 26, 1922

The increase in the number of C.C. members to 50 or even 100 must, in my opinion, serve a double or even a treble purpose: the more members there are in the C.C., the more its work will be studied and the less danger there will be of a split due to some indiscretion. The enlistment of many workers to the C.C. will help the workers to improve our administrative machinery, which is far from perfect. We inherited it, in effect, from the old regime, for it was absolutely impossible to reorganise it in such a short time, especially considering the war, famine, etc. That is why those "critics" who point to the defects of our administrative machinery out of mockery or malice, may be calmly answered that they do not in the least understand the conditions of the revolution today. It is altogether impossible in five years to reorganise the machinery adequately, especially in the conditions in which our revolution took place. It is enough that in five years we have created a new type of state in which the workers are leading the peasants against the bourgeoisie; and in a hostile international environment this in itself is a gigantic achievement. But the knowledge of this must on no account hide from us the fact that, in effect, we took over the old machinery of state from the tsar and the bourgeoisie and that now, with the onset of peace and the satisfaction of the minimum requirements against famine, all our work must be directed towards improving the administrative machinery. . . .

SOVIET INTERNATIONAL POLICY

His years of exile, of close observation of the European scene in peace and war, of gathering data for such works as Imperialism, *together with his sensitivity to factors making for change —technical, organizational and otherwise—probably equipped Lenin better than any other statesman of the immediate postwar period for coping with the problems of foreign policy in a world that had been cast adrift from its moorings. If the Soviets were not more successful in foreign policy by the time of Lenin's death, it was due less to his own limitations than to the severity of the situation which Russia had faced. A bare few years from absolute decline and foreign intervention and still somewhat of a pariah on the international scene, the Soviet Union nevertheless, by 1922, found a place at international conferences and (in its relations with Germany in particular) began to establish the kind of international contacts needed to support the task of societal reconstruction.*

One wonders what the situation would have been had the task of governing been in the hands of, say, Trotsky, with his penchant for seeing revolutions "around the corner." For all of his ideological certainty as to the general drift of international affairs, Lenin was capable of the flexibility of a Talleyrand in the actual conduct of state business. While he took care to cement revolutionary links with the anti-imperialist nationalists of Asia and the Middle East, it is quite clear that (Imperialism notwithstanding) he recognized that, until the Soviet Union was ready to take on the developed capitalist countries in an inevitable conflict, it had to find help in diplomacy and international economics where it could, and pay the price that was demanded.

After Brest-Litovsk, Lenin saw that the only strategy available to a weak state like Soviet Russia was to play off, one against another, the rivalries in the capitalist world—rivalries which he believed to be a permanent feature of the imperialist system.[26]

However much the Anglo-French and American imperialist sharks fume with rage, however much they slander us, . . . *I shall not hesitate a second* to enter into [an] . . . "agreement" with the German imperialist vultures if an attack upon Russia by Anglo-French troops calls for it. . . . Such tactics will ease the task of the socialist revolution, will hasten it, will weaken the international bourgeoisie, will strengthen the position of the working class which is vanquishing the bourgeoisie.

The American people resorted to these tactics long ago to the advantage of their revolution. When they waged their great war of liberation against the British oppressors, they had also against them the French and the Spanish oppressors who owned a part of what is now the United States of North America. In their arduous war for freedom, the American people also entered into "agreements" with some oppressors against others for the purpose of weakening the oppressors and strengthening those who were fighting in a revolutionary manner against oppression, for the purpose of serving the interests of the oppressed *people*. The American people took advantage of the strife between the French, the Spanish and the British; sometimes they even fought side by side with the forces of the French and Spanish oppressors against the British oppressors; first they

[26] From V. I. Lenin, "Letter to the American Workers" (1918), in *Selected Works*, III, 51.

vanquished the British and then freed themselves (partly by ransom) from the French and the Spanish.

Much more strident in tone was the picture of the sources of conflict in international politics which Lenin presented to the Second Congress of the Communist International in 1920.[27]

The economic relations of imperialism constitute the core of the entire international situation as it now exists. Throughout the twentieth century, this new, highest and last stage of capitalism has become fully defined. Of course, you all know that the most characteristic, the most essential feature of imperialism is the enormous dimensions that capital has reached. Free competition has given way to monopoly of gigantic proportions. An insignificant number of capitalists have been able in some cases to concentrate in their hands whole branches of industry; these have passed into the hands of combines, cartels, syndicates and trusts, not infrequently of an international character. . . .

This domination of a handful of capitalists reached its full development when the whole world had been divided up, not only in the sense that the various sources of raw materials and means of production had been captured by the biggest capitalists, but also in the sense that the preliminary division of the colonies had been completed. . . . [I]f we add countries like Persia, Turkey, and China, whose position already at that time was that of semi-colonies, we shall get in round figures a population of a thousand million people oppressed through colonial dependence by the richest, most civilised and freest countries. And you know that, apart from direct state juridical dependence, colonial dependence presumes a number of relations of financial and economic dependence, presumes a number of wars, which were not regarded as wars because very often they amounted to sheer massacres, when European and American imperialist troops, armed with the most up-to-date weapons of destruction, slaughtered the unarmed and defenceless inhabitants of colonial countries.

The inevitable outcome of this partition of the whole world, of this domination of capitalist monopoly, . . . was the first imperialist war of 1914–18. This war was waged in order to repartition the whole world. The war was waged in order to decide which of the tiny groups of biggest states—the British or the German—was to secure the opportunity and the right to rob, strangle and exploit the whole world. You know that

[27] From V. I. Lenin, "Report on the International Situation and the Fundamental Tasks of the Communist International" (July 19, 1920), in *Selected Works*, III, 480–83.

the war settled this question in favour of the British group. And as a result of this war all capitalist contradictions have become immeasurably more acute. The war at one stroke relegated about 250,000,000 of the world's inhabitants to what is equivalent to a colonial position: Russia— whose population must be considered as about 130,000,000, and Austria-Hungary, Germany and Bulgaria—with a population of not less than 120,000,000. That means 250,000,000 people living in countries of which some, like Germany, are among the most advanced, most enlightened, most cultured, and on a level with modern technical progress. By means of the Treaty of Versailles, the war imposed such terms upon these countries that advanced peoples have been reduced to a state of colonial dependence, poverty, starvation, ruin, and loss of rights; for this treaty binds them for many generations, and places [them] in conditions that no civilised nation has ever lived in. You have the following picture of the world: after the war, at one stroke not less than *1,250 million* people are subjected to colonial oppression, to exploitation by brutal capitalism, which boasted of its love for peace, and which had a right to do so some fifty years ago, when the world was not yet divided up, when monopoly did not yet rule, when capitalism could still develop in relative peace, without colossal military conflicts.

Now, following this "peaceful" epoch we see a monstrous intensification of oppression, we see the reversion to a colonial and military oppression that is far worse than before. The Treaty of Versailles has placed Germany and a number of other defeated countries in a position where their economic existence is materially impossible, where they have no rights whatever and are humiliated. . . .

Not only have the colonial and the defeated countries fallen into a state of dependence, but within each victor country contradictions have become more acute, all capitalist contradictions have become aggravated. . . .

Take the national debts. We know that the debts of the principal European states have increased not less than *seven* times in the period from 1914 to 1920. I shall quote an economic source, one of particularly great significance—the British diplomat Keynes, author of *The Economic Consequences of the Peace,* . . . He has arrived at conclusions which are stronger, more striking and more instructive than any a communist revolutionary could draw, . . . Keynes has reached the conclusion that, following the Versailles peace, Europe and the whole world are heading for bankruptcy. He resigned, threw his book in the government's face and said: what you are doing is madness. . . .

Lenin viewed the activities of the Communist International as a vital component of revolutionary foreign policy. At the same

*time, he recognized that considerable allowance had to be made
for national differences in both the direction and the style of work
of the various Communist parties.*[28]

As long as national and state differences exist among peoples and
countries—and these differences will continue to exist for a very long
time even after the dictatorship of the proletariat has been established on
a world scale—the unity of international tactics of the Communist working class movement of all countries demands, not the elimination of
variety, not the abolition of national differences (that is a foolish dream
at the present moment), but such an application of the *fundamental*
principles of Communism (Soviet power and the dictatorship of the proletariat) as will *correctly modify* these principles in *certain particulars,*
correctly adapt and apply them to national and national-state differences. The main task of the historical period through which all the advanced countries (and not only the advanced countries) are now passing is to investigate, study, seek, divine, grasp that which is peculiarly
national, specifically national in the *concrete manner* in which each
country *approaches* the fulfilment of the *single* international task, the
victory over opportunism and "Left" doctrinairism within the working
class movement, the overthrow of the bourgeoisie, and the establishment
of a Soviet republic and a proletarian dictatorship. . . .

*Lenin continued to pay attention to the questions of imperial-
ism and nationalism, and he turned to the Asian and Middle
Eastern nationalist movements as possible allies in outflanking
Western capitalism. He reasserted Russia's longstanding interest in
Persia and Afghanistan, but gave it a new, anti-imperialist twist. In
addition, he sought contacts with the Turkish nationalist movement of Kemal Ataturk and the Chinese Kuomintang of Sun Yat-
sen. In his draft theses on nationalism and colonialism, prepared
for the Comintern Congress of 1920, Lenin developed a rationale for
an end-play in which Communism and revolutionary, anti-imperialist nationalism were to act in unison against their common enemies.*[29]

11) With regard to the more backward states and nations, in which
feudal or patriarchal and patriarchal-peasant relations predominate, it
is particularly important to bear in mind:

[28] From V. I. Lenin, *Left-Wing Communism: An Infantile Disorder*, p. 73.
[29] From V. I. Lenin, "On the National and Colonial Questions" (Lenin's draft theses),
in *Selected Works*, III, 466–67.

first, that all Communist parties must assist the bourgeois-democratic liberation movement in these countries, and that the duty of rendering the most active assistance rests primarily with the workers of the country upon which the backward nation is dependent colonially or financially;

second, the need for struggle against the clergy and other influential reactionary and medieval elements in backward countries;

third, the need to combat the Pan-Islamic and similar trends which strive to combine the liberation movement against European and American imperialism with an attempt to strengthen the positions of the khans, landowners, mullahs, etc.;

fourth, the need, in backward countries, to give special support to the peasant movement against the landowners, against landed proprietorship, and against all manifestations or survivals of feudalism, and to strive to lend the peasant movement the most revolutionary character by establishing the closest possible alliance between the West-European communist proletariat and the revolutionary peasant movement in the East in the colonies, and in the backward countries generally. It is particularly necessary to exert every effort to apply the basic principles of the Soviet system in countries where pre-capitalist relations predominate—by setting up "working people's Soviets," etc.;

fifth, the need for determined struggle against attempts to give a communist colouring to bourgeois-democratic liberation trends in the backward countries; the Communist International should support bourgeois-democratic national movements in colonial and backward countries only on condition that, in these countries, the elements of future proletarian parties, which will be communist not only in name, are brought together and trained to understand their special tasks, i.e., to fight the bourgeois-democratic movements within their own nations. The Communist International must enter into a temporary alliance with bourgeois democracy in colonial and backward countries, but must not merge with it and must under all circumstances uphold the independence of the proletarian movement even if it is in its earliest embryonic form;

sixth, the need constantly to explain and expose among the broadest working masses of all countries, and particularly of the backward countries, the deception systematically practised by the imperialist powers, which, under the guise of politically independent states, set up states that are wholly dependent upon them economically, financially and militarily. Under modern international conditions there is no salvation for dependent and weak nations except in a union of Soviet republics.

The question of relations with the West was, undoubtedly, more complex than the hypothetical question of anti-imperialist conflict during these years. The two sides to this question—the short-run problem of trade relations and economic aid, and the longer-range potential for conflict—are dealt with by Lenin in the following two selections. The first is a pre-NEP justification for seeking to gain Western participation, via economic concessions, in building up the Soviet economy; the second, from his last published article, is a final perspective on the world politics that was emerging out of both the aftermath of World War I and the growing national awareness of colonial revolutionaries.

Comrades, I must say that this trade agreement with Great Britain is connected with one of the most important questions in our economic policy, that of concessions. One of the important acts passed by the Soviet government during the period under review is the law on concessions of November 23, this year. . . . We have published a special pamphlet containing not only the text of the decree but also a list of the chief concessions we are offering: agricultural, timber and mining. We have taken steps to make the published text of this decree available in the West-European countries as early as possible, and we hope that our concessions policy will also be a practical success. We do not in the least close our eyes to the danger which this policy involves for the Socialist Soviet Republic, for a country, moreover, that is weak and backward. As long as the Soviet Republic remains the isolated periphery of the capitalist world, it would be absolutely ridiculous, fantastic and utopian to hope that we can achieve complete economic independence and that all danger will vanish. Of course, as long as the radical contrasts remain, the dangers will also remain, and there is no escaping them. What we have to do is to get firmly on our feet in order to survive these dangers; we must be able to distinguish between big dangers and little dangers, and incur the lesser dangers rather than the greater. . . .

. . . [W]e must say that there is no question of selling Russia to the capitalists. It is a question of concessions; and every concession agreement is limited to a definite period and by definite terms. It is hedged around by every possible guarantee, by guarantees that have been carefully considered and will be considered and discussed with you again and again at the present Congress and at various other conferences. These temporary agreements have nothing to do with selling. There is not a hint in them of selling Russia. What they do represent is a certain economic concession to the capitalists, the purpose of which is to enable us, as soon as possible, to secure the necessary machinery and locomotives without which we cannot effect the restoration of our economy. We have no right to neglect anything that may, in however small a way, help us to improve the conditions of the workers and peasants. . . .

. . . With the aid of industry we shall achieve a great deal, and in a shorter period; but even if the achievements are very great the period will be measured in years, a number of years. It must be borne in mind that although we have now gained a military victory and have secured peace, history teaches us that not a single big question has ever been settled and not a single revolution accomplished without a series of wars. And we shall not forget this lesson. We have already taught a number of powerful countries not to wage war on us, but we cannot guarantee that it will be for long. The imperialist predators will attack us again if there is the slightest change in the situation. We must be prepared for it. Hence, the first thing is to restore the economy and place it firmly on its feet. Without equipment, without machines obtained from capitalist countries, we cannot do this quickly. And we should not grudge the capitalists a little extra profit if only we can effect this restoration. The workers and peasants must share the sentiments of those non-Party peasants who have declared that they are not afraid to face sacrifice and privation. Realising the danger of capitalist intervention, they do not regard concessions from a sentimental point of view, but as a continuation of the war, as the transfer of the ruthless struggle to another plane, they see in them the possibility of fresh attempts on the part of the bourgeoisie to restore the old capitalism. That is fine; it is a guarantee that not only the organs of Soviet power but every worker and peasant will make it his business to keep watch and ward over our interests. We are, therefore, confident that we shall be able to place the protection of our interests on such a basis that the restoration of the power of the capitalists will be totally out of the question even in carrying out the concession agreements; we shall do everything to reduce the danger to a minimum, make it less than the danger of war, so that it will be difficult to resume the war and easier for us to restore and develop our economy in a shorter period, in fewer years (and it is a matter of a good many years).[30]

. . . It is not easy for us, . . . to keep going until the socialist revolution is victorious in more developed countries. . . .

The system of international relationships which has now taken shape is one in which a European state, Germany, is enslaved by the victor countries. Furthermore, owing to their victory, a number of states, the oldest states in the West, are in a position to make some insignificant concessions to their oppressed classes—concessions which, insignificant though they are, nevertheless retard the revolutionary movement in those countries and create some semblance of "social peace."

At the same time, as a result of the last imperialist war, a number of

[30] From V. I. Lenin, "Report of the Council of People's Commissars to the Eighth All-Russian Congress of Soviets" (December 22, 1920), in *Selected Works*, III, 535–37.

countries of the East, India, China, etc., have been completely jolted out of the rut. Their development has definitely shifted to general European capitalist lines. The general European ferment has begun to affect them, and it is now clear to the whole world that they have been drawn into a process of development that must lead to a crisis in the whole of world capitalism. . . .

What tactics does this situation prescribe for our country? Obviously the following. We must display extreme caution so as to preserve our workers' government and to retain our small and very small peasantry under its leadership and authority. We have the advantage that the whole world is now passing to a movement that must give rise to a world socialist revolution. But we are labouring under the disadvantage that the imperialists have succeeded in splitting the world into two camps; and this split is made more complicated by the fact that it is extremely difficult for Germany, which is really a land of advanced, cultured, capitalist development, to rise to her feet. All the capitalist powers of what is called the West are pecking at her and preventing her from rising. On the other hand, the entire East, with its hundreds of millions of exploited working people reduced to the last degree of human suffering, has been forced into a position where its physical and material strength cannot possibly be compared with the physical, material and military strength of any of the much smaller West-European states.

Can we save ourselves from the impending conflict with these imperialist countries? May we hope that the internal antagonisms and conflicts between the thriving imperialist countries of the West and the thriving imperialist countries of the East[31] will give us a second respite as they did the first time, when the campaign of the West-European counter-revolution in support of the Russian counter-revolution broke down owing to the antagonisms in the camp of the counter-revolutionaries of the West and the East, in the camp of the Eastern and Western exploiters, in the camp of Japan and America?

I think the reply to this question should be that the issue depends upon too many factors, and that the outcome of the struggle as a whole can be forecast only because in the long run capitalism itself is educating and training the vast majority of the population of the globe for the struggle.

In the last analysis, the outcome of the struggle will be determined by the fact that Russia, India, China, etc., account for the overwhelming majority of the population of the globe. And it is this majority that, during the past few years, has been drawn into the struggle for emancipation with extraordinary rapidity, so that in this respect there cannot be the slightest doubt what the final outcome of the world struggle will be.

---

[31] [The reference is to Japan and the United States. In many Russian world maps, North America is shown to the far right of the map, i.e., East of Russia–ED.]

In this sense, the complete victory of socialism is fully and absolutely assured.

. . . To ensure our existence until the next military conflict between the counter-revolutionary imperialist West and the revolutionary and nationalist East, between the most civilised countries of the world and the Orientally backward countries which, however, comprise the majority, this majority must become civilised. . . .[32]

[32] From V. I. Lenin, "Better Fewer, But Better" (March 4, 1923). in *Selected Works*, III, 839–41.

LENIN VIEWED BY HIS CONTEMPORARIES

Since 1917, a substantial literature has appeared consisting of reminiscences of Lenin in all his roles: husband, revolutionary, statesman concerned both with high policy and with minutiae of office routine, and as critic (rather conventional) of art and literature. Much of the literature is filled with either more piety or vituperation than insight. The emigré accounts often center on refurbishing ideological debates in the pre-Revolutionary Russian socialist movement. Nevertheless, enough raw material exists to draw a collective portrait of Lenin as viewed by contemporaries.

In Part Two, the first selections present a general overview of Lenin's personality and his significance in the Russian revolutionary movement. These are followed by eyewitness accounts and contemporary appraisals of his role in 1917. Finally, we see Lenin at work after 1917, as architect of the Soviet state and its policies.

4
Personality and Politics

A recurrent historical question concerns the role of the individual actor in historical events. In War and Peace, Tolstoy concluded that historical events are random, chaotic, and confused and that no single factor—least of all, the personality of a leading figure—determines historical outcomes. Marxist historical theory, with its heavy emphasis on primary socioeconomic processes, seemingly weighs against attaching much importance to the historical role of individuals. Yet, in practice, Marxist historians have had to consider the role played by the revolutionary leader—as "midwife" to the historical outcome, and as something more than that. Admittedly, in the case of Lenin, this process is intensified by his position as the central figure in the Soviet state cult. Yet Trotsky, a dissident Communist writing his history of the revolution in exile, found it difficult to reconcile his firsthand view of Lenin as maker of the 1917 October revolution with his own belief, as Marxist theoretician, in the relatively impersonal nature of the historical process. In the *end, he deviated from a puristic position and attached considerable significance to Lenin's character and political skill.*

The importance of Lenin's personality and his impact on the revolution is now generally recognized by critical historians. In one form or another, most would agree with the analysis presented by Sidney Hook, who used the case of Lenin to test the Marxist theory of history (see Hook, The Hero in History *[Boston: Beacon Press, 1955], pp. 184ff.).*

ANNA ULYANOVA-YELIZEROVA: LENIN—CHILDHOOD AND YOUTH [1]

A brief, but revealing impression of the early manifestation of those characteristics that were later noted by both Lenin's associates and his adversaries is contained in the memoirs of his older sister. Anna Ulyanova (1864–1935) became a revolutionary in 1886, served as a writer and editor for a number of Bolshevik publications, and, after her brother's death, helped organize the Lenin Institute in Moscow, a research center that is now part of the Institute of Marxism-Leninism.

Brought up to be conscientious where work was concerned, Volodya,[2] in spite of his mischievousness and high spirits, was always attentive at lessons. This, as his teachers pointed out, together with his excellent memory, enabled him to grasp at once anything he was taught, so that there was hardly any need for him to go over it again at home. In the junior forms he usually finished his homework quickly and began to play all sorts of pranks and to romp about, greatly disturbing us, older ones, who were doing our homework in the same room. Sometimes Father took him to his study to check his lessons and asked him all the Latin words entered in his notebook, but Volodya usually knew every one. He also read a lot. Father received all the new children's books and magazines; we also borrowed books in the library.

Volodya's regular playmate was his sister Olya (born on November 4, 1871). A clever, active and vivacious girl, she learned to read at the age of four together with her brother and like him studied easily and willingly. Moreover, Olya, who in some things resembled her brother Sasha,[3] was exceptionally hard-working. Once, I remember, when Volodya was in senior form at gymnasium, he said to me, listening to Olya's endless

---

[1] From Anna Ulyanova-Yelizerova, *Reminiscences of Ilyich* (Moscow, 1934); reprinted in *Reminiscences of Lenin by his Relatives* (Moscow: Foreign Languages Publishing House, 1956), p. 19.

[2] [Familiar form of Vladimir—ED.]

[3] [Familiar forms of Olga and Alexander—ED.]

exercises on the piano in the next room: "That's diligence for you." And he began to cultivate this quality in himself and, in later years his industry amazed us all and in conjunction with his natural talents helped him to become what he was.

NADEZHDA KRUPSKAYA: LENIN'S MOODS [4]

Nadezhda Krupskaya (1869–1939) first met Lenin while both were participants in a St. Petersburg Marxist circle. The daughter of a Tsarist army officer, she was a teacher by training and later wrote articles on educational problems. In 1898, while she and Lenin were serving terms of exile in Siberia, she became his wife. From then on, she was his closest political assistant, sharing with him the rigors of revolutionary activity. She acted as secretary of the newspaper Iskra *while Lenin was editor; she often served as his messenger, conveying instructions to Bolshevik groups; much of the research for his works was undertaken by her—even his notes on Hobson's* Imperialism *are in her handwriting. After the revolution, she occupied various high positions in the Soviet educational system, and from 1927 until her death, was a member of the Central Committee of the Soviet Communist Party.*

In the main, Krupskaya's reminiscences combine straight narrative of Lenin's activities with extracts from his writings. On occasion, however, she gives us fleeting glimpses of Lenin that are not paralleled elsewhere. The three selections that follow reveal a seldom seen side of Lenin: his various moods. His tranquillity while conducting a training course for Russian underground workers at Longjumeau, near Paris, in 1911 may be contrasted with his reflections on the suicide of Marx's daughter and son-in-law later the same year.

The lessons were held with strict regularity. Vladimir Ilyich read lectures on political economy (thirty lectures), on the agrarian question (ten lectures) and on the theory and practice of socialism (five lectures). The seminars on political economy were conducted by Inessa. Zinoviev and Kamenev lectured on the history of the Party, and Semashko delivered a couple of lectures too. Other lecturers were Ryazanov, who lectured on the history of the West-European labour movement, Charles Rappoport, who lectured on the French movement, Steklov and Finn-Yenotayevsky, who lectured on public law and finance, Lunacharsky—on literature, and Stanislaw Wolski on newspaper printing.

The students studied hard and diligently. In the evenings they sometimes went out into the fields, where they would sing a lot of songs, or

[4] From N. K. Krupskaya, *Reminiscences of Lenin*, trans. Bernard Isaacs (Moscow: Foreign Languages Publishing House, 1959), pp. 223–24, 226, 232–33.

lie about under the haystacks, talking about this and that. Ilyich some-times joined them.

. . . Ilyich was very pleased with the work of the school. In our spare time we went out cycling together as usual, going up the hill and riding out fifteen kilometres to a place where there was an aerodrome. Being further inland, this was much less frequented than the aerodrome at Juvisy. We were often the only spectators, and Ilyich was able to watch the evolutions of the aeroplanes to his heart's content. . . .

In October the Lafargues committed suicide. Their death was a great shock to Ilyich. We recalled our visit to them. Ilyich said: "If you can't do any more work for the Party you must be able to face the truth and die like the Lafargues." . . .

At the beginning of 1912, Lenin's fortunes were at their low-est point. The Tsarist minister, Stolypin, had initiated changes in the landholding system that, by creating a class of peasant pro-prietors with a vested interest in political stability, promised to give the Tsarist regime a renewed basis in the countryside. The Bolshe-viks were reduced to conspiratorial action that had little relation-ship to a wider revolutionary struggle. Robberies and other shady activities were resorted to to raise funds for the party. These, and Lenin's bitter struggles against the Mensheviks, were increasingly isolating Lenin both from Russian socialists and from respectable European social-democrats. In Russia, the ranks of the middle-level Bolshevik leadership were being thinned by police raids (partly the result of the work of Roman Malinovsky, a protégé of Lenin's on the Central Committee and in the Duma who turned out to have been a police spy). Finally, Lenin was having difficulty in maintain-ing leadership over his own followers.

This is the background to the despair which, as Krupskaya re-calls, he had revealed to his sister Anna. Yet, in the spring of the year, when labor unrest flared up in Russia, Lenin was capable of drawing on renewed energy and optimism and looking forward with zest to the political struggles to come.

The uprising was still a long way off, of course, but the Lena gold-fields shootings in the middle of April and the widespread protest strikes vividly revealed the extent to which the proletariat had developed in recent years, and showed that they had forgotten nothing, that the movement was rising to a higher stage, and that quite new conditions of work were being created.

Ilyich became another man. His nerves were steadier, he became more concentrated, and gave more thought to the tasks that now confronted the Russian working-class movement. His mood was perhaps best expressed in his article on Herzen, written in the beginning of May. There was so much of Ilyich in that article, so much of the Ilyich ardour that gripped one and swept one off one's feet.

"In commemorating Herzen we clearly see the three generations, the three classes that were active in the Russian revolution," he wrote. "At first—nobles and landlords, the Decembrists and Herzen. The circle of these revolutionaries was a narrow one. They were very far removed from the people. But their work was not in vain. The Decembrists awakened Herzen. Herzen launched revolutionary agitation.

"This agitation was taken up, extended, strengthened, and tempered by the revolutionary commoners, beginning with Chernyshevsky and ending with the heroes of the *Narodnaya Volya*. The circle of fighters widened, their contacts with the people became closer. 'The young helmsmen of the impending storm,' Herzen said of them. But as yet it was not the storm itself.

"The storm is the movement of the masses themselves. The proletariat, the only class that is revolutionary to the end, rose at the head of the masses and for the first time aroused millions of peasants to open revolutionary struggle. The first onslaught in this storm took place in 1905. The next is beginning to develop before our very eyes." (*Works,* Vol. 18, pp. 14–15.)

Only a few months before this Vladimir Ilyich had said with a touch of sadness to Anna Ilyinichna, who had arrived in Paris: "I do not know whether I'll live to see the next rise of the tide," and now he felt the gathering storm, the movement of the masses themselves, with all his being. . . .

GORKY ON LENIN [5]

In his youth, Maxim Gorky (Aleksei Maksimovich Peshkov, 1868–1936) wandered throughout European Russia, subsisting on odd jobs. Without a formal education, he set out to become a writer, converting his experience of the seamier side of Russian life into a stream of short stories, novels, and plays. By 1907, when he met Lenin, Gorky's writing (particularly his play, The Lower Depths*) had brought him fortune and worldwide acclaim.*

Gorky's relationship with Lenin was ambivalent. He contributed financially to the Bolshevik underground, wrote short stories for

[5] From Maxim Gorky, *Days With Lenin* (New York: International Publishers, 1932), pp. 29–31, 33–41, 44–45, 47–48.

*its publications, and encouraged Lenin to make use of his villa at
Capri. Yet, although he often found himself aligned with the Bolsheviks, he was never completely of their group in either thought
or action. After the revolution, he sought to use his influence to
intercede for intellectual and other victims of the revolution—a role
he maintained, with diminished effect, till his death in the Stalin
period.*

*In the following selection, the portrait of Lenin is highlighted by
the contrast with Gorky's own self-image.*

I have never met in Russia, the country where the inevitability of
suffering is preached as the general road to salvation, nor do I know of,
any man who hated, loathed and despised so deeply and strongly as Lenin
all unhappiness, grief and suffering. In my eyes, these feelings, this hatred
of the dramas and tragedies of life exalted Lenin more than anything,
belonging as he did to a country where the greatest masterpieces have
been gospels in praise and sanctification of suffering, and where youth
begins its life under the influence of books which are in essence descrip-
tions of petty, trivial dramas monotonously unvarying. . . .

Lenin was exceptionally great, in my opinion, precisely because of this
feeling in him of irreconcilable, unquenchable hostility towards the sufferings of humanity, his burning faith that suffering is not an essential
and unavoidable part of life, but an abomination which people ought
and are able to sweep away. . . .

In the years 1917–18 my relations with Lenin were not what I would
have wished them to be, but they could not be otherwise. He was a
politician. He had to perfection that clear-sighted directness of vision
which is so indispensable in the helmsman of so enormous and heavily
burdened a ship as Russia with its dead-weight of peasants. I have an
organic distaste for politics, and little faith in the reasoning powers of
the masses, especially of the peasants. . . .

When in 1917 Lenin on his arrival in Russia published his theses, I
thought that by these theses he was sacrificing to the Russian peasantry
the small but heroic band of politically educated workers and all the
genuine revolutionaries of the intelligentsia. The single active force in
Russia, I thought, would be thrown like a handful of salt into the vapid
bog of village life, . . .

In order to make myself quite clear I will add that all my life, the
depressing effect of the prevalency of the illiteracy of the village on the
town, the individualism of the peasants, and their almost complete lack
of social emotions had weighed heavily on my spirits. The dictatorship
of the politically enlightened workers, in close connection with the scientific and technical intelligentsia, was, in my opinion, the only possible
solution to a difficult situation which the war had made especially complicated by rendering the village still more anarchical. I differed from

the Bolsheviks on the question of the value of the rôle of the intelligentsia in the Russian Revolution, which had been prepared by this same intelligentsia to which belonged all the Bolsheviks who had educated hundreds of workers in the spirit of social heroism and genuine intellectuality. The Russian intelligentsia, the scientific and professional intelligentsia, I thought, had always been, was still, and would long be the the only beast of burden to drag along the heavy load of Russian history. In spite of all shocks and impulses and stimulation which it had experienced, the mind of the masses of the people had remained a force still in need of leadership from without.

So I thought in 1917—and was mistaken. . . .

The duty of true-hearted leaders of the people is superhumanly difficult. A leader who is not in some degree a tyrant, is impossible. More people, probably, were killed under Lenin than under Thomas Münzer; but without this, resistance to the revolution of which Lenin was the leader would have been more widely and more powerfully organized. . . .

The gist of the wailing and complaining of the majority is, "Do not interfere with the way of living to which we are accustomed!" Vladimir Lenin was a man who knew better than anyone else how to prevent people from leading the life to which they were accustomed. . . .

He was venturesome by nature but his was not the mercenary venturesomeness of the gambler. In Lenin it was the manifestation of that exceptional moral courage which can be found only in a man with an unshakable belief in his calling, in a man with a profound and complete perception of his connection with the world, and perfect comprehension of his rôle in the chaos of the world, the rôle of enemy of that chaos.

With equal enthusiasm he would play chess, look through "A History of Dress," dispute for hours with comrades, fish, go for walks along the stony paths of Capri, scorching under the southern sun, feast his eyes on the golden color of the gorse, and on the swarthy children of the fishermen. In the evening, listening to stories about Russia and the country, he would sigh enviously and say, "I know very little of Russia—Simbirsk, Kazan, Petersburg, exile in Siberia and that is nearly all."

He loved fun, and when he laughed it was with his whole body; he was quite overcome with laughter and would laugh sometimes until he cried. He could give to his short, characteristic exclamation, "H'm, h'm," an infinite number of modifications, from biting sarcasm to noncommittal doubt. Often in this "H'm, h'm" one caught the sound of the keen humor which a sharp-sighted man experiences who sees clearly through the stupidities of life.

Stocky and thick set, with his Socratic head and quick eyes, he would often adopt a strange and rather comical posture—he would throw his head back, inclining it somehow on to his shoulder, thrust his fingers under his armpits, in his waistcoat armholes. There was something deliciously funny in this pose, something of a triumphant fighting cock; and at such a moment he beamed all over with joy, a grown-up child in this accursed world, a splendid human being, who had to sacrifice himself to hostility and hatred, so that love might be at last realized. . . .

I did not meet Lenin in Russia, or even see him from afar, until 1918, when the final base attempt was made on his life. I came to him when he had hardly regained the use of his hand and could scarcely move his neck, which had been shot through. When I expressed my indignation, he replied, as though dismissing something of which he was tired: "A brawl. Nothing to be done. Every one acts according to his lights."

We met on very friendly terms, but of course there was evident pity in dear Ilyitch's sharp and penetrating glance, for I was one who had gone astray.

After several minutes he said heatedly: "He who is not with us is against us. People independent of the march of events—that is a fantasy. Even if we grant that such people did exist once, at present they do not and cannot exist. They are no good to any one. All, down to the last, are thrown into the whirl of an actuality which is more complicated than ever before. You say that I simplify life too much? That this simplification threatens culture with ruin, eh?"

Then the ironic, characteristic "H'm, h'm . . ."

His keen glance sharpened, and he continued in a lower tone: "Well, and millions of peasants with rifles in their hands are not a threat to culture according to you, eh? You think the Constituent Assembly could have coped with that anarchy? You who make such a fuss about the anarchy of the country should be able to understand our tasks better than others. We have got to put before the Russian masses something they can grasp. The Soviets and Communism are simple.

"A union of the workers and intelligentsia, eh? Well, that isn't bad. Tell the intelligentsia. Let them come to us. According to you they are true servants of justice. What is the matter then? Certainly, let them come to us. We are just the ones who have undertaken the colossal job of putting the people on its feet, of telling the whole world the truth about life—it is we who are pointing out to the people the straight path to a human life, the path which leads out of slavery, beggary, degradation."

He laughed and said without any trace of resentment: "That is why I received a bullet from the intelligentsia."

When the temperature of the conversation was more or less normal, he said with vexation and sadness: "Do you think I quarrel with the idea that the intelligentsia is necessary to us? But you see how hostile their attitude is, how badly they understand the need of the moment? And they don't see how powerless they are without us, how incapable of reaching the masses. They will be to blame if we break too many heads."

ROSA LUXEMBURG: DICTATORIAL IMPLICATIONS
OF LENIN'S CONCEPT OF THE PARTY [6]

*One of the most scathing contemporary criticisms of Lenin's ap-
proach to revolutionary socialism was made in 1904, in an article
by Rosa Luxemburg (1871–1919). The article was originally published in both the Russian* Iskra *and the German socialist organ,*
Die Neue Zeit *(subsequently reprinted under the title "Leninism
or Marxism?"). Rosa Luxemburg participated in the left-wing of
the socialist movements in the Russian Empire (in particular, Poland) and Germany. In 1919, together with Karl Liebknecht, she
was murdered by German counterrevolutionary soldiers. In recent
years, her writings have attracted renewed interest, largely because
of their undogmatic character.*

Granting, as Lenin wants, such absolute powers . . . to the top
organ of the party, we strengthen, to a dangerous extent, the conserva-
tism inherent in such an organ. If the tactics of the socialist party are
not to be the creation of a Central Committee but of the whole party,
or, still better, of the whole labor movement, then it is clear that the
party sections and federations need the liberty of action which alone
will permit them to develop their revolutionary initiative and to utilize
all the resources of a situation. The ultra-centralism asked by Lenin is
full of the sterile spirit of the overseer. It is not a positive and creative
spirit. *Lenin's concern is not so much to make the activity of the party
more fruitful as to control the party—to narrow the movement rather
than to develop it, to bind rather than to unify it. . . .*
If we assume the viewpoint claimed as his own by Lenin and we fear
the influence of intellectuals in the proletarian movement, we can conceive of no greater danger to the Russian party than Lenin's plan of
organization. *Nothing will more surely enslave a young labor movement
to an intellectual elite hungry for power than this bureaucratic strait
jacket, which will immobilize the movement and turn it into an automa-
ton manipulated by a Central Committee.* On the other hand, there is
no more effective guarantee against opportunist intrigue and personal ambition than the independent revolutionary action of the proletariat, as
a result of which the workers acquire the sense of political responsibility
and self-reliance. . . .
In Lenin's overanxious desire to establish the guardianship of an
omniscient and omnipotent Central Committee in order to protect so
promising and vigorous a labor movement against any misstep, we recog-

[6] From Rosa Luxemburg, *The Russian Revolution and Leninism or Marxism?* (Ann
Arbor: The University of Michigan Press, 1961), pp. 94, 102, 107, 108.

nize the symptoms of the same subjectivism that has already played more than one trick on socialist thinking in Russia. . . .

Let us speak plainly. Historically, the errors committed by a truly revolutionary movement are infinitely more fruitful than the infallibility of the cleverest Central Committee.

LEON TROTSKY: LENIN AS A SPEAKER [7]

Leon Trotsky (1877–1940) was, next to Lenin, the most significant participant in the Bolshevik struggle for power. Prior to 1917, his relationship with Lenin was a stormy one. In 1902, after escaping from Siberian exile, he made his way to London, where Lenin was then living, and for a time was a member of the circle which had gathered around him. But the next year he broke with Lenin—a breach that was more or less maintained until the eve of the Bolshevik seizure of power in 1917. One cause of the breach was Lenin's theory of the party. In scathing, epigrammatic sentences Trotsky suggested that the hegemony of the central committee in a rigid party hierarchy would ultimately pave the way for a single leader to rule over the party, and, through the party, to be a dictator over the people as a whole. As late as 1913, Trotsky condemned Lenin as "the master squabbler . . . the professional exploiter of the backwardness of the Russian working-class movement"; Leninism was "built upon lies and falsifications" and bore within it "the poisoned seed of its own disintegration."

Yet, in 1917, after attempting for a short time to maintain an independent position from either the Bolsheviks or Mensheviks, Trotsky threw in his lot with Lenin. He masterminded the military efforts of the Soviets in the revolution and Civil War. After Lenin's death, he was defeated by Stalin in the political struggle for direction of the Soviet state, became a wanderer in exile, and wrote a voluminous series of historical studies and analyses of contemporary events. In 1940, in Mexico, he was assassinated by a Stalinist agent.

Trotsky's writings are a major source for any assessment of Lenin's political leadership. A number of selections from his works are included in our mosaic. In the extract that follows, Trotsky (writing in 1924, shortly after Lenin's death) analyzes one of the skills that contributed to Lenin's success—his style as a speaker and oral propagandist.

[7] From Leon Trotsky, *Lenin,* trans. Helen G. Smith (New York: G. P. Putnam's Sons, 1925). Reprinted by permission of the publisher.

The leading feature in Lenin's speeches, as in his whole work, is his directness of purpose. He does not build up his speech but guides it to a definite, substantial conclusion. He approaches his listeners in different ways: he explains, convinces, disconcerts, jokes, convinces again, and explains again. What holds his speech together is not a formal plan, but a clear aim formed for today, that pierces the consciousness of his listeners like a splinter. His humor, too, is subordinated to that. His joking is utilitarian. A drastic catch phrase has its practical significance: some it incites, others it curbs. Hence come dozens of winged words, that have long been common property of the country. However, before the speaker uses such a catch phrase, he describes some curves, in order to find just the right point. When he has found it, he applies his nail, measures it with his eye, strikes a mighty blow with his hammer on the head of the nail, once, twice, ten times, until the nail is firm, so that it would be very hard to draw it out if it were no longer needed. Then Lenin again strikes the nail with a witty remark from left and right to loosen it, until he has drawn it out and thrown it in the old iron of the archives—to the great sorrow of all who had become accustomed to the nail.

And now the speech approaches its end. The separate points are established, the conclusions firmly drawn. The speaker looks like an exhausted workman who has finished his work. From time to time he passes his hand over his bald head with its drops of perspiration. His voice has sunk as a camp fire dies away. He is about to close. But one looks in vain for an ascending finale to crown the speech and without which ostensibly one can not leave the platform. Others cannot, but Lenin can. There is no rhetorical winding up with him: he finishes the work and makes a point. "If we understand this, if we act thus, then we shall surely conquer" is a not unusual concluding sentence. Or: "One must strive for that, not in words, but in deeds." Or now and then more simple: "That is all that I wanted to say to you," nothing more. And this conclusion, which entirely corresponds to the nature of Lenin's eloquence and the nature of Lenin himself, by no means cools his audience. On the contrary, after just such a conclusion, "without effect," "pale," the listeners grasp once more, as if with a single blaze of consciousness, all that Lenin had given them in his speech, and the audience breaks out into stormy, grateful, enthusiastic applause.

But Lenin has already gathered up his papers and quickly leaves the speaker's desk in order to escape the inevitable. His head drawn to his shoulders, his chin down, his eyes concealed by his brows, his mustache bristles angrily on the upper lip puckered in annoyance. The roaring handclapping grows, and hurls wave upon wave . . . "Long live . . . Lenin . . . Leader . . . Ilyich . . ."

JOHN REED: LENIN IN THE AFTERMATH OF VICTORY [8]

A brief sketch of Lenin, in the immediate aftermath of the seizure of power, is given by John Reed. Reed was an American correspondent who came to Russia in 1917 after having been involved in the American Socialist movement and as an observer of the Mexican Revolution. He died in 1920, an apparent convert to the Soviet system (though he had allegedly expressed doubts and misgivings to some of his intimates), and was buried in the Kremlin wall.

It was just 8.40 when a thundering wave of cheers announced the entrance of the presidium, with Lenin—great Lenin—among them. A short, stocky figure, with a big head set down in his shoulders, bald and bulging. Little eyes, a snubbish nose, wide, generous mouth, and heavy chin; clean-shaven now, but already beginning to bristle with the well-known beard of his past and future. Dressed in shabby clothes, his trousers much too long for him. Unimpressive, to be the idol of a mob, loved and revered as perhaps few leaders in history have been. A strange popular leader—a leader purely by virtue of intellect; colourless, humourless, uncompromising and detached, without picturesque idiosyncrasies—but with the power of explaining profound ideas in simple terms, of analysing a concrete situation. And combined with shrewdness, the greatest intellectual audacity.

NIKOLAI SUKHANOV: LENIN—POLITICAL GENIUS AND PRIMITIVE DEMAGOGUE [9]

A more knowledgeable and critical assessment of Lenin's personality and influence at the time of the revolution was presented by the left-wing Menshevik, Nikolai Sukhanov. Sukhanov (born 1882) was a revolutionary economist and journalist and, in 1917, a Menshevik member of the Petrograd [10] Soviet; as coeditor with Gorky of the magazine Novaya Zhizn, *he had attempted, for a time, to bridge the gaps between socialists of different views. His wife was a Bolshevik sympathizer; unknown to him, she allowed their apartment to be used as a meeting place for a number of the sessions at which the Bolshevik leaders, in the fall of 1917, planned their seiz-*

---

[8] From John Reed, *Ten Days That Shook the World* (New York: Random House, Inc., 1960), pp. 170–71.

[9] From Nikolai Sukhanov, *The Russian Revolution, 1917: A Personal Record*, edited, abridged, and translated by Joel Carmichael (London, New York, Toronto: Oxford University Press, 1955), pp. 290–92.

[10] On the outbreak of war in 1914, the capital, St. Petersburg, was renamed Petrograd in reaction to the Germanic connotations of its original name.

ure of power. Sukhanov worked as an economist for the Soviet government until 1931; in that year, he was one of the Old Mensheviks who were the subjects of the earliest Stalinist show trials. Sentenced to ten years in a labor camp, he died in the 1930s, a victim of Stalinist repression.

Sukhanov's eyewitness journal of the Revolutionary period is a major historical source. Indeed, Lenin recognized the importance of Sukhanov's analysis and devoted one of his last articles to a rebuttal of one of Sukhanov's historical essays.

First of all—there can be no doubt of it—Lenin is an extraordinary phenomenon, a man of absolutely exceptional intellectual power; he is a first-class world magnitude in calibre. For he represents an unusually happy combination of theoretician and popular leader. If still other epithets were needed I shouldn't hesitate to call Lenin a genius, keeping in mind the content of this notion of genius.

A genius, as is well known, is an abnormal person. More concretely, he is very often a man with an extremely limited area of intellectual activity, in which area this activity is carried on with unusual power and productivity. A genius can very often be extremely narrow-minded, with no understanding or grasp of the simplest and most generally accessible things. Such was the generally accepted genius Leo Tolstoy, who (in the brilliant though paradoxical expression of Merezhkovsky) was simply "not intelligent enough for his own genius."

Lenin was undoubtedly like this too: many elementary truths were inaccessible to his mind—even in politics. This was the source of an endless series of the most elementary errors—in the period of his dictatorship as well as in the epoch of his agitation and demagogy.

But on the other hand, within a certain realm of ideas—a few "fixed" ideas—Lenin displayed such amazing force, such superhuman power of attack that his colossal influence over the Socialists and revolutionaries was secure.

In addition to these internal and, so to speak, theoretical qualities of Lenin's, as well as his genius, the following circumstance also played a primary rôle in his victory over the old Marxist Bolsheviks. In practice Lenin had been historically the exclusive, sole, and unchallenged head of the party for many years, since the day of its emergence. The Bolshevik Party was the work of his hands, and his alone. The very thought of going against Lenin was frightening and odious, and required from the Bolshevik mass what it was incapable of giving.

Lenin the genius was an historic figure—this is one side of the matter. The other is that, except Lenin, there was nothing and no one in the party. The few massive generals without Lenin were *nothing,* like the few immense planets without the sun (for the moment I leave aside Trotsky, who at that time was still outside the ranks of the order, that is, in the camp of the "enemies of the proletariat, lackeys of the bourgeoisie," etc.).

In the First International, according to the well-known description, there was Marx high up in the clouds; then for a long, long way there was nothing; then, also at a great height, there was Engels; then again for a long, long way there was nothing, and finally there was Liebknecht sitting there, etc.

But in the Bolshevik Party Lenin the Thunderer sat in the clouds and then—there was absolutely nothing right down to the ground. And on the ground, amongst the party rankers and officers a few generals could be distinguished—and even then I daresay not individually but rather in couples or combinations. There could be no question of *replacing* Lenin by individuals, couples, or combinations. There could be neither independent thinking nor organizational base in the Bolshevik Party without Lenin. . . .

Lenin's radicalism, his heedless "Leftism," and primitive demagogy, unrestrained either by science or common sense, later secured his success among the broadest proletarian-muzhik masses, who had had no other teaching than that of the Tsarist whip. But the same characteristics of this Leninist propaganda also seduced the more backward, less literate elements of the party itself. Very soon after Lenin's arrival they were faced by an alternative: either keep the old principles of Social-Democracy and Marxist science, but without Lenin, without the masses, and without the party; or stay with Lenin and the party and conquer the masses together in an easy way, having thrown overboard the obscure, unfamiliar Marxist principles. It's understandable that the mass of party Bolsheviks, though after some vacillation, decided on the latter.

But the attitude of this mass could not help but have a decisive influence on the fully-conscious Bolshevik elements too, on the Bolshevik generals, for after Lenin's conquest of the officers of the party, people like Kamenev, for instance, were completely isolated; they had fallen into the position of outlaws and internal traitors. And the implacable Thunderer soon subjected them, together with other infidels, to such abuse that not all of them could endure it. It goes without saying that even the generals, even those who had read Marx and Engels, were incapable of sustaining such an ordeal. And Lenin won one victory after another.

WINSTON CHURCHILL: LENIN—THE GRAND REPUDIATOR [11]

One of Lenin's most formidable enemies was a man he never encountered in person. In 1919 and 1920, as Secretary of State for War

[11] From Winston S. Churchill, *The World Crisis: The Aftermath* (New York: Charles Scribner's Sons, 1929), pp. 63–66. Reprinted by permission of Charles Scribner's Sons, New York, and The Hamlyn Publishing Group Ltd., London.

*and Air in Lloyd George's government, Winston Churchill was one
of the most outspoken advocates of intervention to throttle the
Soviet experiment while it was still in its infancy. In the end, the
collapse of the anti-Bolshevik Russian armies and the British desire
to fully return to a peacetime policy doomed Churchill's efforts.*

In 1928, in an epilogue to The World Crisis, *his multi-volume
history of the First World War, Churchill tried to assess Lenin. The
sketch is more rhetorical than analytical; nevertheless, as an evalua-
tion by one of the twentieth century's most important political
leaders it deserves inclusion here.*

. . . Lenin was to Karl Marx what Omar was to Mahomet. He translated faith into acts. He devised the practical methods by which the
Marxian theories could be applied in his own time. He invented the
Communist plan of campaign. He issued the orders, he prescribed
the watchwords, he gave the signal and he led the attack.

Lenin was also Vengeance. Child of the bureaucracy, by birth a petty
noble, reared by a locally much respected Government School Inspector,
his early ideas turned by not unusual contradictions through pity to
revolt extinguishing pity. Lenin had an unimpeachable father and a
rebellious elder brother. This dearly loved companion meddled in assassination. He was hanged in 1894.[12] Lenin was then sixteen. He was at
the age to feel. His mind was a remarkable instrument. When its light
shone it revealed the whole world, its history, its sorrows, its stupidities,
its shams, and above all, its wrongs. It revealed all facts in its focus—the
most unwelcome, the most inspiring—with an equal ray. The intellect
was capacious and in some phases superb. It was capable of universal
comprehension in a degree rarely reached among men. The execution
of the elder brother deflected this broad white light through a prism:
and the prism was red.

But the mind of Lenin was used and driven by a will not less exceptional. The body, tough, square and vigorous in spite of disease, was well
fitted to harbour till middle age these incandescent agencies. Before they
burnt it out his work was done, and a thousand years will not forget
it. . . .

Lenin has left his mark. He has won his place. And in the cutting off of
the lives of men and women no Asiatic conqueror, not Tamerlane, not
Jenghiz Khan, can match his fame.

Implacable vengeance, rising from a frozen pity in a tranquil, sensible,
matter-of-fact, good-humoured integument! His weapon logic; his mood
opportunist. His sympathies cold and wide as the Arctic Ocean; his
hatreds tight as the hangman's noose. His purpose to save the world: his

---

[12] [The correct date is 1887—ED.]

method to blow it up. Absolute principles, but readiness to change them. Apt at once to kill or learn: dooms and afterthoughts: ruffianism and philanthropy: but a good husband; a gentle guest; happy, his biographers assure us, to wash up the dishes or dandle the baby; as mildly amused to stalk a capercailzie as to butcher an Emperor. The quality of Lenin's revenge was impersonal. Confronted with the need of killing any particular person he showed reluctance—even distress. But to blot out a million, to proscribe entire classes, to light the flames of intestine war in every land with the inevitable destruction of the well-being of whole nations—these were sublime abstractions. . . .

Lenin was the Grand Repudiator. He repudiated everything. He repudiated God, King, Country, morals, treaties, debts, rents, interest, the laws and customs of centuries, all contracts written or implied, the whole structure—such as it is—of human society. In the end he repudiated himself. He repudiated the Communist system. He confessed its failure in an all important sphere. He proclaimed the New Economic Policy and recognised private trade. He repudiated what he had slaughtered so many for not believing. They were right it seemed after all. They were unlucky that he did not find it out before. But these things happen sometimes: and how great is the man who acknowledges his mistake! . . .

Lenin's intellect failed at the moment when its destructive force was exhausted, and when sovereign remedial functions were its quest. He alone could have led Russia into the enchanted quagmire; he alone could have found the way back to the causeway. He saw; he turned; he perished. The strong illuminant that guided him was cut off at the moment when he had turned resolutely for home. The Russian people were left floundering in the bog. Their worst misfortune was his birth: their next worst—his death.

5
Lenin in 1917

Nineteen seventeen marks the zenith of Lenin's career. At the beginning of the year, he was an exile in Switzerland, still uncertain whether revolution would occur in his lifetime. By April, after the fall of Tsarism, he was back in Petrograd—his return made possible because Germany, at war with his country, granted transit rights to Lenin and other revolutionary exiles. By March the following year, he had led his followers to victory, taken Russia out of the war, and begun the consolidation of the Bolshevik grip on the country's policies. Had Lenin done nothing else, his activities between April, 1917, and March, 1918, would have assured him a place in any study of modern history.

At the time, most of Lenin's actions gave rise to great controversy which is still reflected in efforts to interpret his career. At key points, his most important followers were diametrically opposed, as we have seen, to the shifts in policy that he advocated. They questioned whether he was right to push for a more radical stance, leading ultimately to an uprising to seize power. From his own writings and speeches, it appears that Lenin did not believe at first that the revolution in Russia could be sustained on its own; he counted on its sparking upheavals in the more advanced, but equally war-weary countries of Europe.

LENIN AND THE GERMANS

Lenin's relations with the Germans were questioned by his opponents shortly after his return. In recent years, this issue has been somewhat clarified by documents that have become available from the German diplomatic archives. Nevertheless, the ultimate significance of this relationship remains open to interpretation.

As early as 1915, Romberg, the German minister in Berne, was aware of Lenin's activities and outlook through the Estonian nationalist Kesküla. The following report brought the question of supporting Lenin to the attention of German decision-makers. It should be noted, however, that the summary of Lenin's program is that presented by Kesküla. Romberg wished to use Lenin's program mostly for psychological warfare against the French.[1]

---

[1] From Z. A. B. Zeman, ed., *Germany and the Revolution in Russia, 1915–1918* (London, New York, Toronto: Oxford University Press, 1958), pp. 6–7. Reprinted by permission of Z. A. B. Zeman, holder of the copyright.

REPORT NO. 794

A 28659   Bern, 30 September 1915

The Estonian Kesküla[2] has succeeded in finding out the conditions on which the Russian revolutionaries would be prepared to conclude peace with us in the event of the revolution being successful. According to information from the well-known revolutionary Lenin, the programme contains the following points:

1. The establishment of a republic.
2. The confiscation of large land-holdings.
3. The eight-hour working day.
4. Full autonomy for all nationalities.
5. An offer of peace without any consideration for France, but on condition that Germany renounces all annexations and war-reparations.

On Point 5, Kesküla has observed that this condition does not exclude the possibility of separating those national states from Russia which would serve as buffer states.

6. The Russian armies to leave Turkey immediately—in other words, a renunciation of claims to Constantinople and the Dardanelles.
7. Russian troops to move into India.

I leave open the question as to whether great importance should in fact be attached to this programme, especially as Lenin himself is supposed to be rather sceptical of the prospects of the revolution. He seems to be extremely apprehensive of the counter-campaign recently launched by the so-called Social Patriots. According to Kesküla's sources, this counter-movement is headed by the Socialists Axelrod, Alexinsky, Deutsch, Dneveinski, Mark Kachel, Olgin, and Plekhanov. They are unleashing vigorous agitation, and are supposed to have large financial resources, which they appear to draw from the government, at their disposal. Their activities could be all the more dangerous to the revolution as they are themselves old revolutionaries, and are therefore perfectly familiar with the techniques of revolution. In Kesküla's opinion, it is therefore essential that we should spring to the help of the revolutionaries of Lenin's movement in Russia at once. He will report on this matter in person in Berlin. According to his informants, the present moment should be favourable

²Kesküla was a member of the Estonian National Committee, working, in Switzerland and in Sweden, for the independence of his country from the Russian Empire. He was in contact with the German Legation in Bern from September, 1914. Later, he worked with Steinwachs, the German agent. In April 1917 Kesküla apparently negotiated with the representatives of the Allied countries, especially of England and Russia, in Stockholm. When he got to know about these negotiations, Steinwachs dropped him. His activities are well documented in one of the Bern mission files, entitled "Kesküla." Cf. O. H. Gankin and H. H. Fisher, *The Bolsheviks and the World War*, Stanford University Press, 1940, p. 249. [Zeman's note.]

for overthrowing the government. More and more reports of workers' unrest are being received, and the dismissal of the Duma is said to have aroused universal excitement. However, we should have to act quickly, before the Social Patriots gain the upper hand. . . .

Even if, as I have said, the prospects of a revoluton are uncertain and Lenin's programme is therefore of doubtful value, its exploitation could still do invaluable service in enemy territory. If skilfully distributed it could, in my opinion, be especially effective in France, in view of the notorious ignorance of the French in foreign, and particularly Russian affairs. If I receive no instructions from Your Excellency to the contrary, I shall give it to various French confidential agents for distribution among the ranks of the opposition. I can imagine that, by opening the prospect of a separate peace between Germany and the Russian Democrats, which would, of course, involve the loss of the French billions, one could provide the opposition with an extremely valuable trump card to play against M. Delcassé and in favour of a separate peace with us.

Lenin's programme must not, of course, be made public, first because its publication would reveal our source, but also because its discussion in the press would rob it of all its value. I feel that it should be put out in an aura of great secrecy, so that it creates a belief that an agreement with powerful Russian circles is already in preparation.

Quite apart from the French aspect, I would ask you first of all to discuss this information with Kesküla, so that nothing may be spoiled by premature publication.

ROMBERG

Fritz Fischer's book on Germany's objectives in World War I, based on extensive study of the archives, includes a summary of German official assessments at the time of Lenin's return to Russia. The German government clearly viewed it to be in its interest that the extreme radicals gain power in Russia. There was at least a parallelism of interest between Germany and the Bolsheviks. Fischer concludes, however, that to assert that there was a conscious "German-Bolshevik plot" represents "a political rather than an historical judgment." Certainly, the permission to cross Germany was vital to Lenin's activities in 1917. Of equal importance was the fact that, as one of the groups that received German funds, the Bolsheviks were able to continue financing their propaganda even during periods—e.g., the summer of 1917—when they were suffering political reverses. It is possible to argue, however, that in balance Lenin used the Germans more than he was used by them.[3]

As early as March 23 [1917] Romberg, in Berne, had reported that "outstanding" Russian revolutionaries had been pressing to return to Russia since the outbreak of the February revolution and wanted to travel across Germany, and Zimmermann had consented in principle, subject to the agreement of the OHL which arrived two days later. Zimmermann's words prove that he realised that the main purpose was to send back the left Radicals; he thought they should be allowed passage across Germany "because it is in our interest that the radical wing should gain the upper hand in Russia." It is impossible to suppose that the Secretary of State should have taken so momentous a decision without the Chancellor's consent in principle. In fact Bethmann Hollweg, in a report to the Emperor on April 11, claimed as his own work that "immediately after the outbreak of the Russian revolution" he had set on foot the return of the left-wing groups to Russia. This report throws a revealing light on the position of the Emperor. Perhaps because he was expected—as it turned out, quite wrongly—to object, he was left to learn from the newspapers of the possibilities open to German policy, and was only informed of what was really going on after the first transport of emigrants had already passed through Germany. The despatch of Lenin is to be regarded only as one move, if the most successful one, in Germany's policy of revolution, an integral part of her efforts to achieve her war aims through a separate peace.

How strongly Germany was interested in Lenin's journey is shown by the fact that the German government at once accepted his conditions, with one unimportant exception; it also agreed that he should be accompanied by a party of pro-Entente Mensheviks, even larger than the Bolshevik group, so that the Bolsheviks should not be compromised as German agents.

Lenin was anxious to demonstrate his independence, and he therefore concluded a regular treaty with the German authorities, the main condition which he "demanded" of them being that the permission for the group to cross Germany should not be made conditional on "their attitude on the question of war and peace." The help given by the German authorities to him and his group in connection with their journey and the financial support subsequently given by imperial Germany to the Bolsheviks, before and after the October Revolution, inevitably brought Lenin under suspicion of being a paid agent of Germany.

The co-operation between the German government and Lenin has been regarded as a German-Bolshevik plot. This is a political rather than a historical judgment, and one which reflects the standpoint of that "democracy" which had been made an ideological objective of the enemies of the Central Powers by Wilson's welcome to the Russian revolution and his declaration of war on Germany. It was a policy of interests on both sides that brought monarchist Germany and the leaders of the Russian revolution into their short-lived cooperation. The German government was aiming, not simply at achieving any kind of peace, but at realising its definite and far-reaching objectives in the east. For this purpose the Germans needed Lenin, who had declared the question of peace to be central to his political plans and actions. But Lenin, on his side, used the interest of imperial Germany in him and his party to turn the Russian revolution, which was in danger of being frustrated by a Liberal-Social-Democrat coalition, into a victory for the Bolshevik revolution as the first stage of a world revolution. He made use of the peace slogan to get into power, and he needed peace to bring about and consolidate the revolutionary transformation in Russia. Even in Switzerland he had opposed the provisional government, the Mensheviks and even his own adherents in so far as they supported the continuance of the war. After reaching Petersburg on April 16, where he was welcomed enthusiastically by the workers, he at once intervened in the revolution and pressed for conclusion of peace with the Central Powers. His success was delayed by a consolidation of those forces in Russia which wanted the war to be carried on with the moral and financial help of the Entente powers. Bolshevik *putsches* (attempted by Lenin's adherents against his own will) in May, in June, during the First All-Russian Council of Soviets, and finally on July 4 after the failure of the Kerensky offensive, were unsuccessful; their authors failed to turn street demonstrations into a popular upheaval, or to drive the Executive Committee of the Soviets into action against the provisional government. Lenin had to flee. Only after months of agitation did he succeed in gaining a majority in the Soviet of the capital and organising an armed upheaval. In spite of their reverses the Bolsheviks, like the separatist nationalities, enjoyed continuous support from Germany. Thus Zimmermann's successor, Kühlmann, was able to write on December 3, looking back on the successful October Revolution:

> It was only the resources which the Bolsheviks received regularly from our side, through various channels and on various pretexts, that enabled them to develop their chief organ *Pravda,* to carry on a lively agitation, and greatly to expand the originally narrow basis of their party.

NIKOLAI SUKHANOV: LENIN'S ARRIVAL IN PETROGRAD [4]

Lenin's arrival in Petrograd is described in an eyewitness account by Sukhanov.

The throng in front of the Finland Station blocked the whole square, making movement almost impossible and scarcely letting the trams

[4] From Nikolai Sukhanov, *The Russian Revolution, 1917,* 269–74.

through. The innumerable red flags were dominated by a magnificent banner embroidered in gold: "The Central Committee of the R.S.-D.W.P. (Bolsheviks)." [5] Troops with bands were drawn up under the red flags near the side entrance, in the former imperial waiting-rooms.

There was a throbbing of many motor-cars. In two or three places the awe-inspiring outlines of armoured cars thrust up from the crowd. And from one of the side-streets there moved out on to the square, startling the mob and cutting through it, a strange monster—a mounted searchlight, which abruptly projected upon the bottomless void of the darkness tremendous strips of the living city, the roofs, many-storeyed houses, columns, wires, tramways, and human figures. . . . Through the mass of discontentedly grumbling people tightly packed together I made my way right through the station to a platform, and towards the Tsar's waiting-room, where a dejected Chkheidze sat, weary of the long wait. . . .

. . . I passed along the platform. There it was even more festive than in the square. Its whole length was lined with people, mostly soldiers ready to "present A-a-a-r-m-s!" Banners hung across the platform at every step; triumphal arches had been set up, adorned with red and gold; one's eyes were dazzled by every possible welcoming inscription and revolutionary slogan, while at the end of the platform, where the carriage was expected to stop, there was a band, and a group of representatives of the central Bolshevik organizations stood holding flowers.

The Bolsheviks, who shone at organization, and always aimed at emphasizing externals and putting on a good show, had dispensed with any superfluous modesty and were plainly preparing a real triumphal entry. . . .

We waited for a long time. The train was very late.

But at long last it arrived. A thunderous *Marseillaise* boomed forth on the platform, and shouts of welcome rang out. We stayed in the imperial waiting-rooms while the Bolshevik generals exchanged greetings. Then we heard them marching along the platform, under the triumphal arches, to the sound of the band, and between the rows of welcoming troops and workers. The gloomy Chkheidze, and the rest of us after him, got up, went to the middle of the room, and prepared for the meeting. And what a meeting it was, worthy of—more than my wretched pen!

Shlyapnikov, acting as master of ceremonies, appeared in the doorway, portentously hurrying, with the air of a faithful old police chief announcing the Governor's arrival. Without any apparent necessity he kept crying out fussily: "Please, Comrades, please! Make way there! Comrades, make way!"

Behind Shlyapnikov, at the head of a small cluster of people behind whom the door slammed again at once, Lenin came, or rather ran, into the room. He wore a round cap, his face looked frozen, and there was a

[5] I.e., The Russian Social-Democratic Workers' Party (Bolsheviks). . . . (Ed.)

magnificent bouquet in his hands. Running to the middle of the room, he stopped in front of Chkheidze as though colliding with a completely unexpected obstacle. And Chkheidze, still glum, pronounced the following "speech of welcome" with not only the spirit and wording but also the tone of a sermon:

"Comrade Lenin, in the name of the Petersburg Soviet and of the whole revolution we welcome you to Russia . . . But—we think that the principal task of the revolutionary democracy is now the defence of the revolution from any encroachments either from within or from without. We consider that what this goal requires is not disunion, but the closing of the democratic ranks. We hope you will pursue these goals together with us."

Chkheidze stopped speaking. I was dumbfounded with surprise: really, what attitude could be taken to this "welcome" and to that delicious "But——"?

But Lenin plainly knew exactly how to behave. He stood there as though nothing taking place had the slightest connexion with him—looking about him, examining the persons round him and even the ceiling of the imperial waiting-room, adjusting his bouquet (rather out of tune with his whole appearance), and then, turning away from the Ex. Com. delegation altogether, he made this "reply":

"Dear Comrades, soldiers, sailors, and workers! I am happy to greet in your persons the victorious Russian revolution, and greet you as the vanguard of the worldwide proletarian army . . . The piratical imperialist war is the beginning of civil war throughout Europe . . . The hour is not far distant when at the call of our comrade, Karl Liebknecht,[6] the peoples will turn their arms against their own capitalist exploiters . . . The worldwide Socialist revolution has already dawned . . . Germany is seething . . . Any day now the whole of European capitalism may crash. The Russian revolution accomplished by you has prepared the way and opened a new epoch. Long live the worldwide Socialist revolution!"

This was really no reply to Chkheidze's "welcome," and it entirely failed to echo the "context" of the Russian revolution as accepted by everyone, without distinction, of its witnesses and participants.

It was very interesting! Suddenly, before the eyes of all of us, completely swallowed up by the routine drudgery of the revolution, there was presented a bright, blinding, exotic beacon, obliterating everything we "lived by." Lenin's voice, heard straight from the train, was a "voice

---

[6] Liebknecht, Karl (1871–1919): son of Wilhelm Liebknecht, one of the most eminent German Socialists of the end of the 19th century. A pacifist, he played an important rôle in opposition to the official Social-Democratic Party during the war. Continually arrested and imprisoned; after the German Revolution of 1919 he was assassinated, together with Rosa Luxemburg, by Rightists. He was very popular in Russia. (Ed.) [Sukhanov's memoirs.]

from outside." There had broken in upon us in the revolution a note that was not, to be sure, a contradiction, but that was novel, harsh, and somewhat deafening. . . .

NIKOLAI PODVOISKY: PREPARING THE INSURRECTION [7]

In the fall of 1917, the Military-Revolutionary Committee of the Petrograd Soviet, dominated by the Bolsheviks, was formed. Its secretary was Nikolai Ilyich Podvoisky (1880–1948); the chairmanship—sometimes attributed to Podvoisky—was, in fact, held by Trotsky, who served concurrently as Chairman of the Soviet. Earlier, Podvoisky had been one of the organizers of the Red Guards; in the Civil War, he became a military commander at the front and then served, briefly, as People's Commissar for War and Marine in the Soviet Ukrainian government. Podvoisky was purged by Stalin and was not rehabilitated till after Stalin's death.

In the selection that follows, Podvoisky describes how, a few days before the uprising, after having been led by devious routes to a secret hiding place in Petrograd, he was quizzed by Lenin.

I said that the Military Organization was making the most intensive preparations for the uprising, that at one of the recent meetings of the bureau of military organizations it had been decided to send authoritative comrades . . . to prepare our organizations at the front and in the provincial garrisons for the insurrection and to find out what degree of support would be given to Petrograd by troops in other places. . . .

I said that the Military Organization attached great importance to the contacts with the army at the front that had been decided upon, but the fulfilment of the plan required some time. It would therefore be expedient to postpone the insurrection for ten days or so. . . .

The attention with which Vladimir Ilyich listened to my account of the preparations changed to extreme impatience when I spoke about postponement.

"That's just it!" he said, interrupting me, "that's just why it must not be postponed! Every delay on our part will make it possible for the government parties, who are in possession of the powerful state apparatus, to make more resolute preparations to crush us with the aid of reliable troops recalled from the front. They, of course, are most certainly informed of the impending insurrection . . . they are preparing for it. During the period of delay they will make still greater preparations. That's how matters stand! The insurrection must take place before the

[7] From Nikolai Podvoisky's memoirs in the collection, *Petrograd, October, 1917: Reminiscences* (Moscow: Foreign Languages Publishing House, 1957), pp. 29–36.

Congress of Soviets—it is especially important that the congress, confronted with the accomplished fact of the working class having taken power, should immediately give legal strength to the new regime by decrees and the setting up of government machinery. . . ."

Lenin asked me to continue and prepared to listen. . . . I went on to speak about the Red Guards. I pointed out that the workers were becoming more insistent every day in their demands for arms. The number of young workers joining the Red Guards was increasing. Ilyich was particularly pleased that military training, formerly carried out in secret, in places far from the factories and working-class districts, had now been transferred to the factory yards and to the riding-schools of the army units in the neighbourhood. But then his face showed that he was worried about something. Vladimir Ilyich got up from his seat, came over to me, took me by the hand, led me to a sofa standing in the corner of the room, sat me down beside him and asked:

"Are you quite sure the information you have given me is correct? Have you checked up on it?"

I told him that leading members of the Military Organization including myself, were visiting the Red Guard detachment and military units every day. . . .

It seemed to me that Vladimir Ilyich was satisfied with my report. . . . And then Ilyich began asking me for fuller details. Who reported it? When was it reported? Under what circumstances? How did I know that we could rely completely on that factory? Who was the secretary of the Party organization there? What people were there on the factory committee? When was the last election of a company or battalion committee? Who had been sent from the factory or regiment to the Petrogard Soviet after the elections?

I knew that all these questions were "legitimate" but they were so unexpected that I kept going hot and cold. And still Ilyich continued "checking up details." What people were there in the district Duma? In the district Soviet? What connections had such and such a factory with the staff of the Red Guard? How were the factories and the army units linked up? And the district Party committee? How was it linked up with the army units of the district? Where did the Military Organization expect to get arms from? Who was teaching the workers to shoot and how? Lenin then asked questions about the leadership of the Red Guard detachments and battalions, but even here I was no better off and felt as uneasy as an inexperienced boxer in the ring. . . .

"You said that at such and such a factory there is a good military organization, there are 300 men in the Red Guard, there are rifles and cartridges, and, you said, there are even machine-guns. Who is the commander there, do you know him?"

"Yes, I know him." And I told Ilyich all I knew about him.

"You say he is an excellent man? Would give his head for the revolution? And what are his military qualifications? Can he shoot, from a revolver, say? And could he handle a cannon if it were necessary? Could he bring up something essential in a car, in case of need? Can he drive a car? And then, do your Red Guard commanders know anything about the tactics of street fighting?"

It appeared that I knew nothing about any one of the commanders from that point of view. Vladimir Ilyich stood up, placed his fingers in his waistcoat pockets and shook his head reproachfully.

"Ai-ai-ai, and that's the chairman of the Military Organization! How are you going to lead the insurrection if you do not know what your commanders are like? It is not enough for them to be good agitators, good propagandists, that they make good reports and are excellent organizers of the masses. Insurrection is not a meeting to hear reports, insurrection is action with arms in hand. There you not only have to act with self-sacrifice but also with skill, otherwise the slightest mistake may cost the lives of Red Guards, revolutionary sailors and soldiers. . . . A mistake may lead to the defeat of the insurrection." . . .

Noting my confusion, Vladimir Ilyich tried to help me out of the awkward position in which I found myself.

"My dear fellow," he said, "insurrection is the most crucial form of warfare. It is a great art. Of course, bold commanders can do wonders by their own example, audacity and courage. But what sort of commander for an armed uprising is a man who cannot shoot? Such commanders must be immediately replaced by others. Leaders who do not understand the tactics of street fighting will ruin the insurrection. And remember, please, that soldiers are all right in their way, but in our struggle we must depend mostly on the workers."

From that moment on I began to look at insurrection through the eyes of Vladimir Ilyich.

LEON TROTSKY: THE MOMENT OF VICTORY [8]

Trotsky describes the situation at the Bolshevik headquarters— and offers a glimpse of Lenin at the moment he realized that the coup had succeeded.

I began to tell him that the military operations were succeeding rather widely, and that at the moment we had already taken possession of a number of important points in the city. Vladimir Ilyich had seen on a

[8] From Leon Trotsky, *Lenin* trans. Helen G. Smith (New York: G. P. Putnam's Sons, 1925). Reprinted by permission of the publisher.

placard printed the evening before—or perhaps I showed it to him, too —that every one who attempted to make use of the revolution for plundering was threatened with execution on the spot. At first Lenin was thoughtful; it even seemed to me as though he felt misgivings about it. But then he said, "R-i-g-h-t."

He greedily examined all details of the rising. They furnished him with the indisputable evidence that the affair was in full swing, the Rubicon passed, and that no recall and no retreat were possible now. I remember the strong impression made upon Lenin by the news that, by written command, I had ordered out a company of the Pavlovsky regiment in order to assure the appearance of our party and Soviet newspapers.

"Has the company marched out?"

"It has."

"And the newspapers are set up?"

"Yes, indeed."

Lenin was delighted, which he showed by exclamations, laughter, and by rubbing his hands. . . .

Up to the last hour he had feared the enemy might thwart our plans and surprise us. Only now, on the evening of the 25th of October, he composed himself and gave his sanction finally to the course that events had taken. I say "he composed himself,"—but only to again get excited over a whole mass of questions, more and more concrete, big and little, that were connected with the further course of the uprising: "But listen, ought we not do so and so? Ought we not undertake that and that? Ought we not bring up this and that?" These endless questions and suggestions were superficially without any connection, but they had their origin in one and the same intense inner comprehension, which had grasped at once the whole extent of the uprising. . . .

The first session of the Second Council of Soviets took place in Smolny. Lenin was not present at it. He remained in his room at Smolny, which, according to my recollection, had no, or almost no, furniture. Later some one spread rugs on the floor and laid two cushions on them. Vladimir Ilyich and I lay down to rest. . . . Every five or ten minutes some one came running in from the session hall to inform us what was going on there. In addition, messengers came from the city, where, under the leadership of Antonof-Ovsejenko, the siege of the Winter Palace was going on which ended with its capture.

It must have been the next morning, for a sleepless night separated it from the preceding day. Vladimir Ilyich looked tired. He smiled and said: "The transition from the state of illegality, being driven in every direction, to power—is too rough." "It makes one dizzy," he at once added in German, and made the sign of the cross before his face. After this one more or less personal remark that I heard him make about the acquisition of power, he went about the tasks of the day.

MARGARITA FOFANOVA: BAIT FOR THE PEASANTS [9]

The retention of power was an even more difficult problem than its seizure. Even before the victory at Petrograd, Lenin had been puzzling over this question.

Lenin spent the last days before the uprising in hiding in the Petrograd apartment of a recent Bolshevik recruit, the agrarian specialist, Margarita Fofanova (1883–   ). Here he assembled the data on the basis of which he was to make his final appeal for the support of the more radical peasant representatives.

. . . I remember . . . Vladimir Ilyich asking me to bring him all the past issues of *Peasant News,* the organ of the All-Russian Congress of Peasant Deputies, which, of course, I did. I do not remember how many issues there were, only that there were very many of them—a lot of material to study. Vladimir Ilyich worked for two days, sitting up far into the night, and then on the morning after he said to me: "Well, I've gone over all the material of the Left Socialist-Revolutionaries; all I have to do today is to read the peasants' mandate." Two hours later, he called me in and said cheerfully, as he slapped the paper (I could see that it was the *Peasant News* for August 19): "There is the basis for an agreement with the Left Socialist-Revolutionaries. The mandate has been signed by 242 deputies from the localities—that's quite a number. We shall make this the basis of the Decree on Land and then we shall see whether the Left Socialist-Revolutionaries will dare to refuse." He showed me the paper, which had been blue-pencilled in several places, and added: "Now we need only to make sure that their ideas on socialization are implemented in our way. . . ."

TROTSKY: LENIN AND THE REVOLUTION [10]

In 1930, Trotsky assessed, in retrospect, the significance of Lenin for the Russian revolution.

It remains to ask—and this is no unimportant question, although easier to ask than answer: How would the revolution have developed if Lenin had not reached Russia in April 1917? If our exposition demon-

[9] From the memoirs of Margarita Fofanova, as quoted in *Petrograd, October 1917: Reminiscences* (Moscow: Foreign Languages Publishing House, 1957), pp. 15–16.

[10] From Leon Trotsky, *The History of the Russian Revolution* (New York: Simon and Schuster, 1936), I, 329–31; III, 127–30. Reprinted by permission of Esteban Volkov, holder of the copyright.

strates and proves anything at all, we hope it proves that Lenin was not a
demiurge of the revolutionary process, that he merely entered into a
chain of objective historic forces. But he was a great link in that chain.
The dictatorship of the proletariat was to be inferred from the whole
situation, but it had still to be established. It could not be established
without a party. The party could fulfill its mission only after understanding it. For that Lenin was needed. Until his arrival, not one of the
Bolshevik leaders dared to make a diagnosis of the revolution. The leadership of Kamenev and Stalin was tossed by the course of events to the right,
to the Social Patriots: between Lenin and Menshevism the revolution
left no place for intermediate positions. Inner struggle in the Bolshevik
Party was absolutely unavoidable. Lenin's arrival merely hastened the
process. His personal influence shortened the crisis. Is it possible, however, to say confidently that the party without him would have found
its road? We would by no means make bold to say that. The factor of
time is decisive here, and it is difficult in retrospect to tell time historically.
Dialectic materialism at any rate has nothing in common with fatalism.
Without Lenin the crisis, which the opportunist leadership was inevitably bound to produce, would have assumed an extraordinarily sharp
and protracted character. The conditions of war and revolution, however, would not allow the party a long period for fulfilling its mission.
Thus it is by no means excluded that a disoriented and split party might
have let slip the revolutionary opportunity for many years. The rôle of
personality arises before us here on a truly gigantic scale. It is necessary
only to understand that rôle correctly, taking personality as a link in the
historic chain.

The "sudden" arrival of Lenin from abroad after a long absence, the
furious cry raised by the press around his name, his clash with all the
leaders of his own party and his quick victory over them—in a word, the
external envelope of circumstance—make easy in this case a mechanical
contrasting of the person, the hero, the genius, against the objective conditions, the mass, the party. In reality, such a contrast is completely one-
sided. Lenin was not an accidental element in the historic development,
but a product of the whole past of Russian history. He was embedded in
it with deepest roots. . . .

"There is no man more faint-hearted than I am, when I am working
out a military plan," wrote Napoleon. . . . "I exaggerate all dangers and
all possible misfortunes. . . . When my decision is taken everything is
forgotten except what can assure its success." . . . [T]he essence of this
thought applies perfectly to Lenin. In deciding a problem of strategy he
began by clothing the enemy with his own resolution and farsightedness.
The tactical mistakes of Lenin were for the most part by-products of his
strategic power. . . . [H]is hypothetical assumptions, beginning with the

worst possible, are not mistakes but methods of analysis. As soon as the Bolsheviks had got control of the soviets of the two capitals, Lenin said: "Our day is come." In April and July he had applied the brakes; in August he was preparing theoretically the new step; from the middle of September he was hurrying and urging on with all his power. The danger now lay not in acting too soon, but in lagging. "In this matter it is now impossible to be premature." . . .

Lenin very studiously followed all the elections and votings in the country, carefully assembling those figures which would throw light on the actual correlation of forces. The semi-anarchistic indifference to electoral statistics got nothing but contempt from him. At the same time Lenin never identified the indexes of parliamentarism with the actual correlation of forces. He always introduced a correction in favor of direct action. "The strength of a revolutionary proletariat," he explained, "from the point of view of its action upon the masses and drawing them into the struggle, is infinitely greater in an extra-parliamentary than a parliamentary struggle. This is a very important observation when it comes to the question of civil war."

Lenin with his sharp eye was the first to notice that the agrarian movement had gone into a decisive phase, and he immediately drew all the conclusions from this. The muzhik, like the soldier, will wait no longer. "In the face of such a fact as the peasant insurrection," writes Lenin at the end of September, "all other political symptoms, even if they were in conflict with this ripening of an all-national crisis, would have absolutely no significance at all." The agrarian question is the foundation of the revolution. A victory of the government over the peasant revolt would be the "funeral of the revolution. . . ." We cannot hope for more favorable conditions. The hour of action is at hand. "The crisis is ripe. The whole future of the international workers' revolution for socialism it at stake. The crisis is ripe."

6
Lenin in Power

After the Bolshevik seizure of power, Lenin's sole po-
sition was Chairman of the Council of People's Commissars; but
his interests were wide-ranging, and he was the main inspiration for
the regime's decisions across a wide range of issues, from the most
important to the most minute (see Fischer, pp. 182–88).
It is impossible for lack of space to give any comprehensive pic-
ture of Lenin's activities while he was in power. The material pre-
sented contrasts Lenin's use of terroristic methods to his more con-
structive efforts to develop viable policies for the Soviet state.

LEON TROTSKY: EARLY DAYS OF THE SOVIET GOVERNMENT [1]

Until March, 1918, the Soviet capital remained at Petrograd; the
revolutionary headquarters at the Smolny Institute (once a girls'
school) became the site of the Council of People's Commissars. In
March, recognizing the vulnerability of Petrograd to possible attack
by the German armies, the Bolsheviks removed the capital to Mos-
cow. Trotsky describes Lenin's activities during the period when the
government remained at Smolny—and in particular, the way in
which the policies of the Soviet Republic were developed in an
improvised—yet purposeful—fashion.

During the Smolny period, Lenin was eagerly impatient to answer
all problems of economic, political, administrative and cultural life by
decrees. In this he was guided not by any passion for bureaucratic method,
but rather by a desire to unfold the party's programme in the language
of power. . . . No one could tell how much time we would have at our
disposal. During that first period, the decrees were really more propaganda than actual administrative measures. Lenin was in a hurry to tell
the people what the new power was, what it was after, and how it intended to accomplish its aims. He went from question to question with
a magnificent tirelessness; he called small conferences, commissioned experts to make inquiries, and dug into books himself. And I helped him.
Lenin's conviction of continuity in the work that he was doing was

[1] From Leon Trotsky, *My Life* (originally published 1930; New York: Grosset and
Dunlap, 1960), pp. 342–44. Reprinted by permission of Esteban Volkov, holder of the
copyright.

very strong. As a great revolutionary, he understood the meaning of historical tradition. It was impossible to tell in advance whether we were to stay in power or be overthrown. And so it was necessary, whatever happened, to make our revolutionary experience as clear as possible for all men. Others would come, and, with the help of what we had outlined and begun, would take another step forward. That was the meaning of the legislative work during the first period. That was why Lenin insisted impatiently on the earliest possible publication of the classics of socialism and materialism in Russian translation. He was anxious to have as many revolutionary monuments erected as possible, even if they were of the simplest sort, like busts or memorial tablets to be placed in all the towns, and, if it could be managed, in the villages as well, so that what had happened might be fixed in the people's imagination, and leave the deepest possible furrow in memory.

Every meeting of the Soviet of People's Commissaries, which changed its membership often at first, presented a picture of an immense legislative improvisation. Everything had to proceed from the beginning. There were no "precedents," since history had none to offer. Lenin presided indefatigably at the Soviet for five and six hours on end, and the meetings of the People's Commissaries were held every day. As a rule, matters were brought up for consideration without previous preparation, and almost always as urgent business. Often the substance of the question discussed was not known either to the members of the Soviet or to the chairman before the meeting opened. The debates were always condensed, only ten minutes being allowed for the opening report. Nevertheless, Lenin always sensed the necessary course. To save time, he would send very short notes to the members present, asking for information on this or that subject. . . . [A]nd very interesting, . . . the reply in most cases was written on the reverse side of the paper, and the note was usually destroyed at once by the chairman. At the proper moment, Lenin would announce his resolutions, always with an intentional sharpness; after that the debates would cease or else would give way to practical suggestions. In the end, Lenin's "points" were usually taken as the basis for the decree.

Besides other qualities, a great creative imagination was necessary to guide this work. One of the most valuable powers of such an imagination is the ability to visualize people, objects, and events as they really are, even if one has never seen them. To combine separate little strokes caught on the wing, to supplement them by means of unformulated laws of correspondence and likelihood, and in this way to re-create a certain sphere of human life in all its concrete reality, basing everything upon experience in life and upon theory—that is the imagination that a legislator, an administrator, a leader must have, especially in a period of revolution. Lenin's strength was chiefly this power of realistic imagination.

I. Z. STEINBERG: "THE COMMISSARIAT FOR SOCIAL EXTERMINATION" [2]

Isaac Zakharovich Steinberg was one of the left-wing Socialist Revolutionaries whose support Lenin managed to gain in November, 1917. Until March, 1918, Steinberg served as People's Commissar of Justice in Lenin's government, but he resigned when the Brest-Litovsk peace was decided upon. He was arrested when the Civil War terror reached its peak and in 1923 left Russia.

From the very first days of October, Lenin strove to impress his colleagues with the absolute necessity for violence, execution, terror. In his book on Lenin, published in 1924, Leon Trotsky relates a number of incidents that bear witness to this. During the Soviet Congress, which ratified the October rebellion, the Bolshevik Kamenev suggested, with Trotsky's concurrence, the abolition of the Kerensky decree which had reintroduced capital punishment at the front. The decree was duly revoked. When Lenin, a day later, learned of this first action of the Soviet, he was furious. "What nonsense," he exclaimed. "Can you make a revolution without executions? Do you think you'll defeat your enemies by disarming yourselves?" He "feared" the soft-hearted Russian character. He mistrusted its ability to be firm. *"Soft, too soft is the Russian,"* he declared. "He is not capable of applying the harsh measures of revolutionary terror."

Later, during the sessions of the Commissars, Lenin spoke repeatedly in the same spirit. Thus, when the German Army launched its attack in February, 1918, the Government decided to exhort the people with a manifesto (February 21, 1918): "The Socialist Fatherland is in danger!" Its author was Trotsky. And he proposed that this document, which appealed to the heroism of the Russian people, include the threat that all who opposed Government orders would be "destroyed on the spot." When the People's Commissars debated the text, I objected that this cruel threat killed the whole pathos of the manifesto. Lenin replied with derision, "On the contrary, herein lies true revolutionary pathos. Do you really believe that we can be victorious without the very cruelest revolutionary terror?"

It was difficult even to argue with Lenin on this score, and we soon reached an impasse. We were discussing a harsh police measure with far-reaching terroristic potentialities. Lenin resented my opposition to it in the name of revolutionary justice. So I called out in exasperation, "Then

[2] From I. N. Steinberg, *In the Workshop of the Revolution* (New York: Holt, Rinehart and Winston, Inc., 1953), pp. 144–45. Reprinted by permission of the publisher.

why do we bother with a Commissariat of Justice? Let's call it frankly the *Commissariat for Social Extermination* and be done with it!" Lenin's face suddenly brightened and he replied, "Well put . . . that's exactly what it should be . . . but we can't say that."

ALBERT RHYS WILLIAMS: LENIN AND THE EXPERTS [3]

One of the earliest American assessments of Lenin was made by Albert Rhys Williams (1884–1962), a Congregationalist minister, muckraking reformer, and radical journalist who arrived in Petrograd in June, 1917, as correspondent for the New York Evening Post. *He became sympathetic to the Soviet regime and hoped to reconcile it with his conception of American democracy. In the two years that he spent in Russia at this time, Williams assisted in preparing propaganda for distribution to the German troops; he left in 1919 to help mobilize opinion against America's role in the allied intervention. He returned to the Soviet Union on a number of occasions, the last time in 1959, and at the time of his death was completing a new version of his memoirs of the Revolution.[4]*

The following selection includes Wiliams's appraisal of Lenin's views on the use of experts in building a new society and also indicates why Williams believed that Soviet-American cooperation could be established.

. . . In every realm Lenin defers to the expert. He looks to the generals even of the Czar's régime as the authorities in military affairs. If Marx, the German, is Lenin's authority in revolutionary tactics, Taylor, the American, is his authority in efficiency production. And he always was stressing the value of the expert accountant, the big engineer, the specialist in every field of activity. He believed that the Soviet would be a magnet drawing them from around the world. He believed they would see in the Soviet system a wider range for the play of their creative abilities than in any other system. . . .

In his survey of social forces, Lenin made his estimate of the value of all the different elements. The intellectuals had their place before and after the Revolution. As agitators they could help make the Revolution possible. As experts with skill and technic they could help make the Revolution permanent and stable.

American technicians, engineers and administrators Lenin particularly

---

[3] From Albert Rhys Williams, *Lenin: The Man and His Works* (New York: Scott and Seltzer, 1919), pp. 102–103.

[4] *Journey into Revolution: Petrograd, 1917–1918*, ed. Lucita Williams (Chicago: Quadrangle Books, 1969).

held in high esteem. He wanted five thousand of them, he wanted them at once, and was ready to pay them the highest salaries. He was constantly assailed for having a peculiar leaning toward America. Indeed, his enemies cynically referred to him as "the agent of the Wall Street bankers," and in the heat of debate the extreme Left hurled this charge in his face.

BERTRAND RUSSELL: A VISIT TO LENIN 1920 [5]

With the easing of the Allied blockade, many more foreign observers visited the Soviet state. A great many of the books that resulted from these visits are merely of curiosity value today. Still worth reading, however, is the report that Bertrand Russell (1872–1970) wrote after his visit in 1920. The English philosopher was intellectually well equipped to make the journey. He had been imprisoned by the British government for his opposition to the First World War and was not put off by the radicalism of Lenin's ideas. At the same time, he was sure enough in his own radicalism not to be stampeded into a hasty endorsement of Lenin and the Soviet regime. Russell was skeptical of ideologies and was repelled by Marxist fanaticism as much as by any other kind. He believed that Lenin tended to operate on the basis of unwarranted assumptions. For these and other reasons, Russell did not succumb, as did many intellectuals in the 1920s and 1930s, to the lures of the Soviet system.[6]

Soon after my arrival in Moscow I had an hour's conversation with Lenin in English, which he speaks fairly well. An interpreter was present, but his services were scarcely required. Lenin's room is very bare; it contains a big desk, some maps on the walls, two bookcases, and one comfortable chair for visitors, in addition to two or three hard chairs. It is obvious that he has no love of luxury or even comfort. He is very friendly and apparently simple, entirely without a trace of *hauteur*. If one met him without knowing who he was, one would not guess that he is possessed of great power or even that he is in any way eminent. I have never met a personage so destitute of self-importance. He looks at his visitors very closely, and screws up one eye, which seems to increase alarmingly the penetrating power of the other. He laughs a great deal; at first his laugh seems merely friendly and jolly, but gradually I came

[5] From Bertrand Russell, *The Practice and Theory of Bolshevism* (originally published, 1921; New York: Simon and Schuster, 1964), pp. 32–36. Copyright © 1948 by George Allen & Unwin Ltd. Reprinted by permission of Simon and Schuster, Inc., New York, and George Allen & Unwin Ltd., London.

[6] See also *The Autobiography of Bertrand Russell* (Boston, Toronto: Little, Brown, 1968), II, 147–59, 179–81.

to feel it rather grim. He is dictatorial, calm, incapable of fear, extraordinarily devoid of self-seeking, an embodied theory. The materialist conception of history, one feels, is his life-blood. He resembles a professor in his desire to have the theory understood and in his fury with those who misunderstand or disagree, as also in his love of expounding. I got the impression that he despises a great many people and is an intellectual aristocrat.

The first question I asked him was as to how far he recognized the peculiarity of English economic and political conditions. . . . [H]e does not advocate abstention from Parliamentary contests, but participation with a view to making Parliament obviously contemptible. The reasons which make attempts at violent revolution seem to most of us both improbable and undesirable in this country carry no weight with him, and seem to him mere bourgeois prejudices. When I suggested that whatever is possible in England can be achieved without bloodshed, he waved aside the suggestion as fantastic. I got little impression of knowledge or psychological imagination as regards Great Britain. Indeed the whole tendency of Marxianism is against psychological imagination, since it attributes everything in politics to purely material causes.

I asked him next whether he thought it possible to establish communism firmly and fully in a country containing such a large majority of peasants. He admitted that it was difficult and laughed over the exchange the peasant is compelled to make, of food for paper; the worthlessness of Russian paper [money] struck him as comic. But he said—what is no doubt true—that things will right themselves when there are goods to offer to the peasant. For this he looks partly to electrification in industry, which, he says, is a technical necessity in Russia, but will take ten years to complete. . . . Of course he looks to the raising of the blockade as the only radical cure; but he was not very hopeful of this being achieved thoroughly or permanently except through revolutions in other countries. Peace between Bolshevik Russia and capitalist countries, he said, must always be insecure; the Entente might be led by weariness and mutual dissensions to conclude peace, but he felt convinced that the peace would be of brief duration. I found in him, as in almost all leading Communists, much less eagerness than existed in our delegation for peace and the raising of the blockade. He believes that nothing of real value can be achieved except through world revolution and the abolition of capitalism; I felt that he regarded the resumption of trade with capitalist countries as a mere palliative of doubtful value. . . .

. . . He said that two years ago neither he nor his colleagues thought they could survive against the hostility of the world. He attributes their survival to the jealousies and divergent interests of the different capitalist nations; also to the power of Bolshevik propaganda. He said the Germans had laughed when the Bolsheviks proposed to combat guns with leaflets, but that the event had proved the leaflets quite as powerful. . . .

I think if I had met him without knowing who he was, I should not have guessed that he was a great man; he struck me as too opinionated and narrowly orthodox. His strength comes, I imagine, from his honesty, courage, and unwavering faith—religious faith in the Marxian gospel, which takes the place of the Christian martyr's hopes of Paradise, except that it is less egotistical. He has as little love of liberty as the Christians, who suffered under Diocletian and retaliated when they acquired power. Perhaps love of liberty is incompatible with wholehearted belief in a panacea for all human ills. If so, I cannot but rejoice in the skeptical temper of the Western world. . . .

SIMON LIBERMAN: ORIGINS OF THE NEW ECONOMIC POLICY [7]

One of the experts employed by the Soviet government was the Menshevik economist, Simon Liberman. Liberman originally was assigned to help bring order out of chaos in the forest industry. He had a number of meetings with Lenin, and complained frequently at interference by technically incompetent Bolshevik politicians. Liberman's influence, according to his own account, increased; Lenin made him an adviser to the Council of People's Commissars and to the Council of Labor and Defense, which was charged with economic planning. A year prior to the adoption of the New Economic Policy, Liberman claims to have influenced Lenin to consider an easing of the regime's economic policies.

Ever since the critical days of the summer of 1919, . . . I had been friends with a group of old Bolsheviks. . . . Once, in 1920, during a session of the Council of Labor and Defense, I had to wait in the council's anteroom long hours for my turn to appear at the session . . . and, while waiting, I talked with two of these old Bolsheviks, Andrew Lezhava and Gleb Krzhizhanovsky. The former was an assistant to Lenin; his friend was one of the earliest outstanding Soviet planners. We talked of Russia's dire plight, and this led to similar talks in the more private atmosphere of our respective homes. Presently we came to the conclusion that . . . an identical attitude toward the events of 1920 united the three of us. And this was our common position:

Striving to see Russia's economy improved speedily, we should draw the Kremlin's attention to the serious and sharp defects in its economic policy. The country's economy lay expiring in the death-grasp of War Communism, and the whole nation was fast approaching its end. All our private efforts to influence individual commissars into an early correction

[7] From Simon Liberman, *Building Lenin's Russia* (Chicago: University of Chicago Press, 1945), pp. 192–94. Copyright © 1945. Reprinted by permission of the publisher.

of the errors had been without avail; therefore it behooved us to bring our suggestions to the attention of Lenin himself.

We decided not to write any special memoranda or to draw up any formal programs but merely to work toward an interview with Lenin. Since, of the three of us, I was the only one who was an expert and not a Communist politician and could therefore speak to Lenin on such a subject more freely than the others, I was selected as the first one to address him. I also had the advantage of enjoying the trust of both Lenin and the non-Communists.

So once again I went to see Lenin. This talk took place in the same small reception room where I had been received the first time I met him. Lenin was wating for me with an expression which told me that he had been advised beforehand by my friends of the subject I was to broach.

I began the conversation by stating our group's premises and then proceeded to illustrate the main points with examples. . . .

At this point I reminded Lenin that in my capacity as manager of supplies I was in constant touch with persons on the spot—with men coming to Moscow from all the nooks and corners of Russia. Our timber organization reached everywhere, and my work afforded me a contact with the peasantry, the industrial workers, and the party officials heading all manner of local organizations. I knew that all of them were dissatisfied, that all complained of the growing hostility toward the government even on the part of those citizens who had formerly followed the Soviets enthusiastically. And the cause of this hostility, the target of the complaints, was always the same: the fierce behavior of the armed expeditions roaming the countryside in search of the peasants' food.

But I never finished my speech. Lenin interrupted me:

"I understand what brought you here. I agree with you entirely. We are indeed in need of changes. We must broaden the base of our government. We should introduce economic relaxations and concessions. But don't forget, all you comrades, that the civil war is not quite ended yet. It still makes demands upon us. . . . We cannot begin a retreat in our policy when hundreds and thousands of men continue to fall, continue to give their lives, while holding our banner in their hands. We cannot change our banner in the midst of this battle. The least change will kill our soldiers' enthusiasm. First we must vanquish the forces of counter-revolution, and only then will we begin to think of changes. Right now all of us must strive toward a sensible use of everything and anything that may help us in our fight against the Whites. However," he added later, "some of the measures you suggest will be adopted."

When it was time for me to go, he said by way of conclusion: "Leave it to us to decide the basic problems and to set the time and place and method for carrying out our decisions. You experts continue to do your work."

I felt that this was the boss talking; that Lenin could not only listen and argue but also order. And yet I felt, too, that a change was coming, that ideologically Lenin was preparing to change the system, but that he needed time—that he was looking for just the right moment and the most plausible excuse for putting the brakes on the revolution. He had talked to me the way he did on that occasion because he was the head of the government, which always had in store some logical explanation for whatever action it took.

ANGELICA BALABANOFF: THE NEW ECONOMIC POLICY— LENIN ON COMPROMISE AND RETREAT [8]

A different view of the New Economic Policy (NEP) is given by Angelica Balabanoff (1878–1960). Russian in origin, she was truly an international socialist, and, like Rosa Luxemburg, was militantly antiauthoritarian. From the turn of the century, she played an active role in the Italian Socialist Party and contributed to socialist publications in a number of European countries. During World War I, she collaborated with Lenin in establishing the antiwar "Zimmerwald movement." In the spring of 1917, she made a brief visit to Russia but returned to Switzerland to continue work against the war. Expelled in 1918, she went to Russia and, for a time, was Secretary of the Communist International and acting Commissar for Foreign Affairs of the Ukraine.

She was opposed to many of Lenin's policies, and her struggles with the Soviet regime reached a peak at the time of the Kronstadt rising. Yet, in some passages in her writings, she attributes to Lenin a kind of revolutionary purity that seems more a projection of her own ethos than an accurate assessment of Lenin's. In the following passage from memoirs which were first published in Italy in the 1950s, she criticizes the NEP as a betrayal of egalitarianism and relates Lenin's shift in economic policy to the more general theme of compromise and retreat. In 1922, with NEP in full swing, she left Russia for good to resume an active career in the European socialist movement.

I saw Lenin after his announcement of the new economic policy: the compromise that affected Russian life from the political, economic and psychological points of view more deeply than any other—including the peace treaty of Brest Litovsk.

I was staying at the National Hotel in Moscow. . . . In tsarist times there had been at the street level of this hotel a famous confectionery

[8] From Angelica Balabanoff, *Impressions of Lenin*, trans. Isotta Cesari (Ann Arbor: University of Michigan Press, 1964), pp. 62–67. Copyright © 1964. Reprinted by permission of the publisher.

known throughout Europe. . . . The morning the new economic policy was announced, which "rehabilitated" money and authorized commerce, I could hardly believe my eyes. The confectionery, which had been empty and abandoned for years was open and full of light. The shop windows were clean, the counters shiny and full of white bread, pastry, and sweets. Outside the bakery people clutching shopping bags and purses stood in line. . . . The sight of all this was very painful to me. I thought of the workers, the children, and the old people who had not had enough to eat in all these years. How would they feel if they saw what was going on here?

I went immediately to the Kremlin to see Lenin. He was grave and worried and very irascible. "What is the conclusion the workers must draw from all this?" I said to him. "Either that they understood nothing of what we told them about equality, or that they must revolt and send all of us to hell. It is a return to the past made all the more serious by disenchantment, skepticism, and rancor. Now as before, the workers will say, those who have means can get everything, even white bread and sweets. Fine equality!"

Lenin's face darkened more and more as I continued saying what he, no doubt, must have thought himself several times. The repetition irritated him. "You know very well that this was necessary. Russia would not have resisted otherwise. You see how these burghers have sabotaged us. As soon as the announcement was made, they took from their hiding places all the foodstuffs of which we had had to deprive the population. This could not have gone on much longer. We made a minor sacrifice to reach the major goal: the consolidation of the important conquests of the Revolution. The proletariat in other countries does not come to our aid; we cannot hold out alone."

"The way things look in the Workers' Republic," I replied, "will make the proletariat lose faith in the future of socialism."

"Well," Lenin said, in a tone that was sad and ironic at the same time, "if you can suggest another way . . ."

"I certainly did not come to teach you. But, although I do not know the way out, I do know what a proletarian, Socialist government is not allowed to do. It is not allowed to tolerate a minority living in abundance while the overwhelming majority is literally dying of hunger. . . ."

I left, putting an end to that painful conversation. "If you have some concrete proposal," he said, "write to me." And I did write him a long letter. . . .

Lenin on Compromise and Retreat

Contrary to the opinion commonly held about Lenin—especially before his rise to power—he was anything but intransigent in politics. It might be said of him what Turati, with rare insight, had said of himself: "Uncompromising compromise." . . .

Lenin and Turati had one thing in common: moral courage. While unafraid of declaring themselves flexible in politics, they were intransigent regarding their principles of personal conduct. The dichotomy between public and private morals was merely an appearance. The point of departure, the guiding thought, was always to serve the cause which, in their minds, was to bring about the triumph of the highest ideals toward which mankind has ever aspired. The pursuit of these ideals informed their entire lives; they were capable of controlling instincts and feelings and, in Lenin's case, also moral scruples.

To the generally accepted ethics Lenin opposed one of his own, based on the following reasoning: "Contemporary society is deeply immoral because it is based on man's exploitation of man. The few privileged rich owe their privilege to the ill-paid work of the proletarians who, in order to live, that is to eat, must surrender health, energies, technical skills and are thus deprived of the possibility of fulfilling the aspirations to a life fit for human beings. Those who profit from this state of affairs and those who defend it or merely tolerate it, have no right to call themselves ethical. In the struggle against an immoral society like the contemporary one, every means is admissible, since this struggle, implicitly, aims at the uprooting of evil and at the formation of a society that no longer allows man's exploitation of man."

Lenin never deviated from this principle, even if the use of certain means, the causing of suffering, ran counter to his nature. This was his intransigence. It enabled him to apply extremely harsh measures. In time, with the worsening of the country's situation and the increase of those cases which, according to him, required the application of repressive methods, his sensibility atrophied, naturally. A single case, a single human life no longer meant to him what it had meant at the beginning of his career as a statesman invested with responsibilities equaled by few.

This adaptation to reality, this yielding to the exigencies of the moment, Lenin revealed also in private conversations. In the beginning, when harsh repressive methods were first used, he explained to me why the application of severe methods in a specific instance prevented the use of more drastic ones. Thus, he commented, for my benefit, on the shooting of some Mensheviks: "If we had not eliminated these few, we would have been compelled before long to shoot over ten thousand peasants whom these Mensheviks instigated against communist power."

PART THREE

LENIN IN HISTORY

In an essay which surveys the various interpretations of Lenin that have been offered over the last fifty years, Walter Laqueur concludes that

It was in many ways easier to assess Robespierre's rule in 1840 than Lenin's in 1960. Robespierre's rule was a brief interlude; the French Revolution had lasted altogether five years, it was finished even if its repercussions were to be felt for decades to come. Lenin's revolution may have lost some, or much, or all of its original impetus, its character and significance may have changed greatly. But there is enough continuity to regard it as a historical process whose end is not yet in sight. . . .[1]

Thus, in interpreting Lenin and in assessing his significance, historians, to a greater or lesser degree, have to come to grips with the overriding fact that Lenin's revolution still affects our lives. But even independently of the system he created and its ultimate fate, Lenin would still exert a fascination as long as historians and political analysts are interested in the problem of interaction between political leadership (including the personality of the leader) and the exercise of political power. As the subject of a case study, Lenin ranks with such leaders as Napoleon. Napoleon has spawned historical controvery for a full century longer than Lenin; yet, as Pieter Geyl points out in his Napoleon: For and Against,[2] *no definitive and completely accepted assessment of Napoleon has yet emerged —or is likely to emerge. It is in the nature of the problems raised by an historical figure of such significance that ultimate assessments are hard, if not impossible, to come by. Lenin's place in history presents similar problems.*

The four selections that follow are only a miniscule sample of the literature on Lenin. Each typifies one aspect of the problem of historical assessment. Adam Ulam focuses on Lenin's political personality and ideas; he portrays him at the end of the 1905 revolution, in mid-passage, as it were, in his development. Lenin is seen here from the perspective of the nineteenth-century evolution of the Russian intelligentsia, and in reaction to that development. Ulam

---

[1] Walter Laqueur, *The Fate of the Revolution: Interpretations of Soviet History* (New York: Macmillan, 1967), p. 82.
[2] (New Haven: Yale University Press, 1949).

emphasizes Lenin's antipathy to the intellectuals (see Gorky, above, pp. 137–39) and considers it a kind of "reverse snobbery"; Lenin, in Ulam's view, had developed, by 1905, a "real affection" for "the proletarian's simple mentality, untormented by the intellectual's doubts and scruples. . . ."

Louis Fischer, the author of what must be regarded as the most satisfactory biography of Lenin to date, picks up Lenin's story immediately after the revolution. Fischer emphasizes Lenin's role as a political activist, rather than as a theorist; he stresses, as did Angelica Balabanoff, Lenin's pragmatism and his ability to compromise. For Fischer, Lenin's efforts in 1918 represent not an attempt to demonstrate an ideology in practice (see Trotsky, above, pp. 162–63) but rather a practical effort to furnish "a permanent home," to establish "a functioning administration" as part of the struggle to win the civil war. "In power," writes Fischer, Lenin "was not guided by books"; had he attempted to adhere to the ideas of State and Revolution, *Lenin's regime would have probably suffered defeat.*

The selections from Lowenthal and Deutscher touch on the link between Lenin's ideas and policies and the beginning of Stalinist totalitarianism. Richard Lowenthal believes that, though there were some antecedents in the Jacobinism that emerged from the French Revolution, the appearance, under Soviet auspices, of the "first totalitarian single-party State" was sui generis. *He sees Lenin as establishing, first, a terrorist dictatorship, and then, in embryo, the totalitarian state that was to emerge in its full dimensions after his death. This, in his view, was not a corollary to the needs of the period of the revolution and civil war, but was much more closely related to post-civil war decisions about economic development. Here, ideology* did *count—the totalitarian state "was the product of the decision to use the dictatorship . . . to twist the development of society in the preconceived direction indicated by the ideology of the ruling party."*

Isaac Deutscher takes issue with such interpretations. In his view, the totalitarian drift that was becoming evident even to Lenin himself during his final illness was produced by a regression to prerevolutionary modes of bureaucratic and Russian nationalist behavior. Lenin recognized this, wrote against it from his deathbed, but was unable to arrest it; he felt "guilty before the workers of Russia" because he had not acted with determination against these trends when they still might have been stopped.

Now, with the revival of the Left as both a social and cultural force in much of the Western world, Lenin seems to have been relegated to a secondary position, scarcely more than a bracket in the historical period between Marx (who, because of his early writ-

ings on alienation, has been the subject of new intellectual interest) and Mao.

The reader himself may judge whether a reappraisal of Lenin as political thinker and activist is relevant at this juncture in our history. If Lenin is relevant, his relevance may lie less in his specific ideas or in the way that they have been assimilated into the operational code of Communist state ideologies, but rather in the general style of his thought and action, and as a prototypical historical figure whose development can help us understand a portion of what is occurring in our own day. Lenin did not appear ab nihilo; he developed out of a specific social and cultural milieu. His ideas represent a continuity, and they took shape from some of the notions of order, discipline, and progress that had been nurtured in Russia by a small intellectual elite; they were transformed in the interaction of individual perception, the demands of a society in crisis, and the political opportunities that arose at crucial stages in Lenin's career.

There were elements in Lenin's life and career that were certainly unique, but these are secondary when compared to one of the major developments in twentieth-century history: the emergence of the intellectual as a central type of political man. Our objective appraisal of Lenin—as man, as thinker, as revolutionary, and as statesman—may be a touchstone of our ability to understand the problems of our own time and situation.

7

Adam B. Ulam: Lenin and the Intelligentsia[1]

. . . [Nineteen-five] closes another period in Lenin's life and in his development as a political leader. . . .

At this mid-point Lenin was still something of an enigma to his followers as well as to his enemies. His appearance was quite ordinary: a bit shorter than the average (five feet six), though there are inexplicably some references to him as "tiny." He was now bald with a fringe of reddish hair and beard. Nearsighted in one eye, Lenin was wont to squint. Some of his contemporaries remembered Lenin's appearance as either "striking" or "repulsive." A Soviet hagiographer presents it as that of a "wise peasant," . . . With his large head and Kalmyk features he looked not untypical of a Russian from the Volga region. His dress and demeanor . . . were characteristic in a Russian of his class.

[1] From Adam B. Ulam, *The Bolsheviks* (New York: The Macmillan Company, 1965), pp. 208–216. Copyright © 1965 by Adam B. Ulam. Reprinted by permission of The Macmillan Company and of Martin Secker & Warburg Limited.

If it were possible for a moment to forget about his politics, Lenin appears as the very embodiment of the middle-class intelligentsia virtues. He was a devoted son and husband and a solicitous brother. The very avidity with which the biographers seize upon an isolated incident such as his quarrel as a boy with Alexander, or talking back to his parents, is a proof of his irreproachably normal family affections. . . . At every step in his career Lenin sought and found help within his family, from Anna editing his literary works to Maria's care during his last and fatal illness. Even brother Dimitri, not particularly close to Lenin and evidently not held by him in high esteem, was enlisted for advice (he was a doctor) when Krupskaya fell ill. In brief, a thoroughly harmonious and unsensational setting offering no handle for Freudian speculations and conclusions. His sole addictions were chess and books. . . .

Indeed the bohemianism and dissipation not absent in many revolutionaries' lives were alien to Lenin's nature, though his distaste for them never degenerated into an obsession. He viewed philosophically but with evident disapproval the loosening of family and moral bonds, an inevitable side effect of the Revolution and the Civil War. He would not try to impose, as Stalin was to attempt in the 1930s, a code of middle-class moral values on Russia. All this talk and practice of free love, of the abolition of the family, and so on, was for him yet another "infantile disease" of Communism, a necessary if regrettable symptom of the transition from bourgeois to Socialist society. . . .

The same balanced view characterized Lenin on the subject of the arts and literature. "Shameful not to know Turgenev," he used to say, though his favorite author was the very embodiment of "rotten liberalism" in politics. He appreciated even that arch reactionary Dostoevsky, and like almost every Russian, though fearful of Tolstoy's moral and political influence, he paid homage to his genius. Modern art, modern poetry were a closed book. "What do they teach them now," he sighed when the Communist youths proclaimed that they no longer studied Pushkin, a "bourgeois" poet, but were enraptured by the "proletarian" poetry of Mayakovsky. But that too shall pass; and there was nothing in his disapproval of that obsessive rage with which his successors greeted the new, the experimental, and nonconformist in the arts.

In brief, he was a typical cultured Russian gentleman of his generation, with a touch, much as he would have resented the knowledge of it, of bourgeois sentimentality in his tastes. He could listen, he declared, for hours to Tchaikovsky or Beethoven, but at times classical music instead of soothing his nerves excited him. It evoked languor and contentment, and yet there were urgent political tasks calling for concentration and ruthlessness. He seldom could sit through a concert. In contrast there were the stirring popular and revolutionary songs, conducive to alertness rather than lachrymose contemplation.

The words "culture" and "cultured" had long been used by the Russian radicals in a special sense, and so they were by Lenin. Russia was "uncultured" because of her autocracy, because of the peasant, and because of the grossness of her social relations. But in addition to anguish there was an unconscious element of national sensitivity and defiance in this oft-repeated declaration. Just because of her backwardness Russia was going to "show" the world some day. And how really "cultured" was the West with its vast disparities of wealth and its bourgeois hypocrisy? Outwardly, as behooved a Marxist, Lenin was a Westernizer with none of the Populist's guilty passion for the primitiveness of the peasant or other aspects of the Russian scene. But his deeply felt nationalism became evident during his long years in exile. He moved through Paris, London, Cracow, and other cities almost oblivious of his surroundings (except for libraries and parks) as long as they had nothing to do with politics. . . . To be a Russian chauvinist was for Lenin "uncultured," to adhere to the bullying ways of Tsarism. But his very parochialism made him leave an imprint of nationalism on Bolshevism, and thus set the stage for Stalin.

Martov, who had no reason to be tender toward his victorious enemy and knew him better than most, thought Lenin personally modest and devoid of vanity. Hard as it is to endorse this judgment, the fact is that Lenin never tried to create a mystique around himself, strove to exact homage, or posed as a great thinker. A hardened egotist would hardly worship (as he did at times) Plekhanov or the German Social Democracy, or feel so deeply their subsequent betrayal or weakness. There is, with one huge exception to be noted below, no trace of fanaticism about Lenin, no irrational drive or ambition. He was a passionate but prudent politician, always capable of accounting for the possibility of defeat or delay, gauging realistically the strengths and capabilities of his opponents. We do not find in Lenin the sadism and personal vindictiveness characteristic of Stalin. But as the aftermath of the Revolution was to show, he was equally incapable of true generosity toward a defeated enemy, or of gestures of humanitarianism where no political gain was evident.

One must turn now to one great exception to what has been said, . . . Lenin's . . . hatred of the intelligentsia. It runs like a thread through his personal and public life, and provides much if not most of the emotional intensity behind the revolutionary strivings. Phrases such as "the intelligentsia scum," "the scoundrelly intellectuals," "that riffraff," run continually through his writings. . . . His fury was aroused by any concept, any postulate, any phenomenon that in some circuitous way could reflect the mentality of the intelligentsia: liberalism, independence of the judiciary, parliamentarism. Very often while arguing for the very same postulate, say for an alliance between the liberals and the Socialists, Lenin still broke out with the most intemperate abuse of the people he wanted as allies.

In January 1905 Lenin addressed a letter to be smuggled to some Bolsheviks awaiting a public trial in St. Petersburg. . . . His main concern was that the accused should cast good figures in court. The Socialist Revolutionaries, when tried, scorned to plead extenuating circumstances and in the manner of Zhelyabov proudly advertised their beliefs and accused the regime. Now it was important that in the eyes of the revolutionary youth the Social Democrats should also appear as heroic figures braving danger and scorning leniency. . . .

But the most revealing part of the letter is Lenin's almost insane eruption of hatred toward a leading segment of the intelligentsia, lawyers. Their advocates, he helpfully advises the defendants, are to be treated roughly and to be put in an exposed position! Those scoundrels of the intelligentsia are apt to create trouble. The people who are faced with the threat of years at hard labor in Siberia are to instruct their lawyers as follows: "If you son of a bitch will allow yourself the slightest indecency or political opportunism (like talking about the political immaturity of the defendants, the errors of socialism . . . repudiation by the Social Democrats of force, the peaceful nature of their teaching, etc.) then I the accused will give you hell publicly, will denounce you as a scoundrel, and renounce you as my counsel. . . ." [2] Lawyers are not to be believed, *especially* if they declare that they are Socialists themselves. They are to be told: "You little liberal clown cannot understand my convictions." And thus Lenin about his own profession. If there was one institution in Russia that stood up to the Tsarist regime and many of whose members exemplified civic courage, it was the bar. Lenin himself had been a beneficiary of this progressive and civic-minded spirit of the legal profession. But as we shall see repeatedly, personal favors dispensed from the hands of the intelligentsia and liberals only hardened his contempt and hatred of the class.

That there was something elemental and inexplicable in his passion against the intelligentsia was seen and deplored even by those closest to him. . . .

Perhaps a clue may be found in Lenin's awareness of how much he himself belonged to that class and his apparent inability to shake off many of its mannerisms and characteristics. His attempts in that direction often involved him in semicomical dilemmas. The Russian radical could hardly indulge in any activity without gravely considering its "class character." Lenin was extremely fastidious. He cleaned his desk every day, sewed on his buttons, while Krupskaya was busy decoding letters from Russia or at similar work. But while this was a mark of distinction from a *revolutionary intelligent* with his notorious disorderliness, was it not really the kind of behavior appropriate to a bourgeois intellectual? The same with sports. He liked to hunt and to hike in the mountains, at the time rather unusual amusements for an average middle-class person. But weren't those the avocations more befitting a nobleman than a revolutionary? But, as he explained precisely, the revolutionary had to keep in shape, for he might have to overpower or to outrun a policeman.

The same dilemma with manners. By upbringing he was a cultured gentleman. A Russian equivalent of a four-letter word did not come to his tongue as naturally and spontaneously as it does to Mr. Khrushchev's. Yet by design he could be vulgarly abusive, both in speech and in writing. This was the product of a philosophy enunciated to Valentinov: "You are obviously shocked that in the Party we do not use language appropriate in a girl's finishing school. . . . If the Social Democrats in their politics, propaganda, and polemics would employ nothing but tame and nonprovocative language they would be worse than those melancholy Protestant ministers. . . ." [3] And he invoked the highest authority: how vulgar and abusive Marx was when dealing with a political opponent.

Lenin's pathological hatred of the intelligentsia and the middle class was combined, the greatest paradox of all, with a very distinctive intellectual snobbery. He did not believe that either the revolution or the Socialist state could dispense with the leadership of educated and technically qualified people. This never-resolved conflict between his emotions and his practicality will be best illustrated during the Soviet period. There we shall see Lenin intermittently exulting in the sufferings inflicted upon the intelligentsia and pitifully bewailing the lack of educated, "cultured" people to run the institutions of the Socialist state. For the "common man's" ability to run a revolution or a state he had nothing but contempt. But it was not that the realities of power sobered him, for throughout his political life Lenin never forgot that the hated intelligentsia were still the key to the success of the revolutionary or of any political movement in Russia. Lose its sympathy or allegiance and your vaunted masses would be like so many sheep. Any philosophical or religious fad that might turn the interests of the middle class away from politics, Tolstoy's Christian anarchism, the neo-idealist philosophy, became for him an enemy dwarfing even the Mensheviks or autocracy. . . .

Was there one institution of the bourgeois intellectual world that Lenin regarded with awe and the rules of which he was unquestioningly ready to respect? Yes, there was: libraries and library regulations. A fervent book lover, Lenin judged the degree of culture of a given locality according to its library resources. If anything could reconcile him to London, that bastion of plutocracy and imperialism, it was the wonders of the library of the British Museum. In 1920 the Chairman of the Council of the Commissars and virtual dictator of Russia wrote this humble letter to the Rumyantsev Public Library in Moscow: He understands that books are not lent out, but might he have just overnight two Greek dictionaries,

[3] Valentinov, *Meetings with Lenin* (New York, 1953), p. 333.

and he promises to return them first thing in the morning? And practically on his deathbed he addressed an urgent note to Anna: a book lent out to him, again in the way of an exception, has disappeared and it is evidently her adopted son who took it. If so will he return it as soon as possible, for Lenin will be blamed! If the Guild of Librarians, that much-suffering segment of the intelligentsia, needs a patron saint, surely it ought to be Vladimir Ilyich Lenin.

Generations of the Russian radicals have had a love affair with "the people." But by 1900 this love affair had cooled off. Certainly for a Marxist the peasant could not be the object of the naïve worship of the Land and Freedom radicals: the exemplar of moral virtues, an instinctive Socialist, the pillar of future Communist society. In fact he was something of a savage whose ferocity if properly exploited could be turned to use in overthrowing the old regime, but who, by the same token, was going to make trouble when it came to establishing a rational, "cultured" Socialist society. Many Marxists simply disregarded this inconvenient feature of the social scene. But for Lenin the peasants still constituted an overwhelming majority of Russia's population. One could not simply consign them to the category of petty bourgeois, sigh over their invulnerability to Marxism, and let it go at that. The Revolution of 1905 opened the eyes of the Socialists to the still crucial position of the *moujik*. This strange creature at times would show revolutionary zeal: the peasants would seize the gentry's lands, burn their residences, and attack the police. But then they would subside into their age-long lethargy. The peasant soldier would show no compunction when ordered to fire on his fellow peasants.

Lenin viewed the peasant without any sentimentality. For him as to his successors up to this very day, he was the clod standing in the way of progress, his psychology primitive and narrowly materialistic and incompatible with the requirements of socialism. But he saw that one could not approach him, at least in Russia, from the doctrinaire Marxian point of view. A revolution could not be achieved without winning over or at least neutralizing a large segment of the peasantry, if need be by forgetting Marxism and catering to its aspirations. The heirs of the Populists, the Socialist Revolutionaries, were proving to be influential in the countryside. The Marxian Socialists had to compete with them and outbid them for the peasants' affections.

Thus 1905 marks the beginning of the concentrated effort to woo the peasant. From the beginning this effort was marked by insincerity and irritation, for the peasant could not be told what was his final destiny in the Marxist commonwealth: "the idiocy of rural life," as Marx puts it, liquidated, and the villagers assimilated to the status and condition of the industrial workers. No, the peasant has to be promised the satisfaction of his craving: land, more land. Had Lenin's allegiance to Marxism been superficial this need for political maneuvering would not have been felt so hard. But since he took his ideology seriously, this obstinate preference of the peasant to live poorly and primitively on *his own* plot rather than to be a workman in a large scientifically run state farm was felt to be an aberration, a sin against enlightenment and progress. In struggling with the peasant mentality, the Bolsheviks were already beginning to feel that they were struggling against the kingdom of darkness. Here were the seeds of the fury with which the Party under Stalin was to fall upon the countryside to beat and to coerce the peasants into collectivizing, to pay them back for all the temporizing measures and concessions it had granted for a quarter of a century.

For the Socialists the peasant's role of the *noble* savage was assumed by the worker. For Lenin the faith in the natural goodness of the proletarian was the reverse side of his loathing of the intelligentsia. But like the latter it often gave way to practical and political considerations. The workers are heroic and pure but alas, few of them are capable of leadership or of administering the Socialist state. If in their ignorance they should stray from the path of socialism, they have to be dealt with severely. After power was in his hands but a few days Lenin was not squeamish in calling for the suppression of those labor unions that opposed the Bolsheviks. He was to shed no tears over the ruthless massacre of the Kronstadt sailors and proletarians. We shall not be far wrong in attributing to Lenin the sentiments toward the workers that the European officers in the imperial days had toward their native troops: affection, not unmixed with condescension.

That there was real affection and an element of envy, one might almost say, of the proletarian's simple mentality, untormented by the intellectual's doubts and scruples, there can be no doubt. . . . [I]t is not unlikely that his preference of Stalin, which caused headshaking among the Party's intellectuals, also had source in this reverse snobbery. The "wonderful Caucasian" was the son of a shoemaker, and how solid and uncomplicated he appeared compared with the vain and excitable intellectuals! With his bourgeois probity Lenin had no sympathy with the view once held by some Populists that crime (when committed by the lower classes, to be sure) was a primitive form of social protest. But his weakness often made him lenient toward perpetrators of hooliganism or brigandage, when those had their source in an excess of proletarian zeal. The law-abiding, orderly Lenin struggled, not always successfully, with his pleasure at the discomfitures of the middle class; could gloat over how those stuffy and pompous lawyers, professors, and their like, with all their chatter about personal inviolability, legality, and so on were being shoved around by his proletarian "boys."

Such was Lenin in 1905. The subsequent years were to modify his views and affect his tactics; they were not to change the man.

8

Louis Fischer:
"... [Lenin] built the Soviet state, with rifle, trowel, whip, and pen."[1]

All of 1918 was full of the most difficult moments in Lenin's life. Yet he never despaired. Arthur Ransome, British artist-journalist with a gentle sense of humor, said of Lenin, "He struck me as a happy man; every one of his wrinkles is a wrinkle of laughter and not of worry; the reason must be that he is the first great leader who discounts the value of personality." Lenin had wrinkles of laughter and wrinkles of premature sclerosis, and he did not worry because, though he faced a mountain of troubles, he did something about them. He was a doer. Instead of worrying he worked. He had an endless love of work and a mastery of small detail and mammoth undertakings. He shuttled from decisions on whether this military front or that should be reinforced to writing a recommendation for a needy comrade in search of an apartment in crowded Moscow. He possessed prodigious energy and spent it prodigally as if he knew he would not be there long. His vanity was minimal, a quality which no doubt created the impression that he discounted the value of personality. But he was too intelligent to discount the value of his own personality, and if he did, nobody else did, nor can history. . . .

Politics are a major ingredient in all civil wars. The quantity and quality of men and arms decide the issues of battles; but when battles are fought in suburbs and wheat fields rather than on a fixed front, and when citizens can therefore choose sides, the real battlefield is the mind of man, and that is where the tsarist generals lost the civil war and where Lenin won it. They stood for the past. He handed out promissory notes on the future. . . .

If Lenin had had ten brains, twenty eyes, and forty hands he could have used them. Without leaving the capital, except to hunt or rest (there is no record of his having visited a front), he was everywhere. He commanded the army, managed the economy, and ran the state while constructing it from the cellar up. More than anything else, he had to win the civil war by winning popular support among workers, national minorities, and peasants. He did this with cold ruthlessness.

[1] Abridged from Louis Fischer, *The Life of Lenin* (New York: Harper and Row, Publishers, 1964), pp. 245–62. Copyright © 1964 by Louis Fischer. Reprinted by permission of the publisher.

Examples:

In December, 1917, soon after the Bolshevik revolution, the Petrograd directorate of the mining, iron, and steel industry in the Urals was unable or unwilling to transfer money to the plants for workers' wages. The workers sent a delegate to Lenin. After fifteen minutes with the delegate, Lenin ordered Felix Djerzhinsky, chief of the Cheka, and A. G. Shlyiapnikov, Commissar of Labor, to "immediately *arrest* the management of the factories, threaten them with a (revolutionary) trial for creating a crisis in the Urals, and *confiscate* all Ural plants. Prepare a draft of the decree with all possible speed. Lenin." . . .

Further to woo the workers Lenin enlisted them as volunteers of terror; he enabled them to wreak vengeance on those they hated. After the assassination of V. Volodarsky, a prominent Bolshevik, in Petrograd in June, 1918, Lenin was disappointed by the punitive measures. He wrote on June 28, 1918, to Zinoviev, communist boss of the city: "Only today we learned in the Central Committee that Petrograd *workers* wanted to answer the murder of Volodarsky with mass terror but that you (not you personally, the Petrograd Chekists and Petrograd Party Committee) restrained them.

"I resolutely protest.

"We compromise ourselves . . . *we put a brake* on the *perfectly* proper revolutionary initiative of the masses.

"That is im-poss-ible.

"The Terrorists"—the anti-Bolshevik terrorists—"may think we are weak sisters. This is tensest wartime. We must foster energetic action and demonstrations of mass terror against counter-revolutionaries, and especially in Petrograd whose example is decisive." . . .

There remained two large segments of Soviet Russia's population to court and conquer: the national minorities and the peasantry. During the First World War, Lenin stated that Great Russians constituted only 43 percent of Russia's inhabitants; 57 percent were members of ethnic or national minorities: Ukrainians, Byelorussians, Georgians, Armenians, Azerbaijani, Uzbeks, Tadjiks, Turkomans, Tartars, and many others— at least a hundred.

The civil war fronts were fluid, but generally speaking the Bolsheviks held the central Great Russian heart of the country whereas their foes operated, of necessity, in the peripheries inhabited by national minorities. The tsarist generals who dominated the anti-Bolshevik fighting camp were patriots of "undivided Russia," the same centralized Russia that had oppressed the national minorities before the revolution. . . .

. . . Moscow promoted petty-bourgeois nationalists among the ethnic populations—because they had more followers—and discouraged internationalistic communists. . . . War is war and civil war is worse, and Lenin took strength where he found it.

By and large the minorities' politicians accepted the fiction of autonomy and the important posts, however decorative, that came with it, in preference to the Tsar's irritating policy of Great Russian supremacy. Lenin attempted to lend the fiction as much reality as convenient, but this was often little indeed when armies, officers and communist officials obedient to Moscow were present and, of necessity in wartime, predominant on the territories of the national minorities. Lenin himself harbored no prejudices against the minorities, nor did his close collaborators, many of whom—Trotsky, Zinoviev, Kamenev, Rakovsky, Djerzhinsky, Sverdlov, Stalin, and so forth—belonged to racial minority groups. Lack of bias notwithstanding, however, some of these non-Great Russians (Stalin and Djerzhinsky, in particular) tried to out-Great Russian the Great Russians. Lenin once reprimanded Djerzhinsky for this zeal. Nevertheless, the Kremlin's and particularly Lenin's solicitude for the minorities was sensed on Russia's periphery although administrators on the spot were not as virtuous as remote policy-makers. The Kremlin could never be sure of the minorities' loyalty. It could be sure that they hated the White generals. This became a not inconsiderable asset. . . .

Every Soviet problem shriveled by comparison with the peasant problem. Of Russia's 159 million inhabitants in 1913, 18 percent lived in cities, 82 percent in villages.[2] Throughout the civil war lower middle-class and working-class unemployed (many factories had closed) tended to leave the hungry cities for food-producing farm areas. Moreover, most of the ethnic groups were overwhelmingly peasant; the Ukrainians probably 90 percent. Workers, even had they all been pro-Bolshevik, were a small minority.

In the civil war the countryside served a threefold function: it furnished most of the manpower to both sides; it supplied the armies and cities with food; it was the battlefield. The towns were the prizes; the rural areas were the fighting arenas. Victory in the internal war, therefore, would be the gift of the lowly muzhik.

Lenin had become increasingly aware of the crucial role of the peasantry in Russian politics. Before the revolution he wrote copiously about agrarian affairs. But, "I know Russia very little," he admitted to Gorky on Capri. "Simbirsk, Kazan, Petersburg, exile—and that's about all." His experience of Russian village life was even more limited; as boy and teen-ager he spent summers at Kokushkino, a Volga estate of Dr. Blank, his maternal grandfather, which Lenin's mother and her sister Veretennikova, inherited. . . . But he understood the political importance of the land question. When the revolution began, only peace took precedence in Lenin's mind over the peasants.

After removing his wig and makeup on learning that the Winter Palace had been taken at 2 A.M. on November 8, 1917, Lenin appeared briefly

[2] *SSSR v Tsifrakh v 1960 godu* (*The USSR in Figures for 1960*) (Moscow, 1961), p. 65.

before the Petrograd Soviet and went to the private apartment of V. Bonch-Bruevich, his secretary, for some sleep. There was no guard. Bonch fastened the front door with its chain, hook, and lock and loaded and cocked his revolvers. "It's our first night," he thought, "anything might happen." Lenin was given a small bedroom; Bonch was falling asleep when he heard Lenin get out of bed, switch on the electricity, and start writing. He wrote fast, scratched, and seemed to be rewriting. Early in the morning he tiptoed back to bed. He awoke several hours later and appeared in the living room fresh and smiling. "Happy first-day-of-the-revolution," he greeted the family. Breakfast over, Bonch and Lenin began walking to the Smolny Institute, headquarters of the infant Soviet state, but boarded a trolley car for the rest of the journey. "Seeing the exemplary order in the streets, Vladimir Ilyich beamed." In his pocket was the Decree on Land he had drafted in pencil during the night. . . .

When Lenin finished reading [the Decree on Land] he said he had heard delegates shout that this was the policy of the Social Revolutionaries. "So be it," he exclaimed. ". . . Whether this is in the spirit of our [Bolshevik] program or of the Social Revolutionary program is not the essence. The essence is that the peasantry receive a firm guarantee that the landlord has vanished from the village, that the peasants themselves can decide all questions, can arrange their own lives."

The peasants had already been arranging their own lives. Under the Provisional (Kerensky) government, peasants with clubs, stiffened by army deserters with rifles, drove out many landlords, sacked manor houses, and parceled out the estates. Lenin merely sanctioned a mood and a fait accompli. But land is not the only factor in land reform. The peasant, to be prosperous, also needs capital: tools, animals, money, as well as sons and skills. Despite the redistribution of land, therefore, some peasants were poor, others were relatively comfortable; some, the "middle peasants," in between. The Bolsheviks used this stratification to introduce virulent class struggles into the villages. The effect was a civil war within a civil war. . . .

. . . [W]orkers' squads who came from cities to fetch grain by force . . . needed allies within the village. They found them among the peasant poor, organized in Committees of the Poor, who, for varied reasons—envy, power drive, or intimidation by the urban invaders—joined in confiscating whatever food was available, usually in the barns, bins, and concealed pits of the better-off peasants (styled kulaks) and of the middle peasants. The civil-war-within-the-civil-war was thus envenomed. The aggrieved upper strata of the peasantry now favored the anti-Bolshevik White generals; at best they adopted an attitude of a-plague-on-both-your-houses. Or their allegiance changed with the color of the confiscators: when the Whites came to seize grain the muzhiks joined the Reds and when the Reds came for the same purpose they joined the Whites. Small wonder that in this civil-war-squared, which lasted from 1917 to

1921, villages, regions, and towns shuttled back and forth from one side to the other. No military map adequately reflected the chaos.

While Russia wallowed in this welter, Lenin and his aides had to forge a policy and push to victory. The task required almost superhuman faith and fortitude, reliance on the human frailties of the foe, and some luck. For this journey Marx was no Baedeker.

Lenin built his popular backing, and simultaneously he built the Soviet state, with rifle, trowel, whip, and pen. . . .

During February, 1918, . . . Lenin was fighting hard, against Left Communist and Left SR opposition, to achieve a peace treaty with the Germans at Brest-Litovsk. What with party conferences, Soviet conferences, private talks to convert opponents, articles in *Pravda,* and reading reports from Brest and sending instructions to Brest, this would have been a full-time job. Lenin searched N. Karayev's *History of Western Europe* and another book on Napoleon's wars with Germany for data supporting his contention that history did not end with the acceptance of peace at the tip of a conqueror's sword. Every conqueror has his day and death. He pressed these points home. . . .

The Seventh Party Congress met on March 6, 7, and 8, 1918. Lenin spoke several times each day, wrote most of the resolutions. He set himself two goals: approval of the peace treaty and a new party program. Bolsheviks attach supreme importance to program. The party's program is the theoretical ground on which it stands and its plan for the future. The seizure of power in Russia changed the party's role. Lenin therefore proposed a new program and a new name. "Russian Social Democratic Labor Party" no longer suited him. The European socialists' pro-war record, he maintained, had besmirched social democracy. Moreover— echoes of *The State and Revolution*—since every state implied oppression there could be no democratic state and therefore no democracy. He accordingly suggested "The Russian Communist Party (Bolsheviks)." It was adopted by majority vote.

But when the Left Communists, with Bukharin in the van, demanded that the new program define communism or socialism, Lenin replied it was too early. "The materials for a characterization of socialism do not yet exist," he said. "The bricks with which socialism will be built have not yet been made. More than this we cannot say, and we must be as cautious and precise as possible." If they sketched a future beyond their reach the Western proletariat would suspect that "our program is only fantasy." A program, he contended, is a statement of "what we have begun to do and of the next steps that we want to take. We are in no position to describe socialism."

Lenin therefore proposed only two additions to the old party program: first, a description of the imperialism manifested by all the First World War belligerents, and here he referred to his *Imperialism* book as offering the necessary ideas, and, secondly, the assertion, with proof, that the soviets were a new form of government, a new kind of state. On this issue, too, Bukharin challenged Lenin to describe socialism as a society without a state. Lenin refused: "We are now unconditionally for the state, but to say—give a detailed definition of socialism in which there will be no state—here you can think up nothing except that then the principle of: from each according to his abilities, to each according to his needs, will be implemented. But this is still remote, and to say that is to say nothing, except to say that the ground under our feet is weak."

"To proclaim in advance the withering away of the state," Lenin warned, "would be to destroy the perspective of history."

. . . The Seventh Party Congress of March, 1918, gave Lenin what he asked: approval of the Brest treaty, approval of a new program incorporating elements of his two most recent books, *Imperialism* and *The State and Revolution*. He continued the battle for the peace treaty and against bureaucratic "disorganization" and economic bankruptcy. On March 28, 1918, he dictated a draft of an article on the "Current Tasks of the Soviet Government" which stressed the pressing need of "practicality" and "efficiency." To this end, the recruitment of "bourgeois intellectuals" for government service was "indispensable." This implied no retreat from the principles of socialism, he declared. On the contrary, the bourgeois specialists would help the revolution. Meanwhile, the financial situation had become catastrophic. A plan for solvency was presented. Lenin commented on April 18: ". . . even the best financial plan cannot now be fulfilled because we have no apparatus to carry it out." Provincial and local soviets were "not connected with one another" and were "cut off from the central government." They lacked the power to improve their own financial position and often succumbed to "separate groups, partly in conflict with the soviets, which do not obey the soviets and which, unfortunately, dispose of certain rifle strength." Rival organizations levied taxes in the same locality. The state was in a state of dissolution, had withered. He complained.

Throughout March and April, 1918, Lenin concentrated on saving Russia from chaos. He made notes: "raise productivity"; "learn socialism from the big organizers of capitalism, from trusts"; "six hours of physical labor plus four hours running the state" (a sure road to more confusion); "Tailors system, Motion study," he wrote in English—a reference to the Frederick Winslow Taylor labor-saving method reviled by communists and others; "communal feeding"; "one-man management" of industrial plants; "draw with both hands from foreign countries"; "piecework pay according to results"; "don't steal, don't be a slacker . . ."; "the Soviet government plus Prussian railroad efficiency plus American technology and organizations of trusts plus American public school education, etc., etc. plus plus equals socialism." . . .

Lenin seemed to be rushing off in fourteen directions. But there was method in his movements. He was consciously building a state in an administrative desert, building it with old capitalist rubble instead of new socialist bricks. He was preoccupied not only with urgent problems that demanded attention (army, peace treaty, food, management, and so forth) but also with matters that embellish a society. As early as November, 1917, he drafted a memorandum on the libraries in Petrograd. He wanted them reorganized on "principles applied long ago in the free countries of the west, particularly in Switzerland and the United States of America." He ordered the unpaid exchange of books between libraries in Russia and with foreign libraries. The reading room of the Petrograd Public Library, the former Imperial Library, "must be open, as in *private* libraries and in reading rooms for the *rich* in civilized countries, every day, including holidays and Sundays, from 8 a.m. to 11 p.m." On May 25, 1918, he wrote a plan for the establishment of a Socialist Academy of the Social Sciences complete with a publishing department for Marxist books. . . .

. . . When a high official said at a Cabinet meeting that the Bolshoi and Mali theaters were unnecessary to a workers' state, they only wasted fuel and played old bourgeois operas like *Traviata, Carmen,* and *Eugene Onegin,* Lenin demurred and told the official that he "had a somewhat naïve idea of the role and significance of the theater." The theaters were saved. . . .

Lenin and the Bolsheviks were furnishing a permanent home. The Whites or anti-Bolsheviks behaved like temporary tenants. They recruited soldiers, confiscated grain, distributed ministerial portfolios, and printed paper money, but they were essentially an occupational force in transit, not a government. Their goal was Moscow. There they hoped to create a state. One could scarcely establish a national government in Taganrog or Irkutsk or Novocherkassk or Omsk or Archangel. A paramount factor in the Soviets' victory over innumerable enemies in the 1917–1921 civil war was their possession of Russia's capital city, in fact of both capital cities, Moscow and Petrograd. But this would have proved an inert advantage if Lenin had not used it assiduously to build the Soviet state. A revolution occurs when administration breaks down. The Soviet revolution won in November, 1917, because Lenin's "Dual Power" strategy, or the division of power between Kerensky and the soviets, disemboweled the government, just as years, indeed decades, of civil war and the consequent anarchy of administration lifted Mao Tse-tung to the Chinese throne. Similarly, a functioning administration, a state, no matter how rickety, stiffens the army in the field and leads to victory in civil wars. An exception comes to mind: the 1936–1939 Spanish civil war. There the anarchists, the communists, and the touch of anarchism in every Spaniard weakened the government's administration and gave the palm to the stronger, foreign-supported army. Had Lenin adhered to his semianarchistic *The State and Revolution* his regime would have suffered the same fate. But in power he was not guided by books.

9

Richard Lowenthal: Lenin and Totalitarianism[1]

. . . It is as the first totalitarian single-party State, rather than as the first Soviet State, that the new type of government developed by the Bolsheviks has attracted imitators—not only among those who share their ideological goals, but also among their most bitter enemies and among people who are quite indifferent to those goals. . . .

. . . [T]he totalitarian single-party State may be defined by four main institutional characteristics. The first is the monopolistic control of the State by the ruling party, excluding the toleration of other, independent parties in opposition or even as genuine partners in coalition, and leading logically also to a ban on the formation of organised tendencies or "factions" *within* the ruling party; this amounts in effect to a monopoly of political initiative and decision for the inner leadership of that party, and ultimately to a monopoly of decision for a single leader. The second is the party's monopolistic control of all forms of social organisation, depriving these organisations of their role as independent interest groups as exercised in non-totalitarian, "pluralistic" societies and converting them into as many tools for the mobilisation, education, and control of their members by the ruling party; . . . The third is the monopolistic control of all channels of public communication. . . . The fourth is what Lenin himself used as the definition of dictatorship—"the removal of all legal limitations on state power," in other words, the possibility to use state power in arbitrary and terroristic ways whenever this is deemed expedient for the purposes of the régime. . . .

This institutional scheme had not been conceived by the Bolsheviks in advance. We may apply to it the words of J. L. Talmon about another régime with which their rule has often been compared:

> Jacobin dictatorship was an improvisation. It came into existence by stages, and not in accordance with a blueprint. At the same time, it corresponded to, and was the consequence of, a fixed attitude of mind of its authors, intensified and rendered extreme by events.[2]

In the Bolshevik case, however, this attitude of mind had long produced its appropriate body in the centralistic organisational structure of

[1] From Richard Lowenthal, "1917 and After: On The Model of the Totalitarian State," from *The Impact of the Russian Revolution* (introduced by A. J. Toynbee). Published under the auspices of the Royal Institute of International Affairs. (Toronto: Oxford University Press, 1967), pp. 21–273.

[2] J. L. Talmon, *The Origins of Totalitarian Democracy* (London, 1952), p. 122.

the party that seized power on 7 November 1917. Lenin had consciously created his "party of a new type" as an instrument for the revolutionary conquest of power; and even though, in writing *What is to be Done?*, he had been far from envisaging the concrete forms that party's domination was to take fifteen or twenty years later, the possibility of a totalitarian party dictatorship was implied in the shape of that instrument. Without the pre-existing "party of a new type," the first state of the new type could not have been built up; with that party once victorious, the tendency for its leaders to establish dictatorial, monopolistic rule was given—to be brought out "by events."

To understand how the truly epoch-making new system of government became possible, it is therefore necessary to recall how unusual were the basic features of Lenin's concept of the revolutionary party. Up to 1902–3, a party had been generally understood to be the organised expression of a part, a section of society—of a particular economic or social interest or current of ideas. Even the socialist parties of western and central Europe that based themselves on the revolutionary teachings of Karl Marx were supposed merely to express the actual ideas and aspirations of the industrial working class of their respective countries: in Marx's own view, his theories could be assimilated by these parties only gradually in the course of their experience, and it was for each of them to draw its own conclusions on the best road to power in accordance with national conditions. Yet Lenin, in writing *What is to be Done?* as a platform for the reconstruction of the Russian Social-Democratic Party organisation in 1902, and in forming his own "Bolshevik" factions over the question of centralised control during its 1903 congress, started from the assumption that no mere "interest group" of the industrial working class would be able to overthrow Russian Tsarism; that the coalition of all discontented classes and groups necessary for this crucial task could be forged only by a conspiratorial organisation of professional revolutionaries specifically devoted and adapted to the conquest of power; and that this organisation needed links in *all* oppositional classes and groups as well as in the state machine, even though the industrial workers must furnish its main base. Such a party, being not the expression of a social current, but the instrument of a will to power and of a strategy for achieving it, could not grow democratically from its roots, but must be planned and built "centralistically" by its founders. Its local committees must be appointed by the central leadership, its members received only after scrutiny by the local committees, selection from above rather than election from below must be its principle all along the line. Only thus could the historically conscious, "scientifically" Marxist leadership use the party to carry out its strategy and bring about a result which the historical process might fail to yield "spontaneously," that is, without such planned intervention.

As Lenin's Marxist critics—Piekhanov, Axelrod, and Martov, Trotsky and Rosa Luxemburg—protested at once, this concept of the party had its roots not in Marxism, but in the tradition of the Russian revolutionary conspiracies of the 19th century, and particularly in the theories of those of their members who professed so-called "Jacobin" principles, that is, the primacy of the conquest of power and the need to adapt the revolutionary organisation to this overriding purpose. In reply, Lenin proudly accepted the model of such revolutionary organisations as the *Narodnaya Volya* and its predecessor, the (second) *Zemlya i Volya,* pointing out only that they did not confine themselves to conspiratorial activities, but combined those activities (such as the infiltration of the state machine and the preparation for armed insurrection) with open revolutionary propaganda. . . .

Even so, Lenin at first sincerely rejected the implication that he was aiming at a party dictatorship in Russia. We do not know just when he came to regard such a régime as the necessary political form for the "dictatorship of the proletariat," but we do know that up to the First World War, he considered that a dictatorship of the proletariat was not yet on the agenda of Russian history. During the revolution of 1905, he aimed at the overthrow of Tsarism by an alliance of workers and peasants, and at the formation of a coalition government of Social-Democrats and Social-Revolutionaries as its political expression. It was only the shock of the war of 1914 that convinced Lenin that a socialist revolution had become an immediate task internationally, and that it was therefore the duty of socialists even in backward Russia to go beyond the overthrow of Tsarism and the establishment of a "bourgeois-democratic" régime and to set up the power of the proletariat—in order to contribute to the fulfilment of the international task.

When Lenin, after his return to Russia in April 1917, began to propagate this new concept, first within and then beyond his party, he did so under the slogan "All Power to the Soviets." Yet while he emphasised the Soviets as the direct organs of proletarian rule, the opposition of all other socialist parties to this programme convinced him that the establishment of that rule depended on the Bolsheviks acquiring control of the Soviets first. In the course of 1917, the Bolsheviks ceased in Lenin's mind to be merely the most enlightened and energetic representatives of the interests of the Russian working class and became, to him, the *only* party of the Russian proletariat; and this implied that the "dictatorship of the proletariat" must in fact take the form of a Bolshevik party dictatorship.

This crucial identification of party and class appears as a matter of course in all Lenin's writings during the months immediately preceding the seizure of power. It becomes most explicit on the very eve of victory in his pamphlet *Can the Bolsheviks Retain State Power?,* in which the Soviets—the directly elected representatives of the workers, soldiers, and peasants—are openly and unceremoniously treated as the new "state apparatus" by means of which the victorious Bolsheviks will exercise and maintain *their* power and carry out their policy. It was a consequence of this outlook, not yet understood at the time even by many leading Bolsheviks, that Lenin after 7 November consistently rejected all proposals for a coalition with the Mensheviks and accepted as temporary partners in the new régime only those Left Social-Revolutionaries whom he regarded as representing the peasants in the process of agrarian revolution. It was another consequence that he dispersed the Constituent Assembly, elected *after* the Bolshevik assumption of power, when its large non-Bolshevik majority refused to vote a blanket endorsement of all the revolutionary measures already enacted by the new régime.

By the time of the October Revolution, then, Lenin was determined to establish a revolutionary dictatorship of his party. But this did not mean that he had, even then, a plan or blue-print for a totalitarian single-party state. What was clear in his mind was the last of our four characteristics of such a state—the rejection of any legal limitations on the revolutionary power. This was sufficient to enable him to suppress resistance to his policy as the need arose. But as resistance developed into civil war, determination to break it was no longer enough: to maintain and defend the revolutionary government, a new state machine had to be created.

. . . [W]ith the spread of civil war, the creation of a new, revolutionary army, police, and bureaucracy became imperative if the Soviet régime was not to follow the Paris Commune also on the road to defeat. The new, professional state machine had to be staffed with reliable cadres at least in the key positions; and in the conditions of party dictatorship, reliable cadres could only mean Bolsheviks. From being the leading force in the Soviets and the government, the party thus developed into the backbone of a new state machine: its monopolistic control of the new state became entrenched in practice before it was proclaimed in theory. In fact, as Leonard Schapiro has shown,[3] the party was so little prepared for this task that its provincial organisations were temporarily almost paralysed by the absorption of the most active cadres in the work of the new Soviet bureaucracy. When the need for central control of the assignments of party members to state jobs was recognised by the spring of 1919, the central party apparatus was still quite inadequate for this new role: it had to be expanded from a mere 15 persons to 600 within two years.

Even so, during the entire period of the Civil War, the Bolsheviks never argued in principle that they should be the only legal party. Nor was there any hint of that doctrine in the constitution of the RSFSR adopted by the fifth All-Russian Soviet congress in July 1918. But they did argue that they would not tolerate any bourgeois parties opposed to Soviet rule in principle, nor parties working for the armed overthrow of the new régime, even if they professed a socialist programme; and they claimed that the central and local organs of Soviet rule, including the

[3] L. Schapiro, *The Communist Party of the Soviet Union* (London, 1960), pp. 241–6.

Cheka, must not be hampered by any legal safeguards in deciding whether any party, newspaper, or individual was guilty of such counter-revolutionary activity. In practice, this led not only to the suppression of parties and groups that were actually supporting armed insurrection against the Soviet power, . . . It also produced a cat-and-mouse game of arbitrary harassment of parties and groups that explicitly and consistently placed themselves on the ground of the new Soviet Constitution and the defence of the Soviet régime, but claimed the democratic rights of competing for influence and criticising the authorities on that basis, such as the Mensheviks led by Martov and some breakaway groups from the Social-Revolutionaries. In the absence of legal standards, the only maxim underlying that practice was clearly that no party, however loyal to the "Soviet system," must be allowed to become strong enough to endanger the effective power of the Bolsheviks. . . .

Yet while the Bolshevik régime of the Civil War years was clearly a terrorist dictatorship . . . and while the dictatorial party increasingly merged with the new state machine in process of construction, it did not yet create a totalitarian single-party State as we have come to know it since.

As late as 1920, there were many hundreds of Mensheviks in the provincial Soviets, and Martov himself was able in the Moscow Soviet to voice their protest against the arbitrary suppression of "working-class democracy" and to advocate their programme for economic recovery that anticipated the later New Economic Policy of the Bolsheviks. Important trade unions were still under Menshevik control, and the Bolshevik leaders were under no illusion that the influence of their critics among the workers was increasing as the Civil War drew to a close. Discontent and indiscipline had moreover affected so many of the Bolsheviks' own militants that spontaneous co-operation between Mensheviks and those undisciplined Bolsheviks produced surprise majorities against the "party line" in Soviets or trade unions more than once. It was only after the end of the Civil War, in early 1921, at a time of growing unrest among both workers and peasants culminating in the Kronstadt rising, and simultaneously with the decision to introduce the New Economic Policy, that Lenin decided to put his régime on a more secure institutional basis. To understand the decision that produced the first modern totalitarian régime, we must try to envisage the problems that faced him.

The classical task of a Jacobin revolutionary dictatorship had been fulfilled. The counter-revolution had been defeated, the power of the former ruling classes broken for good. But the expectation that the Bolshevik victory in Russia would be the immediate prelude to socialist revolutions in the advanced countries of Europe had not come true. The "dictatorship of the proletariat"—in fact of a minority party claiming to represent the proletariat—had remained isolated in a backward country in which the proletariat formed a minority, and in which, as Lenin knew and recognised, the economic and cultural preconditions for a socialist system were lacking. To overcome the discontent born out of economic paralysis, to begin the work of recovery after the devastations of war and civil war, major economic concessions to all the remaining nonproletarian strata—to the peasant majority above all, but also to the traders and technicians—were inevitable. The "war communist" fantasies of a straight leap into Utopia had to give way to a policy of patiently creating, in co-operation with all classes, the productive resources which elsewhere had been created by capitalism, and which alone could eventually form the basis for a socialist economy. It seemed the typical situation for a "Thermidor"—for liquidating the revolutionary dictatorship that had done its work. That was indeed what the Mensheviks suggested with growing confidence in their own judgment.

Yet Lenin drew a different conclusion. . . . [H]e insisted that the "proletarian" dictatorship must be maintained during the new phase . . . in order to ensure that evolution was accomplished by what he termed state capitalism—under the control of a state which would maintain Russia's independence from the capitalist world and prevent the restoration of a class of capitalist owners, even while accomplishing the task which capitalism had fulfilled in the advanced countries, and would thus preserve the foundations for the later transition to socialism as well as a stronghold for the international revolutionary movement. The Bolsheviks must hold on to their dictatorial power—no longer primarily as a revolutionary dictatorship, but as a special type of a dictatorship of development. It is from this decision that the truly unique course of the Russian Revolution begins. It is from this decision, too, that the need to create a system of totalitarian institutions has resulted.

The new need, as Lenin saw it, was no longer the comparatively simple one of fighting the class enemy arms in hand. It was to harness the economic energies of non-proletarian classes for a constructive task, to grant them a place in society for a whole period—yet to prevent them from influencing the direction of economic and social development. As Lenin had once conceived the "party of a new type" as an instrument to make the social forces of discontent converge in a revolutionary direction which they might not otherwise take, so now he conceived the State of a new type as an instrument to guide the millions of independent peasants, the private traders, the industrial technicians of bourgeois origin, in a socialist direction which ran counter to their natural tendency to evolve a capitalist social structure. To foil that tendency, it was not enough that the state kept firm control of the "commanding heights" of the economy; the alien classes must be permanently excluded from any possible access to the levers of political power. The unique purpose of forcing an entire society to develop not in the direction corresponding to its inherent trend, but in the direction dictated by the ideology of its ruling party, required a unique institutional form, closing all channels of political expression to the existing social forces: no plurality of political parties, however vestigial; no organised interest groups or publishing media free from party control; and finally, as a logical extension of this principle, no plurality of organised tendencies *within* the ruling party, as in the absence of opposition parties such "factions" would tend to become the channels for the pressure of non-proletarian class interests. . . .

The first totalitarian state, thus, did not arise either as an automatic result of revolution and civil war, or as a mere instrument for the accelerated economic development of a backward country. It was the product of the decision to use the dictatorship resulting from the revolution in order to twist the development of society in the preconceived direction indicated by the ideology of the ruling party. . . .

10
Isaac Deutscher: Lenin's Moral Dilemmas[1]

. . . Lenin refused to attribute absolute validity to any ethical principle or law. . . .

It was therefore in a spirit of historical relativism that Lenin approached questions of morality. Yet it would be a mistake to confuse this with moral indifference. Lenin was a man of strong principles; and on his principles he acted with an extraordinary, selfless dedication and with intense moral passion. It was, I think, Bukharin who first said that the Leninist philosophy of historic determinism had this in common with the Puritan doctrine of predestination that, far from blunting, it sharpened the sense of personal moral responsibility.

Cromwell and Robespierre became revolutionaries when they were caught up by the current of actual revolution. . . . Lenin, on the contrary, deliberately entered the path of the revolutionary a full quarter of a century before 1917. Of the thirty years of his political activity, he exercised power in the course of only six years—for twenty-four years he was an outlaw, an underground fighter, a political prisoner, and an exile. During those twenty-four years he expected no reward for his struggle other than moral satisfaction. As late as January 1917 he said at a public meeting that he and men of his generation would probably not live to see the triumph of revolution in Russia. What, then, gave him, a man of political genius and of extraordinary ability in many other fields, the moral strength to condemn himself to persecution and penury in the service of a cause the triumph of which he did not even expect to see?

It was the old dream of human freedom. He himself, the greatest realist among revolutionaries, used to say that it was impossible to be a revolutionary without being a dreamer and without having a streak of romanticism. The enlargement of human freedom implied for him, in the first instance, the freeing of Russia from Tsardom and from a way of life rooted in age-old serfdom. Ultimately it implied the liberation of society at large from the less obvious but not less real domination of man by man inherent in the prevalence of bourgeois property. He saw in the contradiction between the social character of modern production and the unsocial character of bourgeois property the chief source of that irrationalism which condemns modern society to recurrent crises and

[1] Abridged from Isaac Deutscher, *Ironies of History: Essays in Contemporary Communism* (London: Oxford University Press, 1966), pp. 167–173. (Originally published in *The Listener,* London [February 5, 1959].) Copyright © 1966 by Isaac Deutscher. Reprinted by permission of Oxford University Press, Inc.

wars, and makes it impossible for mankind even to begin to master its own destiny. If, to Milton, Englishmen loyal to the King were not free men, and royalism was moral slavery, then to Lenin loyalty to the bourgeois society and its forms of property was also moral slavery. Only that action was moral to him which hastened the end of the bourgeois order and the establishment of the proletarian dictatorship; for he believed that only such a dictatorship could pave the way for a classless and stateless society.

Lenin was aware of the contradiction inherent in this attitude. His ideal was a society free from class domination and state authority; yet immediately he sought to establish the supremacy of a class, the working class, and to found a new state, the proletarian dictatorship. . . . [U]nlike other states, the proletarian dictatorship would have no need of any oppressive government machine—it would not need any privileged bureaucracy which, as a rule, "is separated from the people, elevated above it, and opposed to it.". . .

Here, in this conception, and in its conflict with the realities of the Russian revolution, was the source of the one truly great and crushing moral crisis Lenin ever knew—the crisis at the end of his life. . . .

In . . . some other situations he held that *reculer pour mieux sauter* was a sound maxim. He saw nothing dishonourable in the behaviour of a revolutionary who retreats from his position before overwhelming enemy forces, provided that the revolutionary acknowledges the retreat as a retreat and does not misrepresent it as an advance. This, incidentally, was one of the important differences between Lenin and Stalin; and it is a moral difference, the difference between truthfulness and prestige-ridden, bureaucratic mendacity. It was precisely when he had to bow to expediency, and to act "opportunistically" that Lenin was more than usually anxious to preserve in his party the sense of its direction—a clear awareness of the goal for which it was striving. He had brought up his party in an enthusiasm as ardent and a discipline as severe as were the enthusiasm and the discipline of Cromwell's soldiers. But he was also on guard against the excess of enthusiasm which had more than once led revolutionary parties to quixotry and defeat.

Guided by this astringent realism, Lenin was then for five years engaged in building the Soviet state. The administrative machine he created had little in common with the ideal model of it he had drawn in *State and Revolution*. A powerful army and an awe-inspiring political police came into being. The new administration reabsorbed much of the old Tsarist bureaucracy. Far from merging with a "people in arms," the new state, like the old, was "separated from the people and elevated above it." At the head of the state stood the party's Old Guard, Lenin's Bolshevik Saints. The single-party system took shape. What was to have been a mere para-state was in fact a super-state.

Lenin could not have been unaware of all this. Yet for about five years he had, or appeared to have, a calm conscience, no doubt because he felt that he had retreated from his position under the overwhelming pressure of circumstances. Revolutionary Russia could not survive without a strong and centralized state. A "people in arms" could not defend her against the White Armies and foreign intervention—a severely disciplined and centralized army was needed for that. The Cheka, the new political police, he held, was indispensable for the suppression of counter-revolution. It was impossible to overcome the devastation, chaos, and social disintegration consequent upon civil war by the methods of a workers' democracy. The working class itself was dispersed, exhausted, apathetic, or demoralized. The nation could not regenerate itself by itself—"from below," and Lenin saw that a strong hand was needed to guide it from above, through a painful transition era of unpredictable duration. This conviction gave him what appeared to be an unshakable moral self-confidence in his course of action.

Then, as if suddenly, his self-confidence broke down. The process of state building was already well advanced, and he himself was nearing the end of his active life, when he was seized by acute doubt, apprehension, and alarm. He realized that he had gone too far, and that the new machine of power was turning into a mockery of his principles. He felt alienated from the state of his own making. At a party congress, in April 1922, the last congress he attended, he strikingly expressed this sense of alienation. He said that often he had the uncanny sensation which a driver has when he suddenly becomes aware that his vehicle is not moving in the direction in which he steers it. "Powerful forces," he declared, "diverted the Soviet state from its 'proper road.' " He first threw out this remark as if casually, in an aside; but the feeling behind it then took hold of him until it gripped him completely. He was already ill and suffered from spells of sclerotic paralysis; but his mind still worked with relentless clarity. In the intervals between attacks of illness, he struggled desperately to make the vehicle of the state move "in the right direction." Again and again he failed. He was puzzled by his failures. He brooded over the reasons. He began to succumb to a sense of guilt, and finally, he found himself in the throes of moral crisis, a crisis which was all the more cruel because it aggravated his mortal illness and was aggravated by it.

He asked himself what it was that was transforming the Workers' Republic into an oppressive bureaucratic state. He surveyed repeatedly the familiar basic factors of the situation: the isolation of the revolution; the poverty, the ruin, and the backwardness of Russia; the anarchic individualism of the peasantry; the weakness and demoralization of the working class; and so on.

But something else now also struck him with great force. As he watched his colleagues, followers, and disciples—those revolutionaries turned rulers—their behaviour and methods of government reminded him more

and more of the behaviour and the methods of the old Tsarists bureaucracy. . . . [D]efeated Tsardom was in fact imposing its own standards and
methods on his own party. It was galling for him to have to make this
admission, but he made it: Tsardom was spiritually conquering the
Bolsheviks, because the Bolsheviks were less civilized than even the Tsar's
bureaucracy had been.

Having gained this deep and ruthless insight into what was happening,
he watched his followers and disciples with growing dismay. More and
more often he thought of the *dzierzhymordas* of old Russia, the gendarmes, the leaders of the old police state, the oppressors of national
minorities, and so on. Were they not sitting now, as if resurrected, in the
Bolshevik Politburo? In this mood he wrote his last will, in which he
said that Stalin had already gathered too much power in his hands, and
that the party would be well advised to remove him from the office of
its General Secretary. . . .

On his sick bed, while he was struggling with his paralysis, Lenin
decided to speak up and denounce the *dzierzhymorda,* the big brutish
bully, who was in the name of revolution and socialism, reviving the old
oppression. But Lenin did not absolve himself from responsibility; he
was now a prey to remorse, which was extinguishing the feeble flame of
life left in him but which also aroused him and gave him strength for
an extraordinary act. He decided not merely to denounce Stalin and
Dzerzhinsky but to make a confession of his own guilt.

On 30 December, 1922, cheating his doctors and nurses, he began to
dictate notes on Soviet policy towards the small nations, notes intended
as a message to the next party congress. "I am, it seems, strongly guilty
before the workers of Russia"; these were his opening words, words the
like of which had hardly ever been uttered by any ruler, words which
Stalin subsequently suppressed and which Russia was to read for the
first time only after thirty-three years, after the Twentieth Congress.
Lenin felt guilty before the working class of his country because, so he
said, he had not acted with sufficient determination and early enough
against Stalin and Dzerzhinsky, against their Great Russian chauvinism,
against the suppression of the rights of the small nations, and against
the new oppression, in Russia, of the weak by the strong. He now saw,
he continued, in what "swamp" of oppression the Bolshevik Party had
landed: Russia was ruled once again by the old Tsarist administration
to which the Bolsheviks "had given only a Soviet veneer"; and once again
the national minorities "were exposed to the irruption of that truly Russian man, the Great Russian chauvinist who is essentially a scoundrel
and an oppressor as is the typical Russian bureaucrat."

For thirty-three years this message was to be concealed from the Soviet
people. Yet I think that in these words: "I am, it seems, strongly guilty
before the workers of Russia"—in his ability to utter such words—lay
an essential part of Lenin's moral greatness.

Afterword: The Future of Leninism

> It is not history, as if she were a person apart, that uses men as a means to work out her purposes; rather, history is itself nothing but the activity of men pursuing their purposes.
>
> —KARL MARX

Revolutionaries cannot really be understood apart from their revolutions. When a successful revolutionary's theories of society are projected forward in time, encapsulated in an ongoing postrevolutionary system that seeks its own fulfillment, its own relationship to new times and new problems, there is bound to be distortion: the social "ism" is not quite the same as the living thought of the living man. The closest fidelity to a body of thought occurs not when its postulates are applied as dogmas, but when new problems are tackled in the *spirit* of the original; perhaps, when Jefferson suggested that a new revolution was needed every generation or so, he was suggesting—at least indirectly—that it was necessary, periodically, to break the mold of "Jeffersonianism" so that Jeffersonian ideals could continue to have an impact on American history. So too with almost any revolution one can think of. Successful revolutions all too easily become the subject of fusty analysis in learned institutions; revolutionaries all too readily act as if only the slogans of their predecessors were of value.

Has Leninism a future—a future, that is, other than among the hagiographers or, alternately, among those who would exorcise the devil of social rebelliousness? Do Lenin's ideas, or—more important—his mode of analysis have any value for those who wish to understand not only the past, of which he was a part, but, in their own way, the present in which they themselves must live and act and hope?

If we reexamine Lenin's thought, the two elements that have survived the test of historical development are, on the overt level, the theory of imperialism, and, less explicitly, the concepts of basic dynamism with which he was beginning to grapple, theoretically, in his reassessment of Hegelianism. It is to the scope and limits of these elements in Lenin's thinking that we shall address ourselves in these concluding pages of our study.

Imperialism, as we have already noted, combines analysis at two levels: on the one hand, it studies the internal functioning of advanced industrial society; on the other hand—more conventionally—it attempts to evolve a theory to explain the projection of the power of the advanced capitalist societies on a global scale and to assess the strengths and weaknesses of capitalism as a world system. Lenin's originality (which is obscured by his heavy use of quotations and his interpretation of Hobson,

Hilferding, and Kautsky) lies in the way in which he injected into the analysis of global events his earlier assessment of the expansion of Russian capitalism to bring the Russian peasants into its field of influence and control. Lenin's relationship to the peasantry was ambivalent; however, he implicitly realized that capitalism, having brought peasant society under its sway, then became vulnerable, at the periphery, to the vagaries of rapid social mobilization of a fundamentally recalcitrant social group. This was intrinsic to Leninism (one might almost say it was an element of Lenin's political sensibility, rather than of his political thought) and it ensured his ideas a hospitable reception among nationalist revolutionaries in the countries of Asia, Africa, and Latin America. Mao Tse-tung could build on these concepts, and elaborate the notion of the peasantry as the carrier of the "proletarian" revolution, outflanking capitalism by attacking its most vulnerable outposts. Stalin, seeking to routinize revolution, chose to emphasize the other side of Lenin's stance vis-à-vis the peasantry: his fear of social chaos. To do so, he had to emphasize other elements of Lenin's global view, in particular, his worship of efficiency and of the industrial process.

The concept of the imperative of capitalist expansion (and ultimate vulnerability) accounts for the popularity of Lenin's theory of imperialism among revolutionaries. But it is his views on the *internal* evolution of capitalist society that warrant reconsideration today. It is easy to find fault with specific aspects of his Marxist analysis: in the developed countries, the general welfare of the industrial workers has increased rather than diminished, over the last half-century and this has continued even after colonies have been relinquished. But his emphasis on the significance of large-scale economic organizations, the corporations and the trusts, as an international phenomenon assumes a new significance in the era of the multinational corporation. It has been predicted that by the end of the twentieth century some five hundred firms—or perhaps even fewer—will dominate world manufacturing and trade, and that the multinational corporation may become too powerful to be constrained by national governments or national legal systems or national trade unions. The institutional aspect of transition in today's international economy and global political system leads us back to Lenin's analysis. His conception of the rentier state, dependent more on a return from invested capital than on exports of goods, takes on fresh significance when we read that by 1969 the net return on foreign investment by American companies had reached $5.8 billion a year, and when we compare this to the deteriorating exports of manufactured goods.[1]

The surprising weakness in Lenin's analysis—surprising, that is, in a work of Marxist analysis—is that he did not sufficiently emphasize the

[1] See Laurence B. Krause, "Why Exports are Becoming Irrelevant," *Foreign Policy* (Summer, 1971); reprinted in *The Atlantic Community Quarterly*, IX, no. 3 (Fall, 1971), 337–43.

development of new technology. To a considerable extent, the image of society that emerges in Lenin's mature works implies a rather closed technological system, a system whose technology is basically completed—at least until the socialist revolution can free technology from the organizational fetters of advanced capitalism. Since he stressed the power of the capitalist organization and the significance of return on investment as the basic premises of imperialism, Lenin could not admit that the technological substructure would prove to be a powerful force against the organizational overlay, even though this would have been consistent with classical Marxism. Rather, in his few (and minor) references to technological innovations, Lenin suggested that, in fact, the capitalist trusts will throttle the emergence of any device that is likely to displace existing processes of manufacture, and thus diminish return on capital that is already locked into existing plants and equipment. By de-emphasizing the possibility of autonomous technological development, Lenin sustained the notion of a closed economic system: one in which gains for the capitalist entrepreneur or stockholder had to be made at the expense of the exploited industrial laborer or the colonial native, rather than as a by-product of increased control over the forces of nature. This latter possibility was reserved for the mature socialist society, the society that would have broken through to the "communism" (or advanced stage of socialism) envisaged by Marx and Engels.

Thus, Lenin's statistics deal with the form of capitalist society, with the growth of enterprise, rather than with the material substructure identified in the Marxist system. In a sense, Marxism had been turned upside down; the structure of economic relations, the organizational forms and organizational dynamics of mature capitalism, were seen to be in control—for the time being, at least—of the productive forces. To match the effectiveness of large-scale organization on the part of the capitalists (or, in Russia, the Tsarist regime) required close attention to the organizational forms of modern revolutionary struggle. Social change, in the Leninist schema, was the outcome of a struggle between hierarchically structured organizations, each of which sought to exploit dislocations in the nodal points of societal development over time. War, for example, could be used either to create a synthesis between the state bureaucracy and the capitalist trusts, or to exploit the tensions and dislocations (particularly when the war was leading to defeat) and harness them to the needs of revolutionary struggle. A strong element of voluntarism was injected into Marxism, while at the same time, as we have seen, Lenin had begun to look beyond Marxism to Hegelian logic for a theoretical framework within which to analyze revolutionary change.

Organizational and systemic dynamics were not fully developed in detail in the mature Leninist schema. In contrast to many other statesmen, Lenin realized that the older structure of society could not be re-created; that each critical move in the development of mature industrialism set off a chain of repercussions; that developments which, according to nineteenth-century criteria of power politics (e.g., balance of power) could strengthen the world system could, instead, weaken it—given the global scale of the game that was being played, the interpenetration of international and internal political factors, and the new interrelationship of economics, psychology, and politics. Lenin only dimly perceived this vision of world politics, but its rudiments are discernible in his work. And to this extent, again, his analysis warrants close attention and critical reevaluation, even today, almost fifty years after his death.

At the operational level, Lenin's analysis must be placed in the context of time, place, and situation: it was appropriate to the Russian situation in 1917, but does it hold out any lessons on a wider scale? Only one: that it is possible for governments to lose control of a situation by overextending themselves and by creating a milieu within which wider and wider circles of the population are drawn into the ambience of the extreme revolutionary parties—and that this can occur with comparative rapidity. A few years before World War I, Lenin was the relatively unknown head of a small group of extremists, a group more absorbed in internal struggles than in mobilizing for widespread revolutionary action. By the end of 1917, the follies of those who had started from a more advantageous situation had created the base for his rise to power—societal breakdown, an expansion in the number of those so disadvantaged and discontented that they would follow leaders who could promise a way out of Russia's dilemma, an even wider circle of those who would tacitly acquiesce in the Bolshevik seizure of power while seeking to keep out of the conflict.

But beyond this basic lesson, the question of Lenin's legacy with regard to the strategy and tactics of radical movements admits to no easy answer. Certainly, some of his prescriptions on propaganda and agitation, organization, and the like, have had a lasting influence. But the history of twentieth-century radicalism and of the revolutions since 1917 indicates that, despite similarities, each revolution has had its own unique characteristics. The experience of 1917—an urban revolution *followed by* an extensive civil war, a revolution that took place in the middle of a war, a revolution that occurred in a country which had at least begun to approach industrial take-off—has not really been duplicated. And though Lenin's theories prepared him, psychologically, for revolutionary leadership when the circumstances became favorable, yet the specific strategies and tactics used in 1917 were relatively late outgrowths of his mature theorizing and only partly linked to his earlier conceptions.

As for other countries, Lenin was careful to point out the distinctiveness of the Russian situation (which, however, he felt might be closer to being a prototype for Asian developments) in at least two phases of the development of his theories. In the early 1900s, when he was shaping his concept of the revolutionary party, he conceded that other possibilities might be open in countries like Britain, Germany, and the United States; he justified his conception precisely on the basis of his analysis of the Tsarist system which, he claimed, warranted an exceptional form of revolutionary organization, a deviation from the open Socialist party that prevailed in the West. Again, in 1920, he pointed out to the "ultraleft" communists in the Western countries that armed revolution was not the only form of radical struggle, that where parliamentary politics, open elections, and access to the public were available, then the Left should make use of these political means—if only to build a base for other forms of struggle that might become necessary. It is not possible, then, to read Lenin as if he were a revolutionary doctor prescribing universal nostrums for cases beyond his historical ken. Rather, the fascination of Lenin's strategic and tactical writings lies in their implicit portrayal of a man attempting to come to grips with a complex and changing reality that does not lend itself to formula thinking.

Finally, there is some interest in reading Lenin for the relationship between his personal views (in some respects conservative) and his political orientation. In a period when radical politics and radical life-styles seem to be closely linked, what are we to make of a man in a somewhat staid three-piece suit, a revolutionary polemicist who compiled page after page of statistic-laden notebooks as a background to his propaganda, a man with more than a touch of the provincial schoolteacher in his makeup, a devotee of order and orderliness, a man who cautioned that the best elements of the older culture had to be preserved if a new, post-revolutionary society was to have any chance whatsoever of advancing towards a higher civilization? For some, these aspects of Lenin's personality constitute additional reasons for considering only his historical significance; for others, attempting to make their own syntheses between past and future, they provide a more compelling reason for looking at Lenin from the perspective of contemporary trends.

Social analysis evolves not by discontinuities, but through syntheses. A comprehensive critique of contemporary trends in societal development, on a global scale, will be useless if Lenin's contributions are excluded, or if we accept, uncritically, the caricature of Lenin's ideas enshrined in the various isms. The time has come for serious political thinkers to apply to Lenin the type of original and fundamental analysis that has resulted in a renascence of critical Marxism. The time has come, in other words, to allow Lenin to come in from the cold.

Bibliographical Note

In general, material already cited in the main body of the text is not repeated in this bibliography. For a general review of the appraisals of Lenin that have been made since the Revolution, see Walter Laqueur, *The Fate of the Revolution: Interpretations of Soviet History* (London, 1967), pp. 59–82.

Lenin's *Collected Works* are now available in an English translation (45 volumes; Moscow, 1960–1970); this includes, besides published works, his notebooks on imperialism and philosophical themes and a number of volumes of correspondence. The complete texts of five of the most important pamphlets excerpted in this volume may be found, as follows, in the *Collected Works: What is to be Done?*, in *Collected Works*, vol. 5, 347–529; *Imperialism*, in vol. 22, pp. 185–304; *State and Revolution*, in vol. 25, pp. 381–492; *The Proletarian Revolution and the Renegade Kautsky*, in vol. 28, pp. 227–325; and *"Left-Wing" Communism: An Infantile Disorder*, in vol. 31, pp. 17–118. Lenin, *Selected Works* (3 volumes; Moscow, 1962) contains the most important material, and there are numerous anthologies on special themes (e.g., *On Britain; Against Revisionism; The National Liberation Movement in the East; Marx, Engels, Marxism*). The individual works have been published in numerous editions. Two useful collections, organized by topic, are Stefan Possony, ed., *Lenin: A Reader* (Chicago, 1966), and Howard Selsam and Harry Mendel, eds., *Reader in Marxist Philosophy* (New York, 1963).

Lenin's ideas are placed in the context of Marxist thought in George Lichtheim, *Marxism—A Historical and Critical Survey* (New York, 1961) and Bertram D. Wolfe, *Marxism: One Hundred Years in the Life of a Doctrine* (New York, 1963). Lichtheim follows an essentially chronological order, Wolfe is thematic. For an overview of the background in Russian thought, see S. V. Utechin, *Russian Political Thought* (New York, 1963), and the anthology edited by Hans Kohn, *The Mind of Modern Russia* (New York, reprint 1962). Alfred G. Meyer, *Leninism* (Cambridge, Mass., 1957) is the standard critical introduction. Nathan Leites, *A Study of Bolshevism* (Glencoe, 1953), extracts an "operational code" from Lenin's writings, and combines its exegesis with a controversial psychoanalytical interpretation of Lenin and Bolshevism. John Plamenatz, *German Marxism and Russian Communism* (London, 1954), is a closely reasoned historical and critical study; Plamenatz views Leninism, in the main, as a rather unoriginal vulgarization of Marx's ideas. The philosophical underpinnings of Leninism are examined most thoroughly and perceptively in Gustav Wetter, *Dialectical Materialism* (New York, 1959). For a recent Soviet appraisal, see G. Glezerman and G. Kusanov, *Historical Materialism: Basic Problems* (Moscow, 1968).

The historical background of Leninism is surveyed in Donald W. Treadgold, *Twentieth Century Russia* (Chicago, revised edition, 1971). The early chapters of Pierre Sorlin, *The Soviet People and Their Society* (New York, 1968), should be consulted for social history, while the symposium, *The Russian Intelligentsia*

(New York, 1961), edited by Richard Pipes, is a standard work on this topic. For the background to the Revolution, see Hugh Seton-Watson, *The Decline of Imperial Russia, 1855–1914* (New York, 1962). Sidney Harcave, *First Blood* (New York, 1964), deals with the Revolution of 1905. Among older works on 1917–1921, see William Henry Chamberlin, *The Russian Revolution* (2 volumes, 1935; reprinted, New York, 1965). George Katkov, *Russia, 1917* (London, 1967), deals primarily with the earlier phases of the Revolution; it is based on the more recent documentation, and puts renewed emphasis on conspiratorial aspects. Extensive documentation is found in two collections published under the auspices of the Hoover Institution: Alexander Kerensky and Robert Browder, eds., *The Russian Provisional Government, 1917* (3 volumes; Stanford, 1961), and James Bunyan and H. H. Fisher, eds., *The Bolshevik Revolution, 1917–1918* (reprinted, Stanford, 1961). Robert V. Daniels' most useful collection, *The Russian Revolution* (Englewood Cliffs, N.J., 1972), includes several key documents never before published in English. For developments through 1921, see David Footman, *Civil War in Russia* (New York, 1962). Interpretative history on a grand scale is provided by E. H. Carr's masterwork, *A History of Soviet Russia* (London and New York, 1950–   ); the Lenin period is covered in the subseries "The Bolshevik Revolution" (vols. 1–3) and volume 4, "The Interregnum."

Franco Venturi, *Roots of Revolution* (New York, 1960), is indispensable for the pre-Marxist phase of the Russian Revolutionary movement. For the early history of Russian Marxism and the emergence of Lenin, see Leopold H. Haimson, *The Russian Marxists and the Origins of Bolshevism* (Cambridge, Mass., 1955), and Richard Pipes, *Social Democracy and the St. Petersburg Labor Movement, 1885–1897* (Cambridge, Mass., 1963). The competition among groups within the Russian socialist movement is delineated in Donald W. Treadgold, *Lenin and His Rivals* (New York, 1955), and Allan K. Wildman, *The Making of a Workers' Revolution: Russian Social-Democracy, 1891–1903* (Chicago, 1967). Leonard Schapiro, *The Communist Party of the Soviet Union* (London, New York, revised edition, 1970), is comprehensive, and is based on careful analysis of the evidence. Selected source materials are included in Robert Daniels, ed., *A Documentary History of Communism* (New York, 1960). Various arcane matters, including details of the Bolshevik system of couriers and of Lenin's relations with the Germans, are illuminated in Michael Futtrell, *Northern Underground* (London, 1963).

Taken together, Adam B. Ulam's *The Bolsheviks* and Louis Fischer's *The Life of Lenin* provide the most comprehensive available biographical introduction; Ulam's emphasis is on 1917 and the years leading up to it, while the bulk of Fischer's book is devoted to 1917 and the years during which Lenin held power. A highly critical biography that attempts a psychological interpretation is Stefan Possony, *Lenin: The Compulsive Revolutionary* (Chicago, 1965). For official biography, compare the Stalinist and post-Stalinist examples: Marx-Engels-Lenin Institute, *Vladimir I. Lenin: A Political Biography* (New York, 1943), and P. N. Pospelov, ed., *et al.*, *Vladimir Ilyich Lenin: A Biography* (Moscow, 1966). More specialized biographical studies are Isaac Deutscher, *Lenin's Childhood* (London, New York, Toronto, 1970); Bertram D. Wolfe, *The Bridge and the Abyss: The Troubled Friendship of Maxim Gorky and V. I. Lenin* (New

York, 1967); Moshe Lewin, *Lenin's Last Struggle* (New York, 1968), and E. Victor Wolfenstein, *The Revolutionary Personality: Lenin, Trotsky, Gandhi* (Princeton, 1967).

The role of Lenin in the emergence of totalitarianism is touched on in Carl J. Friedrich and Zbigniew K. Brzezinski, *Totalitarian Dictatorship and Autocracy* (Cambridge, Mass., revised edition, 1965), and forms the implied theme of T. H. von Laue, *Why Lenin? Why Stalin?* (Philadelphia, 1964). For Lenin and the post-1917 Soviet system, see the relevant chapters in the following: Merle Fainsod, *How Russia is Ruled* (Cambridge, Mass., revised edition, 1963); Julian Towster, *Political Power in the U.S.S.R., 1917–1947* (New York, 1948); and Barrington Moore, Jr., *Soviet Politics: The Dilemma of Power* (Cambridge, Mass., 1950). Documentation is included in James H. Meisel and E. S. Kozera, eds., *Materials for the Study of the Soviet System* (Ann Arbor, revised edition, 1953). Special topics are dealt with in the following works: Leonard Schapiro, *The Origin of the Communist Autocracy: Political Opposition in the Soviet State, First Phase, 1917–1922* (Cambridge, Mass., 1955); Robert V. Daniels, *The Conscience of the Revolution: Opposition in the Soviet Union, 1917–1929* (Cambridge, Mass., 1961); Alfred D. Low, *Lenin on the Question of Nationality* (New York, 1958); Richard Pipes, *The Formation of the Soviet Union* (Cambridge, Mass., revised edition, 1964); and Thomas T. Hammond, *Lenin on Trade Unions and Revolution* (New York, 1953). Carr's "The Bolshevik Revolution," volume 2, provides an assessment of Lenin's response to the challenges of the revolutionary economy. From the voluminous essay literature, the following are of special significance: Richard Pipes, "The Origins of Bolshevism: The Intellectual Evolution of Young Lenin," in Pipes, ed., *Revolutionary Russia* (Cambridge, Mass., 1968); and Henry L. Roberts, "Lenin and Power," in Leonard Krieger and Fritz Stern, eds., *The Responsibility of Power: Historical Essays in Honor of Hajo Holborn* (Garden City, 1968).

For Soviet foreign policy during the Lenin period, see the relevant chapters in Adam Ulam, *Expansion and Coexistence: The History of Soviet Foreign Policy, 1917–1967* (New York, 1968). Still useful is Louis Fischer's *The Soviets in World Affairs* (2 volumes; Princeton, 2nd edition, 1951); originally published in 1930, it dealt largely with the period from 1917 to Lenin's death, and was based on extensive research, including interviews with Soviet participants. The third volume of Carr's "The Bolshevik Revolution" deals with foreign policy, as do the relevant chapters of "The Interregnum." Extensive documentation is included in Xenia Joukoff Eudin and Harold H. Fisher, eds., *Soviet Russia and the West, 1920–1927* (Stanford, 1957), and Xenia Joukoff Eudin and Robert C. North, eds., *Soviet Russia and the East* (Stanford, 1957); see also volume 1 of Jane Degras, ed., *Soviet Documents on Foreign Policy* (London and New York, 1951). For critical studies of the earliest phases of Lenin's diplomacy-cum-propaganda, see J. W. Wheeler-Bennett, *Brest-Litovsk: The Forgotten Peace, March, 1918* (London, 1938; reprinted, 1956); and Arno J. Mayer, *Political Origins of the New Diplomacy, 1917–1918* (New Haven, 1958), as well as the appropriate chapters of the latter's *Politics and Diplomacy of Peacemaking: Containment and Counterrevolution at Versailles, 1918–1919* (New York, 1967). For Lenin's policies on China, see (in addition to Eudin and North) Daniel M. Low, *The*

Function of "China" in Marx, Lenin, and Mao (Berkeley and Los Angeles, 1966), and Allen S. Whiting, *Soviet Policies in China, 1917–1924* (New York, 1954). Lenin's relationship to the international socialist and communist movements may be explored in Stanley W. Page, *Lenin and World Revolution* (New York, 1959), and Franz Borkenau, *World Communism: A History of the Communist International* (New York, 1939). For documentation, see Olga Hess Gankin and H. H. Fisher, eds., *The Bolsheviks and the World War* (Stanford, 1940)—also a goldmine of information on Lenin's relations with the pre-1914 Second International—and the first two volumes of Jane Degras, ed., *The Communist International 1919–1943: Documents* (London and New York, 1956, 1960). Elliot R. Goodman, *The Soviet Design for a World State* (New York, 1960), deals, *inter alia*, with Lenin's conception of "proletarian internationalism."

Useful collections are the following: Stanley W. Page, ed., *Lenin: Dedicated Marxist or Revolutionary Pragmatist?* (Lexington, Mass., 1970); Leonard Schapiro, Peter Redaway, and Paul Rosta, eds., *Lenin: The Man, The Theorist, The Leader—A Reappraisal* (London and New York, 1967); and Richard Pipes, ed. *Revolutionary Russia: A Symposium* (Cambridge, Mass., 1968).

Index